D0507542

STL Programming
from the Ground Up

About the Author ...

Herb Schildt is the leading authority on C and C++ and a best-selling author whose books have sold more than 2 million copies. His acclaimed C and C++ books include *Teach Yourself C, C++ from the Ground Up, Teach Yourself C++, C++: The Complete Reference, Borland C++: The Complete Reference,* and *C++ Programmer's Reference* to name a few. Schildt is president of Universal Computing Laboratories, Inc., a software consulting firm in Mahomet, Illinois. He is a member of both the ANSI C and C++ standardization committees. He holds a master's degree in computer science from the Universtiy of Illinois.

STL Programming
from the Ground Up

Herbert Schildt

Osborne/**McGraw-Hill**

Berkeley   New York   St. Louis   San Francisco
Auckland   Bogotá   Hamburg   London   Madrid
Mexico City   Milan   Montreal   New Delhi   Panama City
Paris   São Paulo   Singapore   Sydney
Tokyo   Toronto

Osborne/**McGraw-Hill**
2600 Tenth Street
Berkeley, California 94710
U.S.A.

For information on translations or book distributors outside the U.S.A., or to arrange bulk purchase discounts for sales promotions, premiums, or fund-raisers, please contact Osborne/**McGraw-Hill** at the above address.

STL Programming from the Ground Up

Copyright © 1999 by The McGraw-Hill Companies. All rights reserved. Printed in the United States of America. Except as permitted under the Copyright Act of 1976, no part of this publication may be reproduced or distributed in any form or by any means, or stored in a database or retrieval system, without the prior written permission of the publisher, with the exception that the program listings may be entered, stored, and executed in a computer system, but they may not be reproduced for publication.

1234567890 DOC DOC 90198765432109

ISBN 0-07-882507-5

Publisher	**Copy Editor**
Brandon A. Nordin	Dennis Weaver
Editor in Chief	**Proofreader**
Scott Rogers	Pat Mannion
Acquisitions Editor	**Indexer**
Wendy Rinaldi	Sherry Schildt
Project Editor	**Computer Designers**
Ron Hull	Jani Beckwith
	Ann Sellers
Editorial Assistant	
Monika Faltiss	**Illustrator**
	Beth Young
Technical Editor	
P. J. Plauger	**Series Design**
	Peter Hancik

Information has been obtained by Osborne/**McGraw-Hill** from sources believed to be reliable. However, because of the possibility of human or mechanical error by our sources, Osborne/**McGraw-Hill**, or others, Osborne/**McGraw-Hill** does not guarantee the accuracy, adequacy, or completeness of any information and is not responsible for any errors or omissions or the results obtained from use of such information.

Contents at a Glance

Contents

Acknowledgments

I wish to say special thanks to P. J. Plauger for his advice and suggestions during the preparation of this book. P. J. is one of computing's most accomplished luminaries. He has been at the forefront of much of what forms the basis of modern programming, including C and C++. His input is appreciated.

Preface

The Standard Template Library (STL) is changing the way programs are written. By applying its break-through container technology, it is now possible to do in a few lines of code what once required a few hundred. The preceding statement is not hyperbole. It is literal. Using the STL, storing, retrieving, and manipulating data can be accomplished using standardized, efficient, built-in objects and algorithms. For example, if you need to store data in a list, you can use the **list** class. You don't need to write your own linked-list code. The net effect is that the handling of data has been streamlined. Since the manipulation of data constitutes a significant part of many programs, the STL makes the job of programming a bit easier, and the programs that you write a bit more reliable.

The STL is part of a larger revolution in programming that is centered on component software. In the most general sense, software components are predefined units of functionality that other programs may employ as needed. At the time of this writing, we still tend to think in terms of large, monolithic programs—that is, programs in which all of the functionality is defined within the program itself. In contrast, the component software model lets us think of a program as consisting of many smaller parts (components) that are "wired" together. The STL supplies one specific type: the linkable component.

In the course of this book you will learn how to command the STL and apply it to your own programming tasks. As you will see, the STL is easier to use than one might first expect given its power. For today's professional programmer, proficiency with the STL is no longer optional, but required. STL-based code is the future.

What's Inside

In its 12 chapters and 4 appendices, this book describes the entire Standard Template Library, including all containers, algorithms, and iterators. It also shows you how to create your own containers and algorithms. Its appendices describe several additional classes that are compatible with the STL, but not actually part of it.

Numerous examples are found throughout. They illustrate key concepts or show how the STL can be applied to solve a practical problem. Also included are a number of In Depth boxes that delve deeper into certain topics or present interesting background information. Margin notes highlight key concepts.

You Must Know C++

This book assumes you know C++. You must have a solid working knowledge of classes, templates, and pointers. If you think your C++ skills need a little improving, I suggest the following books of mine:

C++: The Complete Reference, 3rd Ed.

C++ from the Ground Up, 2nd Ed.

Teach Yourself C++, 3rd Ed.

These are published by Osborne/McGraw-Hill.

What Compiler Is Needed

The examples in this book were tested using Microsoft's Visual C++ 6 compiler. In general, to compile this code you will need a modern C++ compiler that supports the version of the STL defined by Standard C++. As explained in Chapter 1, the STL was standardized as part of C++ in late 1997. Prior to that standardization, slightly different versions were implemented by different compiler manufacturers. Thus, older compilers may not accept all of the programs in this book. A modern compiler is required.

Don't Forget: Code on the Web

Remember, the source code for all of the programs in this book is available free-of-charge on the Web at **http://www.osborne.com**. Downloading this code prevents you from having to type in the examples.

For Further Study

STL Programming from the Ground Up is just one of many in the "Herb Schildt" series of programming books. Here is a partial list of Schildt's other books.

If you want to learn more about C++, then you will find these books especially helpful:

C++: The Complete Reference
C++ from the Ground Up
Teach Yourself C++
Expert C++

If you want to learn more about C, the foundation of C++, we recommend:

Teach Yourself C
C: The Complete Reference
The Annotated ANSI C Standard

If you will be developing programs for the Web, you will want to read

Java: The Complete Reference

co-authored by Herbert Schildt and Patrick Naughton.

Finally, if you want to program for Windows, we recommend:

Windows 98 Programming from the Ground Up
Windows NT 4 from the Ground Up
MFC Programming from the Ground Up

When you need solid answers, fast, turn to Herbert Schildt, the recognized authority on programming.

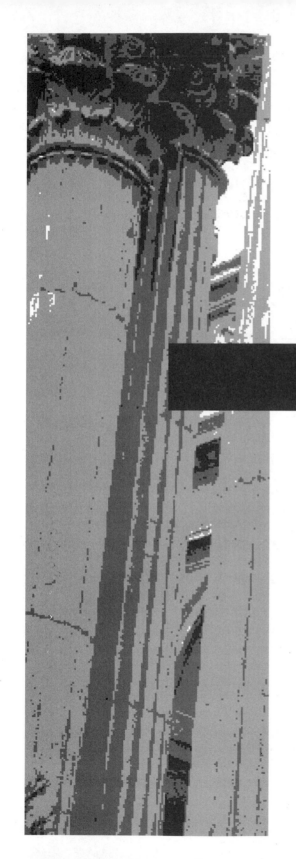

CHAPTER 1

Introducing the Standard Template Library

1

The Standard Template Library (STL) is reshaping the way that programs are written. This is a powerful statement, but then the STL is a powerful library. Although the STL represents some of the newest thought in programming, it is also the culmination of a quest that has engaged programmers for decades: the search for reusable software. While the impact of the STL on programming is just beginning, its effects will be long lasting and profound. When the history of computing in the latter days of the twentieth century is written, the STL will rank as one of programming's major achievements.

This book is first and foremost a practical guide to programming using the STL. As such, it is not overly concerned with the theoretical aspects of the STL except as they directly relate to writing programs. The goal here is to provide a hands-on approach that will have you utilizing the power of the STL as soon as possible. That said, to effectively apply the STL requires that you understand the forces that drove its creation, its design principles and philosophy, and its relationship to C++—and these are the topics of this chapter.

What Is the STL?

In simple terms, the Standard Template Library is a sophisticated set of template classes and functions that implement many popular and commonly used algorithms and data structures. For example, it includes support for vectors, lists, queues, and stacks. It also defines various routines—such as sorting, searching, and transforming—that operate on them. Because the STL is constructed from template classes and functions, the algorithms and data structures can be applied to nearly any type of data. This is, of course, part of its power.

The data structures and algorithms supplied by the STL provide off-the-shelf solutions to a variety of programming problems. For example, instead of having to create your own code for a linked list that holds a mailing list, you could use the STL's **list** class. If your program needs to link a key with a value and provide a means of finding that value given the key (such as in a telephone directory), it could use the STL's **map** class. Because the STL provides solid, debugged implementations of the most commonly used "data engines," you can use one whenever it is needed, without going through the time and trouble to develop your own.

From the preceding description you might be tempted to think of the STL as *only* a library of standard data structures and algorithms, but this is not the case. While the STL does support these elements, it offers a broader programming context in which many diverse programming tasks can be framed. As you will see, the STL gives the programmer a new way to manage the interaction between code and data in a program. Moreover, it provides a new way in which to think about and structure solutions to nearly any programming task. The reason for this is that the STL embodies the concept of *software components*.

The Component Software Revolution

The STL is the vanguard of a larger programming revolution: reusable software components. From the dawn of computing, programmers have sought the ability to reuse their code. Since development and debugging is a costly process, code reuse is highly desirable. In the early days, code reuse was achieved by cutting and pasting source code from one program to another, and, of course, this approach is still used today. The next advance in code reuse took the form of reusable function libraries, such as those provided by C++. This was soon followed by standardized class libraries. While building on the foundation of a class library, the STL takes the concept one important step further: it modularizes the library into components.

A software component is a reusable, self-contained module of code that may be used by another application. One or more can be "plugged into" an application, providing additional control or functionality. Because each component is self-contained, the integrity of one component is unaffected by errors or misuse of another.

A software component is a self-contained module that performs a well-defined function.

In the most general sense, software components take two forms. The first are the executable components typified by ActiveX controls or Java Beans. These components are self-contained entities whose functionality can be accessed at will by other applications. Furthermore, the connection of this kind of component to an application occurs at run time. Taken to its logical conclusion, the bulk of an application could be constructed of nothing but these types of software components "wired" together by the user, with one component feeding into another. As an analogy, an executable software component is like a stand-alone graphic equalizer for your stereo. It is wired in before the amplifier and provides a specific function (it alters the frequency curve), but it is not part of the amplifier itself. Also, the graphic equalizer is a completely independent and self-contained device, with its own power supply, controls, etc. In similar fashion, an executable component exists separately from its client application; it is not compiled into the program that uses it. While executable components are of great value, they are not the type of components defined by the STL.

The second form of software component is the linkable component. This is the type of component defined by the STL. Linkable components, although still self-contained, do not exist as independent executable entities by themselves and they are not "plugged into" another application at run time. Instead, the linkable component must be included during compilation. In essence, a linkable component is an independent subsystem that your program may use at will by incorporating calls to the component in the source code of your program. By analogy, a linkable software component resembles an integrated circuit; it provides substantial functionality, but does not, itself, exist as a separate device. It does not contain its own power supply, for example. It is, however, a large unit of well-defined, modular functionality.

Whether they are executable or linkable, the goal of all software components is the same: to enable the creation of more reliable programs through the better management of complexity. Complexity is the single greatest challenge faced by programmers. Beginners learn early in their programming careers that the longer the program, the longer the debugging time. As program size grows, so usually does its complexity, and there is a limit to the amount of complexity we, as humans, can manage. From a purely combinatoric standpoint, the more individual lines of code there are, the greater the chance for side effects and unwanted interactions. As most programmers today know, programs are growing exceedingly complex.

Software components help us manage complexity through "divide and conquer." By compartmentalizing large blocks of functionality into independent resources, the programmer can reduce the apparent complexity of a program. Towards this end, the STL organizes several common program elements into a set of well-defined building blocks that you can use without being concerned with their implementation details. The net effect of this approach is that complexity is reduced. For example, if I need a linked list for a program I can either write it myself, which may add several hundred lines of code to my program, or I can employ the STL's **list** class, which adds only a few lines of source code. In both cases, the functionality of the linked list is present in the executable version of my program, but by choosing the latter approach, the functionality of the linked list is compartmentalized by the **list** class and I can deal with it as a unit.

As you will see as you progress through this book, the STL gives the programmer a large amount of predefined functionality that may be incorporated into a program. Once you understand the STL, you can think of programs as consisting of a set of components that you connect together. Since these components are still utilized at the source-code level, you, the programmer, are still fully in charge of your program. Thus, the STL gives you the benefits of modular software components while still granting you full source-code control over your program.

The Creation of the STL

1

The Standard Template Library is the brainchild of Alexander Stepanov. In 1979, Stepanov began work on what would ultimately become the STL. Stepanov was soon joined by David Musser of Rensselaer Polytechnic Institute and together they developed and evolved the STL's core concepts. Much of the work was done while Stepanov was at Hewlett-Packard, and for a time the STL was identified with HP. Joining Stepanov and Musser in 1992, Meng Lee (also at HP) made major contributions to the final design of the STL.

As many readers will know, 1979 was also the year in which Bjarne Stroustrup began work on what was originally called "C with Classes" and later named C++. This is important for two reasons. First, while Stepanov did some of the initial design work for the STL in C (and before that, in Ada), its final architecture would require features that C simply did not support, such as generic data types and other object-oriented features. However, these features were being incorporated in C++. Thus, from early in their development, the fates of STL and C++ were closely intertwined.

By the late 1980s, C++ was mature enough to begin what would turn out to be a very long standardization process. Toward that end, a joint American National Standards Institute (ANSI) and International Standards Organization (ISO) committee was formed to create a standard for C++. At that time, the STL was not part of C++. In fact, the draft of the proposed C++ standard dated January 25th, 1994 did not even mention the STL! But this was soon to change.

Late in 1993, Stepanov presented an informal talk on the STL to the C++ committee. Although an initial draft standard for C++ that did not include the STL had already been prepared, the committee decided to consider the prospect of adding the STL to C++. Following further refinements by Stepanov and Lee, in mid 1994, the committee voted to include the STL into the C++ standard, making it part of the C++ language. While the inclusion of the STL dramatically slowed the standardization of C++, it greatly expanded the scope and power of the language.

Before moving on, it is interesting to note that while the STL depended upon the creation of C++ for its existence, its inclusion in C++ ultimately changed fundamental aspects of that language. The combination of Stroustrup's insight into object-oriented programming combined with Stepanov's vision for "plug-compatible" software components yielded a powerful, new software paradigm.

Which Version of the STL?

This book describes the STL as defined by Standard C++. This is important only to the extent that the original version of the STL developed at HP and the version that was finally defined by the C++ standard are slightly different. While the HP version is important for historical perspective (and you might still encounter code written using it), it is the standardized version of the STL that will be used for future projects. Fortunately, the core concepts and many of the details are the same as the original HP version.

The Organization of the STL

While we won't look at any programming examples until the next chapter, it is useful to have a general understanding of how the STL is organized and the purpose of its constituent parts. The Standard Template Library is organized around three foundational items: *containers*, *algorithms*, and *iterators*. Put simply, algorithms act on containers through iterators. More than anything else, the design and implementation of these features determine the nature of the STL. Most of this book will be focused on describing the attributes of these core elements.

In addition to containers, algorithms, and iterators, the STL relies upon three other standard components for support: *allocators*, *adaptors*, and *function objects*. Let's examine each in turn.

Containers

Containers are objects that hold other objects.

Containers are objects that hold other objects. There are several different types of containers. For example, the **vector** class defines a dynamic array, **deque** creates a double-ended queue, and **list** provides a linear list. These containers are called *sequence containers* because in STL terminology, a sequence is a linear list. In addition to the basic containers, the STL also defines *associative containers* that allow efficient retrieval of values based on keys. For example, a **map** provides access to values with unique keys. Thus, a **map** stores a key/value pair and allows a value to be retrieved given its key.

Each container class defines a set of functions that may be applied to the container. For example, a **list** container includes functions that insert, delete, and merge elements. A **stack** includes functions that push and pop values.

Algorithms

Algorithms are functions that act on containers.

Algorithms act on containers. They provide the means by which you will manipulate the contents of containers. Their capabilities include initialization, sorting, searching, and transforming the contents of containers. Many algorithms operate on a *range* of elements within a container.

Iterators

Iterators are pointer-like objects.

Iterators are objects that act more or less like pointers. They give you the ability to cycle through the contents of a container in much the same way that you would use a pointer to cycle through an array. There are five types of iterators:

Iterator	Access Allowed
Random access	Store and retrieve values. Elements may be accessed randomly.
Bidirectional	Store and retrieve values. Forward and backward moving.
Forward	Store and retrieve values. Forward moving only.
Input	Retrieve but not store values. Forward moving only.
Output	Store but not retrieve values. Forward moving only.

In general, an iterator that has greater access capabilities can be used in place of one that has lesser capabilities. For example, a forward iterator can be used in place of an input iterator.

Iterators are handled just like pointers. You can increment and decrement them. You can apply the * operator to them. Iterators are declared using the **iterator** type defined by the various containers.

The STL also supports *reverse iterators*. Reverse iterators are either bidirectional or random access iterators that move through a sequence in the reverse direction. Thus, if a reverse iterator points to the end of a sequence, incrementing that iterator will cause it to point one element before the end.

When referring to the various iterator types in template descriptions, this book will use the following terms:

Term	Represents
BiIter	Bidirectional iterator
ForIter	Forward iterator
InIter	Input iterator
OutIter	Output iterator
RandIter	Random access iterator

Allocators

Allocators manage memory allocation for a container.

Each container has defined for it an *allocator*. Allocators manage memory allocation for a container. The default allocator is an object of class **allocator**, but you can define your own allocators if needed by specialized applications. For most uses, the default allocator is sufficient.

Function Objects

Function objects are classes that define **operator( )**.

Function objects are classes that define **operator( )**. There are several predefined function objects, such as **less( )**, **greater( )**, **plus( )**, **minus( )**, **multiplies( )**, and **divides( )**. Perhaps the most widely used function object is **less( )**, which determines when one object is less than another. Function objects can be used in place of function pointers in the STL algorithms described later. Using function objects rather than function pointers allows the STL to generate more efficient and more flexible code.

Adaptors

Adaptors transform one object into another.

In the most general sense, an *adaptor* transforms one thing into another. There are container adaptors, iterator adaptors, and function adaptors. An example of a container adaptor is **queue**, which adapts the **deque** container for use as a standard queue. As you will see, adaptors simplify a number of difficult situations.

Other STL Entities

Several of the algorithms and containers use a special type of function called a *predicate*. There are two variations of predicates: unary and binary. A unary predicate takes one argument. A binary predicate has two arguments. These functions return true/false results, but the precise conditions that make them return true or false are defined by you. For the rest of this book, when a unary

1

predicate function is required, it will be notated using the type **UnPred**. When a binary predicate is required, the type **BinPred** will be used. In a binary predicate, the arguments are always in the order of *first,second*. For both unary and binary predicates, the arguments will contain values of the type of objects being stored by the container.

A predicate is a function that returns a true/false result.

Some algorithms use a special type of binary predicate that compares two elements. *Comparison functions* return true if their first argument is less than their second. Comparison functions will be notated using the type **Comp**.

Two other entities that populate the STL are binders and negators. A *binder* binds an argument to a function object. A *negator* returns the complement of a predicate. Both increase the versatility of the STL.

Performance Issues

There is one other important aspect to the STL that adds to its power and general applicability: performance guarantees. Although a compiler manufacturer is free to implement the underlying mechanism used by each container and algorithm in its own way, all implementations must conform to the performance guarantees specified by Standard C++. Standard C++ defines the following general performance categories:

◆ Constant
◆ Linear
◆ Logarithmic

Of course, constant time is better than linear time, which is better than logarithmic time. Since different containers store their contents differently, they will have different performance guarantees. For example, insertion into the middle of a vector takes linear time. By contrast, insertion into a list takes constant time. Different algorithms might also behave differently. For example, the **sort( )** algorithm executes proportional to N log N, but the **find( )** algorithm runs in linear time.

In general, the STL specification requires that the containers and algorithms be implemented using techniques that ensure (loosely speaking) optimal runtime performance. This is important because it guarantees to you, the programmer, that the STL building blocks meet a certain level of efficiency no matter what implementation of the STL you are using. Without such a guarantee, the performance of STL-based code would depend entirely upon each individual implementation and could vary widely.

The STL specifies its performance guarantees using the term of *complexity*. Since, for the most part, the STL implements the most commonly used and widely analyzed data structures and algorithms, the general category of complexity for the various components of the STL will be well known to most readers. However, in cases where the complexity of a component may not be obvious, it will be mentioned.

A Review of Terms

This chapter has introduced many terms. They are reviewed here for your convenience.

Term	Definition
Allocator	The component that manages memory allocation in a container.
Algorithm	A function that acts on containers.
Adaptor	Something that transforms one object into another.
Container	An object that holds other objects.
Iterator	A pointer-like object.
Predicate	A function that returns **true** or **false**.
Function Object	A class that defines **operator( )**.

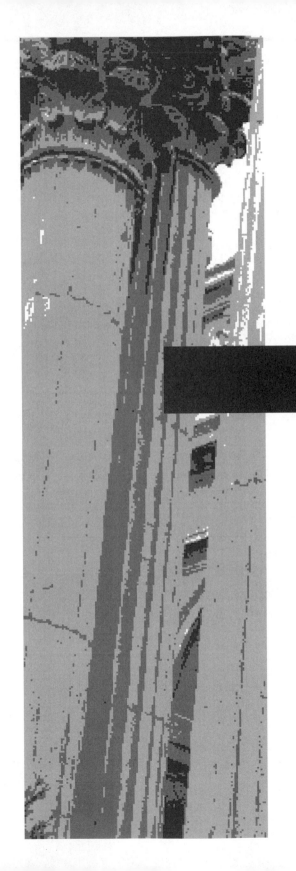

CHAPTER 2

STL Programming Fundamentals

The pieces of the STL do not exist in isolation. Instead, they work together, forming an interrelated programming framework. While this does, of course, make the STL a very powerful system, it also makes it difficult to discuss one aspect of the STL without inherently involving one or more of its other parts. So, before beginning a detailed examination of its various constituents, it is necessary for you to have a general understanding of how the STL works, how its various pieces are used, and the fundamental techniques that you will employ when writing programs. With this goal in mind, this chapter provides a programming overview of the STL.

The Container Classes

At the core of the STL are its containers. As explained in Chapter 1, a container is the component that actually stores data. The containers (and container adaptors) defined by the STL are shown in Table 2-1. Also shown are the headers necessary to use each container. As one might expect, each container has different capabilities and attributes.

Container	Description	Required Header
deque	A double-ended queue.	<deque>
list	A linear list.	<list>
map	Stores key/value pairs in which each key is associated with only one value.	<map>
multimap	Stores key/value pairs in which one key may be associated with two or more values.	<map>
multiset	A set in which each element is not necessarily unique.	<set>
priority_queue	A priority queue.	<queue>
queue	A queue.	<queue>

The Containers Defined by the STL

Table 2-1.

Container	Description	Required Header
set	A set in which each element is unique.	<set>
stack	A stack.	<stack>
vector	A dynamic array.	<vector>

Containers are implemented using template classes. For example, the template specification for the **deque** container is shown here. All containers use similar specifications.

```
template <class T, class Allocator = allocator<T> > class deque
```

Here, the generic type **T** specifies the type of objects held by the deque. The allocator used by the deque is specified by **Allocator**, which defaults to the standard allocator class. For the vast majority of applications, you will simply use the default allocator and that is what all of the code in this book does. However, it is possible to define your own allocator class if a special allocation scheme is ever needed. If you are not familiar with default arguments in templates, just remember that they work in much the same way as default arguments in functions. If the generic type argument is not specified explicitly when an object is created, then the default type is used.

Since the names of the generic placeholder types in a template class declaration are arbitrary (such as **T**, above), the container classes declare **typedef**ed versions of these types. This makes the type names concrete. Some of the most commonly used **typedef** names are shown here:

size_type	Some type of integer.
reference	A reference to an element.
const_reference	A **const** reference to an element.
iterator	An iterator.
const_iterator	A **const** iterator.
reverse_iterator	A reverse iterator.
const_reverse_iterator	A **const** reverse iterator.

value_type	The type of a value stored in a container.
allocator_type	The type of the allocator.
key_type	The type of a key.
key_compare	The type of a function that compares two keys.
value_compare	The type of a function that compares two values.

The sequence containers store objects in some form of linear list. Associative containers store key/value pairs.

There are two broad categories of containers: sequence and associative. The sequence containers are **vector**, **list**, and **deque**. The associative containers are **map**, **multimap**, **set**, and **multiset**. The sequence containers operate on sequences, which are essentially linear lists of objects. The associative containers operate on lists of key/value pairs and allow the retrieval of a value given its key.

The container adaptors are stack, queue, and priority_queue.

The classes **stack**, **queue**, and **priority_queue** are called *container adaptors* because they use (i.e., adapt) one of the sequence containers to hold their elements. Thus, one of the sequence containers underlies the functionality provided by **stack**, **queue**, and **priority_queue**. From the programmer's perspective, the container adaptors look and act much like the other containers and we won't worry about the distinction at this time.

General Theory of Operation

Although the internal operation of the STL is quite sophisticated, using the STL is actually quite easy. First, you must decide on the type of container that you wish to use. Each offers certain benefits and trade-offs. For example, a **vector** is very good when a random-access, array-like object is needed and not too many insertions or deletions are required. A **list** offers low-cost insertion and deletion but trades away speed. A **map** provides an associative container but, of course, incurs additional overhead.

Once you have chosen a container, you will use its member functions to add elements to the container, access or modify those elements, and delete elements. A container will automatically grow as needed when elements are added to it and shrink when elements are removed.

Elements can be added to and removed from a container in a number of different ways. For example, the sequence containers (**vector**, **list**, and **deque**) and the associative containers (**map**, **multimap**, **set**, and **multiset**) provide member functions called **insert( )**, which inserts elements into a container, and **erase( )**, which removes elements from a container. The sequence containers provide **push_back( )** and **pop_back( )**, which add an element to or remove an element from the end, respectively. The **list** and **deque** containers also include **push_front( )** and **pop_front( )**, which add and remove elements from the start of the container.

One of the most common ways to access the elements within a container is through an iterator. The sequence containers and the associative containers provide the member functions **begin( )** and **end( )**, which return iterators to the start and end of the container, respectively. These iterators are very useful when accessing the contents of a container. For example, to cycle through a container you can obtain an iterator to its first element using **begin( )** and then increment that iterator until its value is equal to **end( )**.

Since a **vector** is a dynamic array, it also supports the standard array-indexing syntax for accessing its elements. However, not all other containers can employ the array subscript operator to access their elements.

The associative containers provide the function **find( )**, which is used to locate an element given its key. Since associative containers link a key with its value, **find( )** is the way that most elements in such a container are located.

Once you have a container that holds information, it can be manipulated using one or more of the algorithms. The algorithms not only allow you to alter the contents of a container in some prescribed fashion, but they also let you transform one type of sequence into another.

The remainder of this chapter illustrates how these general techniques can be applied.

IN DEPTH

Are the String Classes Containers?

The Standard C++ Library defines a template string class called **basic_string** and declares two specializations: **string** and **wstring**. The **string** class operates on sequences of characters of type **char** and **wstring** operates on sequences of wide characters of type **wchar_t**. Since both **string** and **wstring** operate on sequences of characters, it should come as no surprise to find out that that they are also containers. Even though they perform the special role of managing character strings, they still meet the minimal requirements for a container. For example, they can be operated upon by algorithms and accessed via iterators.

The string classes were not defined by Stepanov when he designed the STL and are not generally considered to be part of it. But part of the beauty of the STL's design is that any class that meets a certain minimal set of requirements can function as a container, fully integrated into the STL's framework. Thus, the STL is not a closed system; it can be extended, with a little effort, by any programmer who so chooses. In the case of the string classes, the C++ standardization committee decided to make them into containers (and thus compatible with the STL) when the Standard C++ Library was finalized.

Even though neither **string** nor **wstring** is technically part of the STL, they can still be used with it. Most of the techniques described in this book can be applied to them.

Your First STL Program

It is now time to see the STL in action. To do so, we will employ what is perhaps the most commonly used container: **vector**. The **vector** class supports a dynamic array. This is an array that can grow as needed. As you know, in C++ the size of an array is fixed at compile time. While this is by far the most efficient way to implement arrays, it is also the most restrictive because the size of the array cannot be adjusted at run time to accommodate changing program conditions. The **vector** class solves this problem by allocating memory as needed. Although a vector is dynamic, you can still use the standard array subscript notation to access its elements.

The template specification for **vector** is shown here:

template <class T, class Allocator = allocator<T> > class vector

Here, **T** is the type of data being stored and **Allocator** specifies the allocator, which defaults to the standard allocator. Here are some of **vector**'s constructors:

explicit vector(const Allocator &*a* = Allocator( ));

explicit vector(size_type *num*, const T &*val* = T( ),
                const Allocator &*a* = Allocator( ));

vector(const vector<T, Allocator> &*ob*);

The first form constructs an empty vector. The second form constructs a vector that has *num* elements with the value *val*. The value of *val* may be allowed to default. The third form constructs a vector that contains the same elements as *ob*. To use **vector** in a program, you must include **<vector>**.

Although the template syntax looks rather complex, there is nothing difficult about declaring a vector. Here are some examples:

```
vector<int> iv;          // create zero-length int vector
vector<char> cv(20);     // create 20-element char vector
vector<char> cv(5,  'x'); // initialize a 5-element char vector
vector<int> iv2(iv);     // create int vector from an int vector
```

Notice that in all cases, the allocator is allowed to default. As explained, most applications of the STL will use the default allocator.

The following comparison operators are defined for **vector**:

==, <, <=, !=, >, >=

The subscripting operator **[ ]** is also defined for **vector**. This allows you to access the elements of a vector using standard array subscripting notation.

Some of the most commonly used member functions are **size( )**, **begin( )**, **end( )**, **push_back( )**, **pop_back( )**, **insert( )**, and **erase( )**. These are shown in Table 2-2. The **size( )** function returns the current size of the vector. This function is quite useful because it allows you to determine the size of a vector at run time. Remember, vectors will change size as needed, so the size of a vector must be determined during execution, not during compilation.

Member	Description
iterator begin( );	Returns an iterator to the first element in the vector.
iterator end( );	Returns an iterator to the end of the vector.
bool empty( ) const;	Returns **true** if the vector contains no elements.
iterator erase(iterator *i*);	Removes the element pointed to by *i*. Returns an iterator to the element after the one removed.
iterator erase(iterator *start*, iterator *end*);	Removes the elements in the range *start* to *end*. Returns an iterator to the element after the last element removed.
iterator insert(iterator *i*, const T &*val*);	Inserts *val* immediately before the element specified by *i*. An iterator to the element is returned.
void insert(iterator *i*, size_type *num*, const T & *val*)	Inserts *num* copies of *val* immediately before the element specified by *i*.
template <class InIter> void insert(iterator *i*, InIter *start*, InIter *end*);	Inserts the sequence defined by *start* and *end* immediately before the element specified by *i*.
void pop_back( );	Removes the last element in the vector.
void push_back(const T &*val*);	Adds an element with the value specified by *val* to the end of the vector.
size_type size( ) const;	Returns the number of elements currently in the vector.

Some Commonly Used Member Functions Defined by **vector**
Table 2-2.

The **begin( )** function returns an iterator to the start of the vector. The **end( )** function returns an iterator to the end of the vector. The **push_back( )** function puts a value onto the end of the vector. If necessary, the vector is increased in length to accommodate the new element. You can add elements to the middle using **insert( )**. A vector can also be initialized. In any event, once a vector contains elements, you can use array subscripting to access or modify those elements. You can remove elements from a vector using **erase( )**. You can remove an element from the end using **pop_back( )**.

Here is a program that illustrates the basic operation of **vector**:

```cpp
// Demonstrate a vector.
#include <iostream>
#include <vector>
using namespace std;

int main()
{
  vector<int> v(10); // create a vector of length 10
  int i;

  // display original size of v
  cout << "Size = " << v.size() << endl;

  // assign the elements of the vector some values
  for(i=0; i<10; i++) v[i] = i;

  // display contents of vector
  cout << "Current Contents:\n";
  for(i=0; i<v.size(); i++) cout << v[i] << " ";
  cout << "\n\n";

  cout << "Expanding vector\n";
  /* put more values onto the end of the vector,
     it will grow as needed */
  for(i=0; i<5; i++) v.push_back(i + 10);

  // display current size of v
  cout << "Size now = " << v.size() << endl;

  // display contents of vector
  cout << "Current contents:\n";
  for(i=0; i<v.size(); i++) cout << v[i] << " ";
  cout << "\n\n";
```

```
    // change contents of vector
    for(i=0; i<v.size(); i++) v[i] = -v[i];

    cout << "Modified Contents:\n";
    for(i=0; i<v.size(); i++) cout << v[i] << " ";
    cout << endl;

    return 0;
}
```

The output of this program is shown here:

```
Size = 10
Current Contents:
0 1 2 3 4 5 6 7 8 9

Expanding vector
Size now = 15
Current contents:
0 1 2 3 4 5 6 7 8 9 10 11 12 13 14

Modified Contents:
0 -1 -2 -3 -4 -5 -6 -7 -8 -9 -10 -11 -12 -13 -14
```

Let's look at this program carefully. The first thing to notice is that the header **<vector>** is included. As explained, this is the header that supports the **vector** container. It must be included in any program that uses a **vector**. Since the STL (like the entire Standard C++ library) is defined within the **std** namespace, the statement

```
using namespace std;
```

is used to bring the **std** namespace into view. While not technically necessary, this simplifies access to the C++ standard library, and all of the programs in this book will be using this approach.

In **main( )**, an integer vector called **v** is created with an initial capacity of 10. That is, **v** initially contains ten elements. This is confirmed by calling the **size( )** member function. Next, these ten elements are assigned the values 0 through 9 and the contents of **v** are displayed. Notice that the standard array subscripting notation is employed. Next, five more elements are added to the end of **v** using the **push_back( )** function. This causes **v** to grow in order to accommodate the new elements. As the output shows, its size after these additions is 15. Finally, the values of **v**'s elements are altered using standard subscripting notation.

Notice that **v** was expanded by adding elements to it using **push_back( )**. The size of a vector can be increased only when elements are added to it using functions such as **push_back( )** or **insert( )**. It cannot be increased by assigning values to nonexistent array elements through the normal array-subscripting notation. For example, the following sequence is invalid:

2

```
vector<int> num(10);

num[10] = 100; // wrong
num[11] = 101; // wrong
```

Here, **num** is a vector that initially contains only ten elements, and it is not possible to index past the tenth element. Attempting to do so will *not* increase the size of **num**. It will simply cause an error.

Indexing a vector beyond its end will not cause the vector to increase in size.

There is one other point of interest in this program. Notice that the loops that display the contents of **v** use **v.size( )** as their target value. One of the advantages that vectors have over arrays is that it is possible to find the current size of a vector. As you can imagine, this is quite useful in a variety of situations.

A Second STL Program

As the preceding example showed, vectors will grow when elements are added to them. They will also shrink when elements are removed. The following program illustrates this fact. It uses the **pop_back( )** function to remove elements from the end of a vector until it is completely empty.

```
// Use pop_back() and empty().
#include <iostream>
#include <vector>
using namespace std;

int main()
{
  vector<char> v;
  int i;

  for(i=0; i<10; i++)
    v.push_back(i + 'A');
```

```
  cout << "Vector's original contents:\n";
  for(i=0; i<v.size(); i++)
    cout << v[i] << " ";

  cout << "\n\n";

  do {
    v.pop_back(); // remove an element from the end

    cout << "Vector now contains:\n";
    for(i=0; i<v.size(); i++)
      cout << v[i] << " ";
    cout << endl;

  } while(!v.empty());

  return 0;
}
```

The output produced by the program is shown here:

```
Vector's original contents:
A B C D E F G H I J

Vector now contains:
A B C D E F G H I
Vector now contains:
A B C D E F G H
Vector now contains:
A B C D E F G
Vector now contains:
A B C D E F
Vector now contains:
A B C D E
Vector now contains:
A B C D
Vector now contains:
A B C
Vector now contains:
A B
Vector now contains:
A
Vector now contains:
```

As the output shows, the **pop_back( )** function is the reverse of **push_back( )**: it removes elements from the end of the vector. Each time an element is removed, the size of **v** is decreased. (Remember: containers will expand and contract dynamically during program execution.) The **empty( )** function determines when the vector is empty. It returns **true** once all of the elements have been removed from **v**.

Iterators

In the preceding examples we used the array-subscripting operator **[ ]** to access the elements stored in a vector. However, the use of array-style indexing is not allowed by all of the other containers. Most often, you will access the elements in a container through an iterator. Iterators are generalized pointers that can point to elements stored within a container. They work like standard C++ pointers and are used much the same way. For example, iterators are manipulated using the same operators as those used by pointers.

The Five Iterator Types

As explained in Chapter 1, there are five types of iterators: random access, bidirectional, forward, input, and output. Since the type of iterator determines its capabilities, let's take a closer look at what these categories imply.

The most powerful iterator is the random access iterator. It can be used to store and retrieve values and it supports the following operations: **++, − −, +,** and **−** A random access iterator can also be indexed via the **[ ]** operator. A random access iterator is the type used by the **vector** container.

The next most powerful iterator is bidirectional. It can store and retrieve values and can move in both the forward and backward direction. It supports **++** and **− −**, but not **+** or **−**. Bidirectional iterators are used by **list**, for example.

A forward iterator can store and retrieve values, but it can move only in a forward direction. An input iterator can obtain values, but not alter them. It can move in a forward direction only. An output iterator can store values, but not obtain them. It, too, can move in a forward direction only. These iterators support only **++**.

In general, an iterator that has greater access capabilities can be used in place of one that has lesser capabilities. For example, a random access iterator can be used in place of a bidirectional iterator.

Remember that throughout this book when a template specification requires a generic iterator type, the following type names will be used: **RandIter** (random access), **BiIter** (bidirectional), **ForIter** (foward), **InIter** (input), **OutIter** (output).

Using an Iterator to Access the Contents of a Vector

The contents of a vector may be accessed through either array-style indexing or iterators.

Although vectors allow array-style indexing, you can also access a vector's elements through an iterator. This parallels the way that the elements of a standard C++ array can be accessed via indexing or through a pointer. As you will find when using the STL, even though **vector** supports the subscripting operator, most of the time you will be operating on vectors through iterators since iterators are the common thread that binds the STL together.

The following example shows how to use an iterator to cycle through the entire contents of a vector:

```cpp
// Access the elements of a vector through an iterator.
#include <iostream>
#include <vector>
using namespace std;

int main()
{
  vector<int> v(10); // create a vector of length 10
  vector<int>::iterator p; // create an iterator
  int i;

  // assign elements in vector a value
  p = v.begin();
  i = 0;
  while(p != v.end()) {
    *p = i; // assign i to v through p
    p++; // advance the iterator
    i++;
  }

  // display contents of vector
  cout << "Original contents:\n";
  p = v.begin();
  while(p != v.end()) {
    cout << *p << " ";
    p++;
  }
  cout << "\n\n";
```

```
// change contents of vector
p = v.begin();
while(p != v.end()) {
  *p = *p * 2;
  p++;
}

// display contents of vector
cout << "Modified Contents:\n";
p = v.begin();
while(p != v.end()) {
  cout << *p << " ";
  p++;
}
cout << endl;

return 0;
}
```

The output from this program is shown here:

```
Original contents:
0 1 2 3 4 5 6 7 8 9

Modified Contents:
0 2 4 6 8 10 12 14 16 18
```

In the program, notice how the iterator **p** is declared. The type **iterator** is defined by the container classes. Thus, to obtain an iterator for a particular container, you will use a declaration similar to that shown in the example: simply qualify **iterator** with the name of the container. In the program, **p** is initialized to point to the start of the vector by using the **begin( )** member function. This iterator can then be used to access the vector an element at a time by incrementing it as needed. This process is directly parallel to the way a pointer can be used to access the elements of an array. To determine when the end of the vector has been reached, the **end( )** member function is employed. Thus, when **p** equals **v.end( )**, the end of the vector has been encountered.

The **iterator** type is defined by each of the containers.

While the preceding program demonstrates the use of an iterator to access the elements of a vector, the same general principle can be applied to any container.

Understanding end( )

The **end( )**
function returns
an iterator that
points one
element past
the end of the
container.

Now is a good time to explain a somewhat unexpected attribute of the **end( )** container function. **end( )** does not return a pointer to the last element in a container. Instead, it returns a pointer *one past* the last element. Thus, the last element in a container is pointed to by **end( )** – 1. As the previous example showed, this feature allows us to write very efficient algorithms that cycle through all of the elements of a container, including the last one, using an iterator. When the iterator has the same value as the one returned by **end( )**, we know that all elements have been accessed. However, you must keep this feature in mind since it may seem a bit counterintuitive. For example, consider the following program, which displays a vector forward and backward:

```
// Understanding end().
#include <iostream>
#include <vector>
using namespace std;

int main()
{
  vector<int> v; // create an empty vector
  int i;

  for(i=0; i<10; i++) v.push_back(i);

  cout << "Vector printed forwards:\n";
  vector<int>::iterator p = v.begin();
  while(p != v.end()) {
    cout << *p << " ";
    p++;
  }
  cout << "\n\n";

  cout << "Vector printed backwards:\n";
  p = v.end();
  while(p != v.begin()) {
    p--; // decrement iterator before using
    cout << *p << " ";
  }

  return 0;
}
```

The output produced by this program is shown here:

```
Vector printed forwards:
  0 1 2 3 4 5 6 7 8 9

Vector printed backwards:
  9 8 7 6 5 4 3 2 1 0
```

The code that displays the vector in the forward direction is the same as the earlier example. But pay special attention to the code that displays the vector in reverse order. The iterator **p** is initially set to the end of the vector through the use of the **end( )** function. Since **end( )** returns an iterator to an object that is one past the last object actually stored in the list, **p** must be decremented before it is used. This is why **p** is decremented before rather than after the **cout** statement inside the loop. Remember: **end( )** does not return a pointer to the last object in the container; rather, it returns a pointer that is one past the last value.

Using Iterators

A range is a subset of a sequence.

The role of iterators in the STL must not be understated. Iterators are used by the STL's algorithms and by many of the container member functions. For example, the **vector** member functions **insert( )** and **erase( )** both use iterators to point to the location at which elements are inserted or deleted. To program using the STL implies the use of iterators, so it is good to become comfortable with them from the start. Fortunately, since they directly parallel pointers, most readers will have no trouble.

A pair of iterators is frequently used to define a *range* within a container, with one iterator pointing to the start and the other to the end. For example, consider this version of the **erase( )** function defined by **vector**:

iterator erase(iterator *start*, iterator *end*);

Here, *start* points to the first element in the range to erase and *end* points to the last element. As you will see, ranges specified by iterators are very common in STL programming.

The following program demonstrates **vector::insert( )** and **vector::erase( )**. Pay close attention to the use of the iterators.

```
// Demonstrate insert and erase.
#include <iostream>
#include <vector>
using namespace std;
```

```cpp
int main()
{
  vector<char> v(10);
  vector<char> v2;
  char str[] = "<Vector>";
  int i;

  // initialize v
  for(i=0; i<10; i++) v[i] = i + 'a';

  // copy characters in str into v2
  for(i=0; str[i]; i++) v2.push_back(str[i]);

  // display original contents of vector
  cout << "Original contents of v:\n";
  for(i=0; i<v.size(); i++) cout << v[i] << " ";
  cout << "\n\n";

  vector<char>::iterator p = v.begin();
  p += 2; // point to 3rd element

  // insert 10 X's into v
  v.insert(p, 10, 'X');

  // display contents after insertion
  cout << "Size after inserting X's = " << v.size() << endl;
  cout << "Contents after insert:\n";
  for(i=0; i<v.size(); i++) cout << v[i] << " ";
  cout << "\n\n";

  // remove those elements
  p = v.begin();
  p += 2; // point to 3rd element
  v.erase(p, p+10); // remove next 10 elements

  // display contents after deletion
  cout << "Size after erase = " << v.size() << endl;
  cout << "Contents after erase:\n";
  for(i=0; i<v.size(); i++) cout << v[i] << " ";
  cout << "\n\n";
```

```
    // Insert v2 into v
    v.insert(p, v2.begin(), v2.end());
    cout << "Size after v2's insertion = ";
    cout << v.size() << endl;
    cout << "Contents after insert:\n";
    for(i=0; i<v.size(); i++) cout << v[i] << " ";
    cout << endl;

    return 0;
}
```

2

This program produces the following output:

```
Original contents of v:
a b c d e f g h i j

Size after inserting X's = 20
Contents after insert:
a b X X X X X X X X X X c d e f g h i j

Size after erase = 10
Contents after erase:
a b c d e f g h i j

Size after v2's insertion = 18
Contents after insert:
a b < V e c t o r > c d e f g h i j
```

This program demonstrates two forms of **insert( )**. The first time it is used, it inserts ten X's into **v**. The second time, it inserts the contents of a second vector, **v2**, into **v**. This second use is the most interesting. It takes three iterator arguments. The first specifies the point at which the insertion will occur within the invoking container. The last two point to the beginning and ending of the range to be inserted.

The characters inserted by the first call to **insert( )** are removed by the form of **erase( )** just described. It is called with iterators that point to the beginning and end of the range of characters to be removed.

A Second Container

Although the STL's containers have distinctive, unique traits, they all share many similarities. This is part of what makes the STL a cohesive subsystem whose individual components can work together. To illustrate some of the similarities and differences between containers, we will look at another of the sequence containers: **list**.

The **list** class supports a bidirectional, linear list. Like a vector, a list is a dynamic container that can grow or shrink during use. Unlike **vector**, which supports random access, **list** can be accessed sequentially only. Since lists are bidirectional, they may be accessed front to back or back to front.

A **list** has this template specification. Notice that it is quite similar to the specification for **vector**.

> template <class T, class Allocator = allocator<T> > class list

Here, **T** is the type of data stored in the list. The allocator is specified by **Allocator**, which defaults to the standard allocator. Here are two of **list**'s constructors:

> explicit list(const Allocator &*a* = Allocator( ));

> explicit list(size_type *num*, const T &*val* = T ( ),
>   const Allocator &*a* = Allocator( ));

The first form constructs an empty list. The second form constructs a list that has *num* elements with the value *val*, which can be allowed to default. To use **list** in a program, you must include **<list>**.

The following comparison operators are defined for **list**:

> ==, <, <=, !=, >, >=

Some of the commonly used **list** member functions are shown in Table 2-3. Notice that several of the functions are similar to those supported by **vector**. Since both are sequence containers, they have many operations in common. For example, both provide **begin( )** and **end( )**. Of course, **list** defines some member functions that are not defined by **vector**, which makes sense because **vector** and **list** implement two different types of data structures.

Member	Description
iterator begin( );	Returns an iterator to the first element in the list.
bool empty( ) const;	Returns **true** if the invoking list is empty and **false** otherwise.
iterator end( );	Returns an iterator to the end of the list.
iterator erase(iterator *i*);	Removes the element pointed to by *i*. Returns an iterator to the element after the one removed.
iterator erase(iterator *start*, iterator *end*);	Removes the elements in the range *start* to *end*. Returns an iterator to the element after the last element removed.
iterator insert(iterator *i*, const T &*val*);	Inserts *val* immediately before the element specified by *i*. An iterator to the element is returned.
void insert(iterator *i*, size_type *num*, const T &*val*)	Inserts *num* copies of *val* immediately before the element specified by *i*.
template <class InIter> void insert(iterator *i*, InIter *start*, InIter *end*);	Inserts the sequence defined by *start* and *end* immediately before the element specified by *i*.
void merge(list<T, Allocator> &*ob*); template <class Comp> void merge(list<T, Allocator> &*ob*, Comp *cmpfn*);	Merges the ordered list contained in *ob* with the ordered invoking list. The result is ordered. After the merge, the list contained in *ob* is empty. In the second form, a comparison function can be specified that determines when one element is less than another.
void pop_back( );	Removes the last element in the list.
void pop_front( );	Removes the first element in the list.
void push_back(const T &*val*);	Adds an element with the value specified by *val* to the end of the list.

Some Commonly Used **list** Member Functions
Table 2-3.

Member	Description
void push_front(const T &*val*);	Adds an element with the value specified by *val* to the front of the list.
size_type size( ) const;	Returns the number of elements currently in the list.

void sort( );
template <class Comp>
  void sort(Comp *cmpfn*);
	Sorts the list. The second form sorts the list using the comparison function *cmpfn* to determine when one element is less than another.

void splice(iterator *i*, list<T, Allocator> &*ob*);	The contents of *ob* are inserted into the invoking list at the location pointed to by *i*. After the operation, *ob* is empty.

void splice(iterator *i*,
    list<T, Allocator> &*ob*,
    iterator *el*);
	The element pointed to by *el* is removed from the list *ob* and stored in the invoking list at the location pointed to by *i*.

void splice(iterator *i*,
    list<T, Allocator> &ob,
    iterator *start*, iterator *end*);
	The range defined by *start* and *end* is removed from *ob* and stored in the invoking list beginning at the location pointed to by *i*.

Some Commonly Used **list** Member Functions *(continued)*

Table 2-3.

Syntactically, the **list** class is used in much the same way as **vector**. Many of the programming constructs that apply to one can be applied to the other. For example, here is a simple program that uses **list**. As you can see, much of the code in this program is similar to that found in the **vector** examples.

```cpp
// Using a list.
#include <iostream>
#include <list>
using namespace std;

int main()
{
```

```
list<int> lst; // create an empty list
int i;

for(i=0; i<10; i++) lst.push_back(i);

cout << "Size = " << lst.size() << endl;

cout << "Contents: ";
list<int>::iterator p = lst.begin();
while(p != lst.end()) {
  cout << *p << " ";
  p++;
}
cout << "\n\n";

// change contents of list
p = lst.begin();
while(p != lst.end()) {
  *p = *p + 100;
  p++;
}

cout << "Contents modified: ";
p = lst.begin();
while(p != lst.end()) {
  cout << *p << " ";
  p++;
}

  return 0;
}
```

The output produced by this program is shown here:

```
Size = 10
Contents: 0 1 2 3 4 5 6 7 8 9

Contents modified: 100 101 102 103 104 105 106 107 108 109
```

This program creates a list of integers. First, an empty **list** object is created. Next, ten integers are put into the list. This is accomplished using the **push_back( )** function, which puts each new value on the end of the existing list. Next, the size of the list and the list itself are displayed. Then, the contents of the list are modified and displayed again.

Notice that the list is displayed via an iterator, using the following code:

```
list<int>::iterator p = lst.begin();
while(p != lst.end()) {
  cout << *p << " ";
  p++;
}
```

Here, the iterator **p** is initialized to point to the start of the list. Each time through the loop, **p** is incremented, causing it to point to the next element. The loop ends when **p** points to the end of the list. This code is essentially the same as was used to cycle through a vector using an iterator. Loops like this are common in STL code, and the fact that the same constructs can be used to access different types of containers is part of the power of the STL.

Lists vs. Vectors

As the preceding example illustrates, the general techniques that you used to work with **vector** also apply to **list**. Because of the way the STL is designed, for many operations, using one container is much like using another. Of course, different containers support differing data structures and this means that not all operations that apply to one will apply to all. Thus, while lists and vectors have much in common, they also differ in several regards. The biggest difference is, of course, that you can index a vector, but not a list.

Lists and vectors differ in other, less dramatic ways, too. For example, lists can be spliced and merged using **list** member functions. No such functions are defined by **vector**. To illustrate these capabilities, the following program demonstrates the **merge( )** and **splice( )** functions defined by **list**:

```
// Merge and splice lists.
#include <iostream>
#include <list>
using namespace std;

int main()
{
  list<char> lst1, lst2, lst3;
  int i;

  for(i=0; i<10; i+=2) lst1.push_back(i + 'A');
  for(i=1; i<11; i+=2) lst2.push_back(i + 'A');
```

```
  cout << "Contents of lst1:\n";
  list<char>::iterator p = lst1.begin();
  while(p != lst1.end()) {
    cout << *p << " ";
    p++;
  }
  cout << "\n\n";

  cout << "Contents of lst2:\n";
  p = lst2.begin();
  while(p != lst2.end()) {
    cout << *p << " ";
    p++;
  }
  cout << "\n\n";

  // now, merge the two lists
  lst1.merge(lst2);
  if(lst2.empty())
    cout << "lst2 is now empty\n";

  cout << "Contents of lst1 after merge:\n";
  p = lst1.begin();
  while(p != lst1.end()) {
    cout << *p << " ";
    p++;
  }
  cout << "\n\n";

  // create another list using push_front()
  char str[] = "-splicing-";
  for(i=0; str[i]; i++) lst3.push_back(str[i]);

  cout << "Contents of lst3:\n";
  p = lst3.begin();
  while(p != lst3.end()) {
    cout << *p << " ";
    p++;
  }
  cout << "\n\n";

  // now, splice the two lists
  p = lst1.begin();
  while(p != lst1.end()) {
    if(*p == 'F') lst1.splice(p, lst3);
```

```
  p++;
}

cout << "Contents of lst1 after splice:\n";
p = lst1.begin();
while(p != lst1.end()) {
  cout << *p << " ";
  p++;
}

return 0;
}
```

The output from this program is shown here:

```
Contents of lst1:
A C E G I

Contents of lst2:
B D F H J

lst2 is now empty
Contents of lst1 after merge:
A B C D E F G H I J

Contents of lst3:
- s p l i c i n g -

Contents of lst1 after splice:
A B C D E - s p l i c i n g - F G H I J
```

When the program begins, two lists of characters are created that contain alternating characters of the alphabet. These two lists are then merged into one through the use of **merge( )**. Two lists can be merged only if both are in sorted order. The result is an ordered list that contains the contents of the two original lists. The new list is left in the invoking list and the merged list is left empty.

The program next creates a third list that contains unsorted characters that comprise the string "-splicing-". This list is then spliced into **lst1** immediately before the letter F. Sorted lists are not required when splicing lists. The outcome of the splice is left in the invoking list and the spliced list is left empty.

Another difference between **list** and **vector** is found in how elements can be pushed onto and popped from an object. The **vector** class defines only the **push_back( )** and **pop_back( )** functions, which allow elements to be added to or removed from the end of a vector. While still supporting these functions, **list** adds **push_front( )** and **pop_front( )**, which allow you to add elements to or remove elements from the start of a list. The following program illustrates the difference:

```cpp
/* Demonstrating the difference between
   push_back() and push_front(). */
#include <iostream>
#include <list>
using namespace std;

int main()
{
  list<int> lst1, lst2;
  int i;

  for(i=0; i<10; i++) lst1.push_back(i);
  for(i=0; i<10; i++) lst2.push_front(i);

  list<int>::iterator p;

  cout << "Contents of lst1:\n";
  p = lst1.begin();
  while(p != lst1.end()) {
    cout << *p << " ";
    p++;
  }
  cout << "\n\n";

  cout << "Contents of lst2:\n";
  p = lst2.begin();
  while(p != lst2.end()) {
    cout << *p << " ";
    p++;
  }

  return 0;
}
```

2

The output produced by this program is shown here:

```
Contents of lst1:
0 1 2 3 4 5 6 7 8 9

Contents of lst2:
9 8 7 6 5 4 3 2 1 0
```

Since **lst2** is built by putting elements onto its front, the resulting list is in the reverse order of **lst1**, which is built by putting elements onto its end.

There is one other difference between vectors and lists that is not apparent on the surface: the type of operations that may be performed on iterators. As mentioned, the **iterator** type defined by **vector** is random access. This means that it allows the full range of pointer operations, including the addition of an integer. However, the **iterator** type defined by **list** is bidirectional. This means that it allows only increment or decrement operations. For example, consider the following:

```
list<int> lst;
vector<int> v;
list<int>::iterator lp;
vector<int>::iterator vp;

// ...

lp = lst.begin();
lp++; // OK
//   lp += 2; // Error!

vp = v.begin();
vp++; // OK
vp += 2; // OK, too
```

Here, both iterators can be incremented, but only **vp** can have an integer added to it. Thus, while the addition of 2 to **vp** is perfectly valid, it is not allowed on **lp**.

The reason that **list** and **vector** define **iterator** differently is because the fundamental capabilities of the two containers differ. A **vector** is a random-access object. A **list** is a sequential object. Requiring **list** to support random-access iterators, while possible, would introduce substantial inefficiencies. Thus, each container defines the type of iterator that is most appropriate.

Although we have only compared **vector** and **list**, the same general pattern of similarities and differences will be found between any two containers. All containers share a certain fundamental set of traits that make them containers, but each defines its own unique characteristics.

Algorithms

2

Algorithms act on containers. Although each container provides support for its own basic operations, the standard algorithms provide more extended or complex actions. They also allow you to work with two different types of containers at the same time. To have access to the STL algorithms, you must include **<algorithm>** in your program.

The STL defines a large number of algorithms, which are summarized in Table 2-4. All of the algorithms are template functions. This means that they can be applied to any type of container. Although we will examine the algorithms in detail later in this book, their general operation and principles are described here. In the process, a few representative algorithms are demonstrated.

Algorithm	Purpose
adjacent_find	Searches for adjacent matching elements within a sequence and returns an iterator to the first match.
binary_search	Performs a binary search on an ordered sequence.
copy	Copies a sequence.
copy_backward	Same as **copy( )** except that it moves the elements from the end of the sequence first.
count	Returns the number of elements in the sequence.
count_if	Returns the number of elements in the sequence that satisfy some predicate.

The STL
Algorithms
Table 2-4.

Algorithm	Purpose
equal	Determines if two ranges are the same.
equal_range	Returns a range in which an element can be inserted into a sequence without disrupting the ordering of the sequence.
fill and fill_n	Fills a range with the specified value.
find	Searches a range for a value and returns an iterator to the first occurrence of the element.
find_end	Searches a range for a subsequence. It returns an iterator to the end of the subsequence within the range.
find_first_of	Finds the first element within a sequence that matches an element within a range.
find_if	Searches a range for an element for which a user-defined unary predicate returns true.
for_each	Applies a function to a range of elements.
generate and generate_n	Assign elements in a range of the values returned by a generator function.
includes	Determines if one sequence includes all of the elements in another sequence.
inplace_merge	Merges a range with another range. Both ranges must be sorted in increasing order. The resulting sequence is sorted.
iter_swap	Exchanges the values pointed to by its two iterator arguments.

The STL
Algorithms
(continued)
Table 2-4.

Algorithm	Purpose
lexicographical_compare	Alphabetically compares one sequence with another.
lower_bound	Finds the first point in the sequence that is not less than a specified value.
make_heap	Constructs a heap from a sequence.
max	Returns the maximum of two values.
max_element	Returns an iterator to the maximum element within a range.
merge	Merges two ordered sequences, placing the result into a third sequence.
min	Returns the minimum of two values.
min_element	Returns an iterator to the minimum element within a range.
mismatch	Finds the first mismatch between the elements in two sequences. Iterators to the two elements are returned.
next_permutation	Constructs next permutation of a sequence.
nth_element	Arranges a sequence such that all elements less than a specified element *E* come before that element and all elements greater than *E* come after it.
partial_sort	Sorts a range.
partial_sort_copy	Sorts a range and then copies as many elements as will fit into a resulting sequence.
partition	Arranges a sequence such that all elements for which a predicate returns true come before those for which the predicate returns false.

2

The STL
Algorithms
(continued)
Table 2-4.

Algorithm	Purpose
pop_heap	Exchanges the first and last-1 elements and then rebuilds the heap.
prev_permutation	Constructs previous permutation of a sequence.
push_heap	Pushes an element onto the end of a heap.
random_shuffle	Randomizes a sequence.
remove, remove_if, remove_copy, and remove_copy_if	Removes elements from a specified range.
replace, replace_copy, replace_if, and replace_copy_if	Replaces elements within a range.
reverse and reverse_copy	Reverses the order of a range.
rotate and rotate_copy	Left-rotates the elements in a range.
search	Searches for subsequence within a sequence.
search_n	Searches for a sequence of a specified number of similar elements
set_difference	Produces a sequence that contains the difference between two ordered sets.
set_intersection	Produces a sequence that contains the intersection of the two ordered sets.
set_symmetric_difference	Produces a sequence that contains the symmetric difference between the two ordered sets.
set_union	Produces a sequence that contains the union of the two ordered sets.
sort	Sorts a range.
sort_heap	Sorts a heap within a specified range.

The STL Algorithms *(continued)*

Table 2-4.

2

Algorithm	Purpose
stable_partition	Arranges a sequence such that all elements for which a predicate returns true come before those for which the predicate returns false. The partitioning is stable. This means that the relative ordering of the sequence is preserved.
stable_sort	Sorts a range. The sort is stable. This means that equal elements are not rearranged.
swap	Exchanges two values.
swap_ranges	Exchanges elements in a range.
transform	Applies a function to a range of elements and stores the outcome in a new sequence.
unique and unique_copy	Eliminates duplicate elements from range.
upper_bound	Finds the last point in a sequence that is not greater than some value.

The STL
Algorithms
(continued)
Table 2-4.

Counting

One of the most basic operations that you can perform on a sequence is to count its contents. To do this you can use either **count( )** or **count_if( )**. Their general forms are shown here:

```
template <class InIter, class T>
    size_t count(InIter start, InIter end, const T &val);

template <class InIter, class UnPred>
    size_t count_if(InIter start, InIter end, UnPred pfn);
```

The **count( )** algorithm returns the number of elements that match *val* in the sequence beginning at *start* and ending at *end*. The **count_if( )** algorithm returns the number of elements in the sequence beginning at *start* and ending at *end* for which the unary predicate *pfn* returns true. Recall that a unary predicate is a function that takes one parameter and returns a true/false result.

Notice that the prototypes of **count( )** and **count_if( )** specify that *start* and *end* must be input iterators. As explained, an iterator that has greater access capabilities can be used in place of one that has lesser capabilities. For example, a forward iterator can be used in place of an input iterator. The **iterator** types specified by all of the various STL containers are suitable for use by **count( )**.

The following program demonstrates **count( )**:

```
// Demonstrate count().
#include <iostream>
#include <vector>
#include <cstdlib>
#include <algorithm>
using namespace std;

int main()
{
  vector<bool> v;
  int i;

  for(i=0; i < 10; i++) {
   if(rand() % 2) v.push_back(true);
   else v.push_back(false);
  }

  cout << "Sequence:\n";
  for(i=0; i<v.size(); i++)
    cout << boolalpha << v[i] << " ";
  cout << endl;

  i = count(v.begin(), v.end(), true);
  cout << i << " elements are true.\n";

  return 0;
}
```

This program displays the following output:

```
Sequence:
true true false false true false false false false false
3 elements are true.
```

The program begins by creating a vector comprised of randomly generated true and false values. Next, **count( )** is used to count the number of true values.

This next program demonstrates **count_if( )**. It creates a vector containing the numbers 1 through 19. It then counts those that are even. To do this, it creates a unary predicate called **isEven( )** that returns true if its argument is even.

```cpp
// Demonstrate count_if().
#include <iostream>
#include <vector>
#include <algorithm>
using namespace std;

/* This is a unary predicate that determines
   if number is even. */
bool isEven(int i)
{
  return !(i%2);

  return false;
}

int main()
{
  vector<int> v;
  int i;

  for(i=1; i < 20; i++) v.push_back(i);

  cout << "Sequence:\n";
  for(i=0; i<v.size(); i++)
    cout << v[i] << " ";
  cout << endl;

  i = count_if(v.begin(), v.end(), isEven);
  cout << i << " numbers are evenly divisible by 2.\n";

  return 0;
}
```

This program produces the following output:

```
Sequence:
1 2 3 4 5 6 7 8 9 10 11 12 13 14 15 16 17 18 19
9 numbers are evenly divisible by 2.
```

Notice how the unary predicate **isEven( )** is coded. All unary predicates receive as a parameter an object that is of the same type as that stored in the container upon which the predicate is operating. The predicate must then return a true or false result based upon this object.

Removing and Replacing Elements

Sometimes it is useful to generate a new sequence that consists of only certain items from an original sequence. One algorithm that does this is **remove_copy( )**. Its general form is shown here:

> template <class InIter, class OutIter, class T>
>   OutIter remove_copy(InIter *start*, InIter *end*,
>   OutIter *result*, const T &*val*);

The **remove_copy( )** algorithm copies elements from the specified range, removing those that are equal to *val*. It puts the result into the sequence pointed to by *result* and returns an iterator to the end of the result. The output container must be large enough to hold the result.

To replace one element in a sequence with another when a copy is made, use **replace_copy( )**. Its general form is shown here:

> template <class InIter, class OutIter, class T>
>   OutIter replace_copy(InIter *start*, InIter *end*,
>   OutIter *result*, const T &*old*, const T &*new*);

The **replace_copy( )** algorithm copies elements from the specified range, replacing elements equal to *old* with *new*. It puts the result into the sequence pointed to by *result* and returns an iterator to the end of the result. The output container must be large enough to hold the result.

The following program demonstrates **remove_copy( )** and **replace_copy( )**. It creates a sequence of characters. It then removes all of the spaces from the sequence. Next, it replaces all spaces with + signs.

```cpp
// Demonstrate remove_copy and replace_copy.
#include <iostream>
#include <vector>
#include <algorithm>
using namespace std;

int main()
{
  char str[]="Algorithms operate on containers through iterators.";
  vector<char> v, v2(100);
  vector<char>::iterator p;
  int i;

  for(i=0; str[i]; i++) v.push_back(str[i]);

  // **** demonstrate remove_copy ****
  cout << "Input sequence:\n";
  for(i=0; i<v.size(); i++) cout << v[i];
  cout << endl;

  // remove all spaces
  p = remove_copy(v.begin(), v.end(), v2.begin(), ' ');

  cout << "Result after removing spaces:\n";
  for(i=0; i<p-v2.begin(); i++) cout << v2[i];
  cout << "\n\n";

  // **** now, demonstrate replace_copy ****
  cout << "Input sequence:\n";
  for(i=0; i<v.size(); i++) cout << v[i];
  cout << endl;

  // replace spaces with +'s
  p = replace_copy(v.begin(), v.end(), v2.begin(), ' ', '+');

  cout << "Result after replacing spaces with +'s:\n";
  for(i=0; i<p-v2.begin(); i++) cout << v2[i];
  cout << "\n\n";

  return 0;
}
```

2

The output produced by this program is shown here:

```
Input sequence:
Algorithms operate on containers through iterators.
Result after removing spaces:
Algorithmsoperateoncontainersthroughiterators.

Input sequence:
Algorithms operate on containers through iterators.
Result after replacing spaces with +'s:
Algorithms+operate+on+containers+through+iterators.
```

Reversing a Sequence

An often useful algorithm is **reverse( )**, which reverses a sequence. Its general form is

> template <class BiIter> void reverse(BiIter *start*, BiIter *end*);

The **reverse( )** algorithm reverses the order of the range specified by *start* and *end*.

The following program demonstrates **reverse( )**:

```cpp
// Demonstrate reverse.
#include <iostream>
#include <vector>
#include <algorithm>
using namespace std;

int main()
{
  vector<int> v;
  int i;

  for(i=0; i<10; i++) v.push_back(i);

  cout << "Initial: ";
  for(i=0; i<v.size(); i++) cout << v[i] << " ";
  cout << endl;

  reverse(v.begin(), v.end());
```

```
    cout << "Reversed: ";
    for(i=0; i<v.size(); i++) cout << v[i] << " ";

    return 0;
}
```

The output from this program is shown here:

```
Initial:  0 1 2 3 4 5 6 7 8 9
Reversed: 9 8 7 6 5 4 3 2 1 0
```

Transforming a Sequence

One of the more interesting algorithms is **transform( )**. It modifies each element in a range according to a function that you provide. The **transform( )** algorithm has these two general forms:

> template <class InIter, class OutIter, class Func)
>   OutIter transform(InIter *start*, InIter *end*, OutIter *result*, Func *unaryfunc*);

> template <class InIter1, class InIter2, class OutIter, class Func)
>   OutIter transform(InIter1 *start1*, InIter1 *end1*, InIter2 *start2*,
>   OutIter *result*, Func *binaryfunc*);

The **transform( )** algorithm applies a function to a range of elements and stores the outcome in *result*. In the first form, the range is specified by *start* and *end*. The function to be applied is specified by *unaryfunc.* This function receives the value of an element in its parameter, and it must return its transformation. In the second form, the transformation is applied using a binary operator function that receives the value of an element from the sequence to be transformed in its first parameter and an element from the second sequence as its second parameter. Both versions return an iterator to the end of the resulting sequence.

The following program uses a simple transformation function called **reciprocal( )** to transform the contents of a list of numbers into their reciprocals. Notice that the resulting sequence is stored in the same list that provided the original sequence.

```
// An example of the transform algorithm.
#include <iostream>
#include <list>
#include <algorithm>
using namespace std;
```

```
// A simple transformation function.
double reciprocal(double i) {
  return 1.0/i; // return reciprocal
}

int main()
{
  list<double> vals;
  int i;

  // put values into list
  for(i=1; i<10; i++) vals.push_back((double)i);

  cout << "Original contents of vals:\n";
  list<double>::iterator p = vals.begin();
  while(p != vals.end()) {
    cout << *p << " ";
    p++;
  }

  cout << endl;

  // transform vals
  p = transform(vals.begin(), vals.end(),
                vals.begin(), reciprocal);

  cout << "Transformed contents of vals:\n";
  p = vals.begin();
  while(p != vals.end()) {
    cout << *p << " ";
    p++;
  }

  return 0;
}
```

The output produced by the program is shown here:

```
Original contents of vals:
1 2 3 4 5 6 7 8 9
Transformed contents of vals:
1 0.5 0.333333 0.25 0.2 0.166667 0.142857 0.125 0.111111
```

As you can see, each element in **vals** has been transformed into its reciprocal.

IN DEPTH

The Power of Algorithms

Part of the power of the STL comes from the fact that many of its algorithms operate through iterators. In some cases, this fact allows operations on two different containers at the same time. For example, consider the **copy( )** algorithm, which has this prototype:

```
template <class InIter, class OutIter>
        OutIter copy(InIter start, InIter end, OutIter result);
```

This algorithm copies the range defined by *start* and *end* into the target sequence beginning at *result*. It returns a pointer to the end of the resulting sequence. But here is the important point: there is no requirement that *result* point into the same container as *start* and *end*. Thus, using **copy( )**, you can copy the contents of one type of container into another. For example, the following program copies the contents of a list into a vector:

```cpp
// Copy a list to a vector.
#include <iostream>
#include <vector>
#include <list>
#include <algorithm>
using namespace std;

int main()
{
  vector<char> v(20);
  list<char> lst;
  int i;

  // initialize vector
  for(i=0; i<20; i++) v[i] = 'A' + i;

  cout << "Original contents of vector:\n";
  for(i=0; i<v.size(); i++) cout << v[i] << " ";
  cout << "\n\n";
```

IN DEPTH

CONTINUED

```
// initialize list
char str[] = "-STL Power-";
for(i = 0; str[i]; i++) lst.push_back(str[i]);

// copy lst into v
copy(lst.begin(), lst.end(), v.begin());

// display result
cout << "Contents of vector after copy:\n";
for(i=0; i<v.size(); i++) cout << v[i] << " ";

return 0;
}
```

The output produced by this program is shown here:

```
Original contents of vector:
A B C D E F G H I J K L M N O P Q R S T

Contents of vector after copy:
- S T L   P o w e r - L M N O P Q R S T
```

As you can see, the contents of **lst** are copied into **v**, overwriting the first part of its original contents. Even though **lst** and **v** are different containers, through the use of iterators **copy( )** is able to make them work together.

As you learn more about the STL, you will find that iterators are the glue that holds it together. They offer a convenient means of working with two or more STL objects at the same time.

Function Objects

The last component that we will look at before starting our in-depth examination of the STL is the function object. The STL supports (and extensively utilizes) function objects. Recall that function objects are simply classes that define **operator( )**. The STL provides many built-in function objects, such as **less**, **minus**, etc. You can also define your own function objects, but you will have to wait until later to learn how. It is, however, quite easy to use the built-in ones.

Unary and Binary Function Objects

Just as there are unary and binary predicates, there are unary and binary function objects. A unary function object requires one argument; a binary function object requires two. You must use the correct type of object. For example, if an algorithm is expecting a binary predicate, you must pass it a binary function object.

Using the Built-in Function Objects

The STL provides a rich assortment of built-in function objects. The binary function objects are shown here:

plus	minus	multiplies	divides	modulus
equal_to	not_equal_to	greater	greater_equal	less
less_equal	logical_and	logical_or		

Here are the unary function objects:

logical_not	negate

The function objects perform the operations specified by their names. The only one that may not be self-evident is **negate,** which reverses the sign of its argument.

The built-in function objects are template classes that overload **operator( )**, which returns the result of the specified operation on whatever type of data you select. When a container function or algorithm requires a function object, you can pass it one by calling the function object's default constructor. For example, to construct the binary function object **plus** for use on **float**, use this syntax:

```
plus<float>()
```

The built-in function objects use the header **<functional>**.

Here is an example that uses a unary function object. The following program uses the **transform( )** algorithm (described in the preceding section) and the **negate** function object to reverse the sign of a list of values:

```
// Use a unary function object.
#include <iostream>
#include <list>
#include <functional>
#include <algorithm>
using namespace std;

int main()
{
  list<double> vals;
  int i;

  // put values into list
  for(i=1; i<10; i++) vals.push_back((double)i);

  cout << "Original contents of vals:\n";
  list<double>::iterator p = vals.begin();
  while(p != vals.end()) {
    cout << *p << " ";
    p++;
  }
  cout << endl;

  // use the negate function object
  p = transform(vals.begin(), vals.end(),
                vals.begin(),
                negate<double>()); // use function object

  cout << "Negated contents of vals:\n";
  p = vals.begin();
```

```
    while(p != vals.end()) {
      cout << *p << " ";
      p++;
    }

    return 0;
}
```

This program produces the following output:

```
Original contents of vals:
1 2 3 4 5 6 7 8 9
Negated contents of vals:
-1 -2 -3 -4 -5 -6 -7 -8 -9
```

In the program, notice how **negate** is used. Since **vals** is a list of **double** values, **negate** is passed using **negate<double>( )**. The **transform( )** algorithm automatically calls **negate::operator( )** for each element in the sequence. Thus, the single parameter to **negate::operator( )** receives as its argument an element from the sequence.

The next program demonstrates the use of the binary function object, **divides**. It creates two lists of **double** values and has one divide the other. This program uses the binary form of the **transform( )** algorithm.

```
// Use a binary function object.
#include <iostream>
#include <list>
#include <functional>
#include <algorithm>
using namespace std;

int main()
{
  list<double> vals;
  list<double> divisors;
  int i;

  // put values into list
  for(i=10; i<100; i+=10) vals.push_back((double)i);
  for(i=1; i<10; i++) divisors.push_back(3.0);

  cout << "Original contents of vals:\n";
  list<double>::iterator p = vals.begin();
```

```
while(p != vals.end()) {
  cout << *p << " ";
  p++;
}

cout << endl;

// transform vals
p = transform(vals.begin(), vals.end(),
              divisors.begin(), vals.begin(),
              divides<double>()); // use function object

cout << "Divided contents of vals:\n";
p = vals.begin();
while(p != vals.end()) {
  cout << *p << " ";
  p++;
}

return 0;
}
```

The output from this program is shown here:

```
Original contents of vals:
10 20 30 40 50 60 70 80 90
Divided contents of vals:
3.33333 6.66667 10 13.3333 16.6667 20 23.3333 26.6667 30
```

In this case, the binary function object **divides** divides the elements from the first sequence by their corresponding elements from the second sequence. Thus, **divides::operator( )** receives arguments in this order: *first, second.* This order can be generalized. Whenever a binary function object is used, its arguments are ordered *first, second.*

CHAPTER 3

The deque Container

Beginning here and extending through the next several chapters we will examine the STL container classes in detail. We will begin our tour with the most general-purpose container: **deque**. The **deque** class implements a double-ended queue. This means that elements can be pushed onto both the front and rear of the container. (Elements can also be inserted into the middle.) Because of **deque**'s flexibility, it is used as the default container that underlies the container adaptors **queue** and **stack**.

deque Fundamentals

The template specification for **deque** is

    template <class T, class Allocator = allocator<T> > class deque

Here, **T** is the type of data stored in the **deque** and **Allocator** specifies the allocator, which defaults to the standard allocator. Here are **deque**'s constructors:

    explicit deque(const Allocator &a = Allocator( ));

    explicit deque(size_type num, const T &val = T ( ),
        const Allocator &a = Allocator( ));

    deque(const deque<T, Allocator> &ob);

    template <class InIter> deque(InIter start, InIter end,
        const Allocator &a = Allocator( ));

The first form constructs an empty deque. The second form constructs a deque that has *num* elements with the value *val*. The third form constructs a deque that contains the same elements as *ob*. This is **deque**'s copy constructor. The fourth form constructs a deque that contains the elements in the range specified by *start* and *end*. To use **deque** include **<deque>**.

The **deque** class defines the assignment operator and the following comparison operators:

    ==, <, <=, !=, >, >=

deque supports random-access iterators and the **[ ]** is overloaded. This means that a **deque** object can be indexed like an array. **deque** contains the member functions shown in Table 3-1.

Member	Description
template <class InIter> void assign(InIter *start*, InIter *end*);	Assigns the deque the sequence defined by *start* and *end*.
void assign(size_type *num*, const T &*val*);	Assigns the deque *num* elements of value *val*.
reference at(size_type *i*); const_reference at(size_type *i*) const;	Returns a reference to the specified element specified by *i*.
reference back( ); const_reference back( ) const;	Returns a reference to the last element in the deque.
iterator begin( ); const_iterator begin( ) const;	Returns an iterator to the first element in the deque.
void clear( );	Removes all elements from the deque.
bool empty( ) const;	Returns **true** if the invoking deque is empty and **false** otherwise.
const_iterator end( ) const; iterator end( );	Returns an iterator to the end of the deque.
iterator erase(iterator *i*);	Removes the element pointed to by *i*. Returns an iterator to the element after the one removed.
iterator erase(iterator *start*, iterator *end*);	Removes the elements in the range *start* to *end*. Returns an iterator to the element after the last element removed.
reference front( ); const_reference front( ) const;	Returns a reference to the first element in the deque.
allocator_type get_allocator( ) const;	Returns deque's allocator.
iterator insert (iterator *i*, const T &*val*);	Inserts *val* immediately before the element specified by *i*. An iterator to the element is returned.

The **deque**
Member
Functions
Table 3-1.

Member	Description
void insert (iterator *i*, size_type *num*, const T &*val*)	Inserts *num* copies of *val* immediately before the element specified by *i*.
template <class InIter> void insert (iterator *i*, InIter *start*, InIter *end*);	Inserts the sequence defined by *start* and *end* immediately before the element specified by *i*.
size_type max_size( ) const;	Returns the maximum number of elements that a deque can hold.
reference operator[ ](size_type *i*); const_reference operator[ ](size_type *i*) const;	Returns a reference to the *i*th element.
void pop_back( );	Removes the last element in the deque.
void pop_front( );	Removes the first element in the deque.
void push_back(const T &*val*);	Adds an element with the value specified by *val* to the end of the deque.
void push_front(const T &*val*);	Adds an element with the value specified by *val* to the front of the deque.
reverse_iterator rbegin( ); const_reverse_iterator rbegin( ) const;	Returns a reverse iterator to the end of the deque.
reverse_iterator rend( ); const_reverse_iterator rend( ) const;	Returns a reverse iterator to the start of the deque.
void resize(size_type *num*, T *val* = T ( ));	Changes the size of the deque to that specified by *num*. If the deque must be lengthened, those elements with the value specified by *val* are added to the end.

The **deque** Member Functions *(continued)*

Table 3-1.

Member	Description
size_type size( ) const;	Returns the number of elements currently in the deque.
void swap(deque<T, Allocator> &*ob*)	Exchanges the elements stored in the invoking deque with those in *ob*.

3

The **deque** class defines the following concrete types:

size_type	Some type of integer.
difference_type	Some type of integer that can hold the difference between two addresses.
reference	A reference to an element (i.e., **T** &).
const_reference	A **const** reference to an element (i.e., **const T** &).
iterator	An iterator.
const_iterator	A **const** iterator.
reverse_iterator	A reverse iterator.
const_reverse_iterator	A **const** reverse iterator.
value_type	The type of a value stored in a container; same as **T**.
allocator_type	The type of the allocator.
pointer	A pointer to an element (i.e., **T** *).
const_pointer	A **const** pointer to an element (i.e., **const T** *).

The following program demonstrates the basic operation of **deque**.

```
// Demonstrate a deque.
#include <iostream>
#include <deque>
#include <cstring>
using namespace std;
```

```
int main()
{
  deque<char> q1;
  char str[] = "Using a deque.";
  int i;

  for(i=0; str[i]; i++) {
    q1.push_front(str[i]);
    q1.push_back(str[i]);
  }

  cout << "Original q1:\n";
  for(i=0; i<q1.size(); i++)
    cout << q1[i];
  cout << "\n\n";

  // remove backward string
  for(i=0; i<strlen(str); i++) q1.pop_front();
  cout << "q1 after popping front:\n";
  for(i=0; i<q1.size(); i++)
    cout << q1[i];
  cout << "\n\n";

  deque<char> q2(q1); // construct a copy of q1
  cout << "q2 original contents:\n";
  for(i=0; i<q2.size(); i++)
    cout << q2[i];
  cout << "\n\n";

  // transpose q2
  for(i=0; i<q2.size(); i++)
    q2[i] = q2[i]+1;

  cout << "q2 transposed contents:\n";
  for(i=0; i<q2.size(); i++)
    cout << q2[i];
  cout << "\n\n";

  // get iterator to first occurrence of 'a'
  deque<char>::iterator p = q1.begin();
  while(p != q1.end()) {
    if(*p == 'a') break;
    p++;
  }
```

```
    // insert transposed q2 into q1
    q1.insert(p, q2.begin(), q2.end());

    cout << "q1 after insertion:\n";
    for(i=0; i<q1.size(); i++)
      cout << q1[i];
    cout << "\n\n";

    return 0;
}
```

The output from the program is shown here:

```
Original q1:
.euqed a gnisUUsing a deque.

q1 after popping front:
Using a deque.

q2 original contents:
Using a deque.

q2 transposed contents:
Vtjoh!b!efrvf/

q1 after insertion:
Using Vtjoh!b!efrvf/a deque.
```

As the program illustrates, a deque can be accessed via array-style subscripting or, of course, through iterators. The container can also be built from either end.

Performance Characteristics

Insert or deletion from either end of a deque is very efficient, taking place in constant time.

Pushing or popping elements from either end of a deque takes place in constant time. When occurring in the middle, insertions or erasures of elements take place in linear time. Access of an element via the subscript operator takes place in constant time. Since adding or deleting elements from the ends of a deque is quite efficient, deques make an excellent choice when these types of operations will occur frequently.

Exploring deque

As the workhorse of the STL, **deque** offers a substantial amount of built-in functionality through its member functions. In this section, we will explore some of the more interesting ones.

Working with the Head and Tail of a deque

Although **deque** has several similarities with **vector**, it differs in one important respect: you can manipulate both ends of a **deque**. For example, **deque** provides **push_front( )**, **pop_ front( )**, **push_back( )**, and **pop_back( )**, which add and remove elements from either the front or back end of the container. These functions were described in Chapter 2. Another set of functions are **front( )** and **back( )**, which return a reference to the element stored at the head and tail of the **deque**, respectively. Collectively, these functions allow you to perform operations on both ends of a **deque** container. This is the reason why **deque** is the default container for the **queue** and **stack** container adaptors.

The following program demonstrates how **push_front( )**, **pop_front( )**, and **front( )** can be used together to reverse the contents of a **deque** when it is copied:

```cpp
// One way to reverse-copy a deque.
#include <iostream>
#include <deque>
using namespace std;

int main()
{
  deque<char> q;
  deque<char> rev_q;
  int i;

  for(i=0; i<10; i++) q.push_back('A'+i);

  cout << "Contents of q: ";
  for(i=0; i<q.size(); i++)
    cout << q[i];
  cout << "\n";

  /* Remove elements from q and put them
     into rev_q in reverse order. */
```

```
  while(!q.empty()) {
    rev_q.push_front(q.front());
    q.pop_front();
  }

  cout << "Contents of rev_q: ";
  for(i=0; i<rev_q.size(); i++)
    cout << rev_q[i];

  return 0;
}
```

3

The output from this program is shown here:

```
Contents of q: ABCDEFGHIJ
Contents of rev_q: JIHGFEDCBA
```

The interesting part of this program occurs in the following loop:

```
/* Remove elements from q and put them
   into rev_q in reverse order. */
while(!q.empty()) {
  rev_q.push_front(q.front());
  q.pop_front();
}
```

With each iteration, the element at the start of **q** is pushed onto the start of **rev_q** and then the first element in **q** is removed. This process continues until **q** is empty.

Because **deque** allows easy, low-cost manipulations of both the head and tail of the list, it is the perfect container to use if you will be frequently moving elements from one end to the other, such as when rotating the contents of the container. While the STL provides a general-purpose algorithm called **rotate( )** that rotates the contents of most containers, it is easy to write your own, high-performance rotation functions that are designed specifically for **deque** containers. For example, the following program defines the functions **lrot( )** and **rrot( )** that left-rotate and right-rotate the contents of a deque by one position. Since they are template functions, they will work with any type of deque.

```
// Rotating deques
#include <iostream>
#include <deque>
#include <string>
```

```
using namespace std;

// Left-rotate a deque.
template <class T> lrot(deque<T> &q)
{
  q.push_back(q.front());
  q.pop_front();
}

// Right-rotate a deque.
template <class T> rrot(deque<T> &q)
{
  q.push_front(q.back());
  q.pop_back();
}

int main()
{
  deque<string> w;
  int i, n;

  w.push_back("Rotation");
  w.push_back("is");
  w.push_back("easy");
  w.push_back("using");
  w.push_back("deque.");

  cout << "This is the original sentence:\n";
  for(i=0; i<w.size(); i++)
    cout << w[i] << " ";
  cout << "\n\n";

  cout << "First, left rotate:\n";
  for(n=0; n<w.size(); n++) {
    lrot(w);
    for(i=0; i<w.size(); i++)
      cout << w[i] << " ";
    cout << "\n";
  }

  cout << "\nNow, right rotate:\n";
  for(n=0; n<w.size(); n++) {
    rrot(w);
    for(i=0; i<w.size(); i++)
      cout << w[i] << " ";
    cout << "\n";
  }
```

3

```
  return 0;
}
```

The output produced by the program is shown here:

```
This is the original sentence:
Rotation is easy using deque.

First, left rotate:
is easy using deque. Rotation
easy using deque. Rotation is
using deque. Rotation is easy
deque. Rotation is easy using
Rotation is easy using deque.

Now, right rotate:
deque. Rotation is easy using
using deque. Rotation is easy
easy using deque. Rotation is
is easy using deque. Rotation
Rotation is easy using deque.
```

While the **lrot( )** and **rrot( )** functions rotate only one position, you could easily change these functions so that the number of positions to rotate is passed as a second argument. You might find this interesting to try on your own.

Using Reverse Iterators

A reverse iterator moves in the opposite direction from a regular iterator.

The **deque** class supports *reverse iterators*. Reverse iterators work just like regular iterators except for one important fact: they move in the opposite direction. For example, if **p** is a reverse iterator, then **p++** decrements the iterator and **p – –** increments it! This property is especially useful when you want some operation to proceed in reverse.

You can obtain a reverse iterator to the end of a deque by calling **rbegin( )**. A reverse iterator to the start of the container is returned by **rend( )**. Here is a program that demonstrates reverse iterators:

```
// Use reverse iterators.
#include <iostream>
#include <deque>
using namespace std;
```

```
int main()
{
  deque<int> q;
  deque<int>::reverse_iterator rp;
  int i;

  for(i=0; i<10; i++) q.push_back(i);

  cout << "Contents printed backward:\n";
  rp = q.rbegin();
  while(rp != q.rend()) {
    cout << *rp << " ";
    rp++;
  }
  cout << "\n\n";

  cout << "Contents printed forward:\n";
  rp = q.rend();
  while(rp != q.rbegin()) {
    rp--;
    cout << *rp << " ";
  }

  return 0;
}
```

The output from the program is shown here:

```
Contents printed backward:
9 8 7 6 5 4 3 2 1 0

Contents printed forward:
0 1 2 3 4 5 6 7 8 9
```

As explained, a reverse iterator operates backwards from a normal iterator. For example, consider this loop from the program:

```
cout << "Contents printed backward:\n";
rp = q.rbegin();
while(rp != q.rend()) {
  cout << *rp << " ";
  rp++;
}
```

rbegin( )
returns an
iterator to the
end of the
container and
rend( ) returns
an iterator to
the start of the
container.

Here, **rp** is initialized to the end of the container via the call to **rbegin( )**. Remember, **rbegin( )** returns a reverse iterator to the *end of the container*. That is, the last element in the container is the beginning of the container for reverse iterators. Each time **rp** is incremented, it moves towards the head of the container. The value returned by **rend( )** is an iterator that points one element past the start of the container.

Reverse iterators can be quite useful. For example, if you pass a reverse iterator to many of the algorithms, then those algorithms will "run backwards." For example, consider the **copy( )** algorithm that was discussed briefly in Chapter 2. It has the following prototype:

```
template <class InIter, class OutIter>
        OutIter copy(InIter start, InIter end, OutIter result);
```

It copies the range defined by *start* and *end* into the target sequence beginning at *result*. It returns a pointer to the end of the resulting sequence. However, if *start* and *end* are reverse iterators, the range they specify will be copied into the target object in reverse. Here is a program that demonstrates this fact. The program copies a container, first using regular iterators and then using reverse iterators.

```
// Reverse iterators and copy.
#include <iostream>
#include <deque>
#include <algorithm>
#include <cstring>
using namespace std;

int main()
{
  deque<char> q1(30), q2, q3;
  int i;

  char str1[] = "forward";
  for(i=0; str1[i]; i++) q2.push_back(str1[i]);

  // copy in forward direction
  copy(q2.begin(), q2.end(), q1.begin());

  cout << "Contents q1 after forward copy:\n";
  for(i=0; i<q1.size(); i++)
    cout << q1[i];
  cout << "\n\n";
```

```
char str2[] = "backward";
for(i=0; str2[i]; i++) q3.push_back(str2[i]);

// copy in reverse direction
copy(q3.rbegin(), q3.rend(), q1.begin()+strlen(str1));

cout << "Contents q1 after reverse copy:\n";
for(i=0; i<q1.size(); i++)
  cout << q1[i];

return 0;
}
```

The output from this program is shown here:

```
Contents q1 after forward copy:
forward

Contents q1 after reverse copy:
forwarddrawkcab
```

When **copy( )** is called the first time, it copies the contents of **q2** to **q1** in the normal fashion. When **copy( )** is called the second time, with reverse iterators, it copies the contents of **q3** to **q1** in reversed order.

Assignment and the assign( ) Function

Like all containers, it is possible to assign one entire **deque** object to another through the use of the assignment operator. After an assignment takes place, the object on the left will contain the same elements as the object on the right. The left-side object will also be of the same size as the object on the right. Thus, if the target container is smaller than the source, the target's size is automatically increased. For example,

```
deque<T> x(10), y;
// ...
y = x;
```

After the assignment, **y** will also be 10 elements long.

A deque can also be assigned values through the use of the member function **assign( )**. The **assign( )** function has two forms. The first assigns a range of elements to the invoking container. The second assigns one or more copies of an element to the container. In both cases, the size of the target container is changed, if necessary, to accommodate the assignment. The second form is especially useful when you want to reinitialize the container. The first form is, however, the most interesting because it provides a convenient way to assign part of one deque to another.

The following example demonstrates the ways in which a **deque** container can be assigned a value:

3

```cpp
// Assigning deque objects.
#include <iostream>
#include <deque>
using namespace std;

int main()
{
  deque<char> q1(10), q2;
  int i;

  for(i=0; i<10; i++) q1[i] = i + 'A';
  cout << "Contents of q1 are: ";
  for(i=0; i<q1.size(); i++)
    cout << q1[i];
  cout << "\n\n";

  // assign one deque to another
  q2 = q1;

  cout << "Size of q2 is " << q2.size() << "\n";
  cout << "Contents of q2 are: ";
  for(i=0; i<q2.size(); i++)
    cout << q2[i];
  cout << "\n\n";

  // assign a range from q1 to q2
  q2.assign(q1.begin()+2, q1.end()-2);

  cout << "Size of q2 is " << q2.size() << "\n";
  cout << "Contents of q2 are: ";
  for(i=0; i<q2.size(); i++)
    cout << q2[i];
  cout << "\n\n";

  // assign elements to q2
  q2.assign(8, 'X');
```

```
cout << "Size of q2 is " << q2.size() << "\n";
cout << "Contents of q2 are: ";
for(i=0; i<q2.size(); i++)
  cout << q2[i];

rcturn 0;
}
```

This program produces the following output:

```
Contents of q1 are: ABCDEFGHIJ

Size of q2 is 10
Contents of q2 are: ABCDEFGHIJ

Size of q2 is 6
Contents of q2 are: CDEFGH

Size of q2 is 8
Contents of q2 are: XXXXXXXX
```

In the program, **q1** is first assigned the values A through J. Next, **q1** is assigned in its totality to **q2** through the use of an assignment statement. Although **q2** has an initial length of zero, its size is increased to 10 when the assignment takes place. Next, a subrange of these values, C through H, is assigned to **q2** by using **assign( )**. Notice that the size of **q2** is automatically decreased to 6, which is the number of values **q2** now contains. Finally, **q2** is assigned 8 X's and its size is changed to 8.

Swapping deque Containers

The STL provides two ways to exchange the contents of two **deque** containers. First, you can use the **swap( )** member function, which is shown here:

   void deque::swap(deque<T, Allocator> &*ob*);

This function exchanges the contents of *ob* with those of the invoking object.

Second, you can use the **swap( )** algorithm, which has a specialization defined expressly for **deque** objects. The prototype for this specialization is shown here:

   void swap(deque<T, Allocator> &*a*, deque<T, Allocator> &*b*);

This algorithm exchanges the contents of *a* and *b*.

For both versions of **swap( )**, the sizes of the objects are adjusted as needed to accommodate the exchange. The following program demonstrates both versions of **swap( )**:

```cpp
// Demonstrate swap().
#include <iostream>
#include <deque>
using namespace std;

int main()
{
  deque<char> q1, q2;
  int i;

  for(i=0; i<26; i++) q1.push_back(i+'A');
  for(i=0; i<10; i++) q2.push_front(i+'0');

  cout << "Size of q1 and q2: ";
  cout << q1.size() << " " << q2.size() << "\n";

  cout << "q1: ";
  for(i=0; i<q1.size(); i++)
    cout << q1[i];
  cout << "\n";

  cout << "q2: ";
  for(i=0; i<q2.size(); i++)
    cout << q2[i];
  cout << "\n\n";

  // swap deques using member function.
  q1.swap(q2);

  cout << "Size of q1 and q2 after first swap: ";
  cout << q1.size() << " " << q2.size() << "\n";

  cout << "q1 after first swap: ";
  for(i=0; i<q1.size(); i++)
    cout << q1[i];
  cout << "\n";

  cout << "q2 after first swap: ";
  for(i=0; i<q2.size(); i++)
    cout << q2[i];
  cout << "\n\n";
```

```
// swap deques using algorithm
swap(q1, q2);

cout << "Size of q1 and q2 after second swap: ";
cout << q1.size() << " " << q2.size() << "\n";

cout << "q1 after second swap: ";
for(i=0; i<q1.size(); i++)
  cout << q1[i];
cout << "\n";

cout << "q2 after second swap: ";
for(i=0; i<q2.size(); i++)
  cout << q2[i];
cout << "\n";

return 0;
}
```

The following output is produced:

```
Size of q1 and q2: 26 10
q1: ABCDEFGHIJKLMNOPQRSTUVWXYZ
q2: 9876543210

Size of q1 and q2 after first swap: 10 26
q1 after first swap: 9876543210
q2 after first swap: ABCDEFGHIJKLMNOPQRSTUVWXYZ

Size of q1 and q2 after second swap: 26 10
q1 after second swap: ABCDEFGHIJKLMNOPQRSTUVWXYZ
q2 after second swap: 9876543210
```

Notice that each time an exchange takes place, the sizes of the two objects are altered to reflect the change.

Understanding size( ), max_size( ), and resize( )

Sometimes newcomers to the STL are confused by the precise meaning of the **size( )**, **max_size( )**, and **resize( )** container functions. The **size( )** function returns the number of elements currently stored in the container. The **max_size( )** function returns the maximum number of elements that a container of that type can hold. The **resize( )** function changes the size of a container. When resizing, elements will be added to or subtracted from the end of the container as needed.

The **resize( )** function is particularly valuable when working with algorithms. In general any container that is the target of an algorithm must be large enough to hold all the elements that it will be given—the container will not automatically be increased in size. In some cases, this size may be available only at run time. When this happens, you can use **resize( )** to increase the size of the target container before calling the algorithm. The following program illustrates this point. It asks the user for a series of angles (specified in radians) and then computes their sines. It does this through the use of the **transform( )** algorithm. Since the number of sines to be computed is determined by the user, the size of the deque receiving the sines is set at run time.

3

```
// Demonstrate resize()
#include <iostream>
#include <deque>
#include <algorithm>
#include <cmath>
using namespace std;

int main()
{
  deque<double> radians, sines;
  double num;
  int i;

  for(;;) {
    cout << "Enter angles (0 to stop): ";
    cin >> num;
    if(num == 0.0) break;
    radians.push_back(num);
  }

  /* resize sines so that it can
     hold all of the results */
  sines.resize(radians.size());

  transform(radians.begin(), radians.end(),
            sines.begin(), sin);

  for(i=0; i<sines.size(); i++) {
    cout << "Angle and sine: ";
    cout << radians[i] << " " << sines[i];
    cout << "\n";
  }
  cout << "\n";

  return 0;
}
```

Sample output is shown here:

```
Enter angles (0 to stop): 0.1
Enter angles (0 to stop): 0.2
Enter angles (0 to stop): 0.3
Enter angles (0 to stop): 0.4
Enter angles (0 to stop): 0.5
Enter angles (0 to stop): 0
Angle and sine: 0.1 0.0998334
Angle and sine: 0.2 0.198669
Angle and sine: 0.3 0.29552
Angle and sine: 0.4 0.389418
Angle and sine: 0.5 0.479426
```

As an experiment, try removing the call to **resize( )** in the preceding program. This will usually result in a runtime error because the **sines** container is not large enough to hold the values that **transform( )** attempts to give it.

If you want to resize a deque to zero length, the best way to do this is by using the **clear( )** member function.

IN DEPTH

Iterator and Reference Invalidation

Consider the following scenario. You have a **deque** container holding several elements. You also have an iterator that points to an element within that container. Next, you insert one or more elements into the middle of the container. After the insertion is complete, to what element does the iterator now point: to the original element or to a different one? The answer to this question reflects a fundamental design aspect of the **deque** class.

IN DEPTH
CONTINUED

According to Standard C++, an insertion into the middle of a **deque** container invalidates all iterators and references to the contents of that container. Because a deque is implemented as a double-ended dynamic array, an insertion implies that existing elements will be "spread apart" to accommodate the new elements. Thus, if an iterator is pointing to an element prior to an insertion, there is no guarantee that it will be pointing to the same element after the insertion. The same applies to references.

An insertion at the head or the tail of a deque invalidates iterators but not references. An erasure to the middle invalidates both iterators and references. An erasure limited to either end invalidates only those iterators and references that point to the elements that are being erased.

Here is a short example that demonstrates the invalidation of iterators when an insertion occurs.

```
// Watch Out! Iterator values may change.
#include <iostream>
#include <deque>
using namespace std;

int main()
{
  deque<char> q;
  deque<char>::iterator p1, p2;
  int i;

  for(i=0; i<5; i++) q.push_back(i + 'A');

  cout << "Original sequence: ";
  for(i=0; i<q.size(); i++)
    cout << q[i] << " ";
  cout << "\n";
```

```
p1 = q.begin() + 2;
p2 = q.begin() + 3;
cout << "*p1: " << *p1 << ", ";
cout << "*p2: " << *p2 << "\n";
cout << "\n";

// now, insert an element into the sequence
q.insert(p1, 'X');

cout << "Sequence after insert: ";
for(i=0; i<q.size(); i++)
  cout << q[i] << " ";
cout << "\n";

// these now point to different elements
cout << "*p1: " << *p1 << ", ";
cout << "*p2: " << *p2 << "\n";

return 0;
}
```

The output from this program is shown here:

```
Original sequence: A B C D E
*p1: C, *p2: D

Sequence after insert: A B X C D E
*p1: X, *p2: C
```

As you can see, the elements pointed to by **p1** and **p2** are changed after the insertion.

Storing Class Objects in a deque

A **deque** container can store objects of classes that you create as long as you follow two simple rules. First, your class must define a default constructor. Second, your class must overload any relational operators used by your program, either directly or indirectly through calls to container functions or algorithms. Typically, you will need to overload at least the < and often the = = operators.

NOTE: Technically, for trivial uses of the STL, neither of the preceding two rules needs to be followed, but for all practical purposes they apply.

3

Here is an example that uses a deque to reassemble packets of information that might arrive out of order. This situation can occur with some types of networking schemes, for example. The program uses a deque to store the packets as they are received, putting each packet into its proper order, which might be at the start, middle, or end of the container. Since a deque can perform all of these actions and is especially efficient when elements are added to the start or the end, a deque makes an excellent choice for this application.

For use with **deque**, classes that you create should overload at least the < and = = operators.

In this example, each packet consists of a packet number, which determines its order, and the information associated with that packet, which in this case is a **string**. Each packet is encapsulated by the **packet** class. When the packets are assembled in their correct order, the strings will make a complete sentence.

```cpp
/* Using a deque to reassemble out-of-order
   information packets. */
#include <iostream>
#include <deque>
#include <algorithm>
#include <string>
using namespace std;

class packet {
  int pnum;      // packet number
  string info; // information
public:
  packet() { pnum = -1; info = ""; }
  packet(int n, string i) {
    pnum = n;
    info = i;
  }

  int getpnum() const { return pnum; }
  string getinfo() { return info; }
};

// Compare two packets for less than.
```

```cpp
bool operator<(const packet &a, const packet &b) {
  return a.getpnum() < b.getpnum();
}

// Compare two packets for equality.
bool operator==(const packet &a, const packet &b) {
  return a.getpnum() == b.getpnum();
}

/* Obtain the next packet.
   Returns true if packet available
   and false otherwise.  */
bool getpacket(packet &pkt)
{
  static packet message[] = {
    packet(2, "is"),
    packet(4, "Programming"),
    packet(0,"The"),
    packet(3, "Power"),
    packet(1, "STL"),
    packet(-1, "") // end of transmission mark
  };
  static int i=0;

  if(message[i] == packet(-1, "")) return false;

  pkt = message[i];

  cout << "Sending: " << pkt.getinfo() << "\n";

  i++;
  return true;
}

int main()
{
  deque<packet> pack;
  deque<packet>::iterator p;
  packet pkt;

  getpacket(pkt); // get first packet
  pack.push_back(pkt); // put first packet in deque

  // read and store remaining packets
  while(getpacket(pkt)) {
```

```
      if(pkt.getpnum() <= pack.front().getpnum())
        pack.push_front(pkt);
      else if(pkt.getpnum() >= pack.back().getpnum())
        pack.push_back(pkt);
      else {
        p = lower_bound(pack.begin(), pack.end(), pkt);
        pack.insert(p, pkt);
      }
    }

    cout << "\nPackets reassembled:\n";
    for(int i=0; i<pack.size(); i++)
      cout << pack[i].getinfo() << " ";

    return 0;
  }
```

3

The output from this program is shown here:

```
Sending: is
Sending: Programming
Sending: The
Sending: Power
Sending: STL

Packets reassembled:
The STL is Power Programming
```

Let's examine this program carefully. The **packet** class defines two private members, **pnum**, which contains the packet number, and **info**, which contains the information associated with the packet. Both a default constructor and a parameterized constructor are defined. The function **getpnum( )** returns the packet number. The function **getinfo( )** returns the string. Notice that the operators < and = = are overloaded. The < is used by the **lower_bound( )** algorithm and = = is used by the **getpacket( )** function.

The **getpacket( )** function defines an array of out-of-order packets. Each time the function is called, it obtains the next packet from the array and returns **true**. When no packets remain, it returns **false**. In **main( )**, the packets are reassembled in their proper order. Each time a packet is received, the program determines if the packet goes at the start of the container, the end of the container, or somewhere in the middle. Since additions to the head or tail of a deque are the most efficient, the program checks these two possibilities first. If neither is the case, the **lower_bound( )** algorithm is employed to find the right location in which to insert the packet.

The prototype for the form of the **lower_bound( )** algorithm used in the program is shown here:

```
template <class ForIter, class T>
    ForIter lower_bound(ForIter start, ForIter end, const T &val);
```

The **lower_bound( )** algorithm finds the first point in the ordered sequence defined by *start* and *end* that is not less than *val*. It returns an iterator to this point. The program uses the returned iterator as the point at which to insert the next packet.

In the next chapter we will examine a close relative of **deque**: **vector**.

CHAPTER 4

The vector Class

Possibly the most commonly used container class is **vector.** The **vector** class supports dynamic arrays and, as you will see, it has several similarities to the **deque** described in the preceding chapter. However, **vector** is more efficient when array-like capabilities are needed.

vector Fundamentals

The template specification for **vector** is shown here:

    template <class T, class Allocator = allocator<T> > class vector

Here, **T** is the type of data being stored and **Allocator** specifies the allocator, which defaults to the standard allocator. **vector** has the following constructors:

    explicit vector(const Allocator &a = Allocator( ));

    explicit vector(size_type num, const T &val = T ( ),
            const Allocator &a = Allocator( ));

    vector(const vector<T, Allocator> &ob);

    template <class InIter> vector(InIter start, InIter end,
            const Allocator &a = Allocator( ));

The first form constructs an empty vector. The second form constructs a vector that has *num* elements with the value *val*. The third form is **vector**'s copy constructor. The fourth form constructs a vector that contains the elements in the range specified by *start* and *end*. To use **vector** include **<vector>**.

The **vector** class overloads the assignment operator. In addition, the following comparison operators are defined for **vector**:

    ==, <, <=, !=, >, >=

vector supports random-access iterators and the **[ ]** is overloaded. This means that a **vector** object can be indexed like an array.

The **vector** class defines the following concrete types:

size_type	Some type of integer.
difference_type	Some type of integer that can hold the difference between two addresses.
reference	A reference to an element (i.e., **T** &).
const_reference	A **const** reference to an element (i.e., **const T** &).

iterator	An iterator.
const_iterator	A **const** iterator.
reverse_iterator	A reverse iterator.
const_reverse_iterator	A **const** reverse iterator.
value_type	The type of a value stored in a container; same as **T**.
allocator_type	The type of the allocator.
pointer	A pointer to an element (i.e., **T ***).
const_pointer	A **const** pointer to an element (i.e., **const T ***).

4

The **vector** class defines the member functions shown in Table 4-1.

Member	Description
template <class InIter> void assign(InIter *start*, InIter *end*);	Assigns the vector the sequence defined by *start* and *end*.
void assign(size_type *num*, const T &*val*);	Assigns the vector *num* elements of value *val*.
reference at(size_type *i*); const_reference at(size_type *i*) const;	Returns a reference to the element specified by *i*. Throws an **out_of_range** exception if *i* is out-of-bounds.
reference back( ); const_reference back( ) const;	Returns a reference to the last element in the vector.
iterator begin( ); const_iterator begin( ) const;	Returns an iterator to the first element in the vector.
size_type capacity( ) const;	Returns the current capacity of the vector. This is the number of elements it can hold before it will need to allocate more memory.

The Member
Functions
Defined by
vector
Table 4-1.

Member	Description
void clear( );	Removes all elements from the vector.
bool empty( ) const;	Returns **true** if the invoking vector is empty and **false** otherwise.
iterator end( ); const_iterator end( ) const;	Returns an iterator to the end of the vector.
iterator erase(iterator *i*);	Removes the element pointed to by *i*. Returns an iterator to the element after the one removed.
iterator erase(iterator *start*, iterator *end*);	Removes the elements in the range *start* to *end*. Returns an iterator to the element after the last element removed.
reference front( ); const_reference front( ) const;	Returns a reference to the first element in the vector.
allocator_type get_allocator( ) const;	Returns vector's allocator.
iterator insert(iterator *i*, const T &*val*);	Inserts *val* immediately before the element specified by *i*. An iterator to the element is returned.
void insert (iterator *i*, size_type *num*, const T & *val*)	Inserts *num* copies of *val* immediately before the element specified by *i*.

template <class InIter>
    void insert (iterator *i*, InIter *start*,
            InIter *end*);
	Inserts the sequence defined by *start* and *end* immediately before the element specified by *i*.

size_type max_size( ) const;	Returns the maximum number of elements that the vector can hold.
reference operator[ ](size_type *i*); const_reference operator[ ](size_type *i*) const;	Returns a reference to the element specified by *i*.

The Member
Functions
Defined by
vector
(*continued*)

Table 4-1.

Member	Description
void pop_back( );	Removes the last element in the vector.
void push_back(const T &*val*);	Adds an element with the value specified by *val* to the end of the vector.
reverse_iterator rbegin( ); const_reverse_iterator rbegin( ) const;	Returns a reverse iterator to the end of the vector.
reverse_iterator rend( ); const_reverse_iterator rend( ) const;	Returns a reverse iterator to the start of the vector.
void reserve(size_type *num*);	Sets the capacity of the vector so that it is equal to at least *num*.
void resize(size_type *num*, T val = T ( ));	Changes the size of the vector to that specified by *num*. If the vector must be lengthened, then elements with the value specified by *val* are added to the end.
size_type size( ) const;	Returns the number of elements currently in the vector.
void swap(vector<T, Allocator> &*ob*)	Exchanges the elements stored in the invoking vector with those in *ob*.

The Member
Functions
Defined by
vector
(continued)
Table 4-1.

4

The following program demonstrates the various ways that a vector can be constructed:

```
// Demonstrating the four ways that vectors can be created.
#include <iostream>
#include <vector>
using namespace std;

int main()
{
  vector<char> a; // empty
  vector<char> b(5, 'X'); // size and initialize
  vector<char> c(b); // initialize with another vector
  int i;
```

```
// give a the values A through E
for(i=0; i<5; i++) a.push_back('A'+i);

// create a vector from a range
vector<char> d(a.begin()+1, a.end()-1);

// display contents of each
for(i=0; i<a.size(); i++)
  cout << "a[" << i << "]: " << a[i] << "  ";
cout << "\n\n";

for(i=0; i<b.size(); i++)
  cout << "b[" << i << "]: " << b[i] << "  ";
cout << "\n\n";

for(i=0; i<c.size(); i++)
  cout << "c[" << i << "]: " << c[i] << "  ";
cout << "\n\n";

for(i=0; i<d.size(); i++)
  cout << "d[" << i << "]: " << d[i] << "  ";

return 0;
}
```

The output from the program is shown here:

```
a[0]: A  a[1]: B  a[2]: C  a[3]: D  a[4]: E

b[0]: X  b[1]: X  b[2]: X  b[3]: X  b[4]: X

c[0]: X  c[1]: X  c[2]: X  c[3]: X  c[4]: X

d[0]: B  d[1]: C  d[2]: D
```

Notice the way that **d** is created. It is constructed from a range of elements within **a**. The ability to create a new vector from a subset of another is an often-useful feature.

Performance Characteristics

Inserting or deleting elements at the end of a vector takes place in amortized constant time. (See the In-depth box.) When occurring at the beginning or in

4

Insertion or deletion at the end of a vector takes place in amortized constant time.

the middle, insertions or deletions take place in linear time. Access of an element via the subscript operator takes place in constant time. In general, element access in a vector is faster than it is with a deque, or any other container. This is why **vector** is used for dynamic arrays.

When a vector's size is exceeded, a memory reallocation occurs.

In all cases, when an insertion occurs, references and iterators to elements after the point of the insertion will be invalid. However, in some cases, including those in which the element is added to the end via a call to **push_back( )**, all references and iterators to elements may be invalid. This situation occurs only if the vector needs to allocate more memory. In this case, a *reallocation* occurs, and the contents of the vector may have to be moved to a new location. If the vector is physically moved, previous iterators and references are no longer valid. Thus, for all practical purposes, it is best to assume that iterators and references are not valid after insertions.

A reallocation causes iterators and references to be invalidated.

When an element is deleted from a vector, iterators and references to elements that are after the point of the erasure are invalid.

IN DEPTH

Understanding Amortized Constant Time

As mentioned, insertions to and deletions from the end of a vector occur in what is called *amortized constant time*. This is the term used to describe a situation in which an operation usually takes constant time of X but occasionally requires longer, such as 10X. If the longer operation is rare enough, then it can be thought of as being amortized over a number of shorter operations. For example, if every tenth operation requires 100 CPU cycles and the other operations take only 10 cycles, then in amortized time, each operation takes 19 cycles. By referring to the complexity of such an operation as amortized constant time, we most accurately reflect its true nature since its worst-case performance occurs only sporadically.

In the case of a vector, if an element can be added to the end without causing additional memory to be allocated, then that insertion occurs in constant time. However, if more memory must be allocated, then the insertion will take place in linear time. Since reallocation occurs only occasionally, **vector**'s insertion-at-end complexity is rightly described as amortized constant time.

IN DEPTH

CONTINUED

It is possible to reserve additional space in a vector by using the **reserve( )** function. By preallocating extra memory you will prevent reallocations from occurring. Thus, if you manage your vectors correctly, most insertions will occur in constant time.

Exploring vector

The **vector** class is the container of choice when a dynamic array is needed. Although similar to **deque**, **vector** provides faster random access to its elements. This makes the **vector** better for array-based applications. Since many of **vector**'s member functions and features are exactly like those provided by **deque** and described in the previous chapter, we will not duplicate those discussions here. Instead, we will focus on the unique aspects of **vector** or those that are mostly applicable to **vector**.

Using capacity( ) and reserve( )

Two member functions of **vector** which are not supported by **deque** are **capacity( )** and **reserve( )**. Their prototypes are shown here:

    size_type capacity( ) const;

    void reserve(size_type *num*);

The capacity of a vector is the number of elements it can hold before it must allocate more memory.

The **capacity( )** function returns the current capacity of the invoking vector. This is the number of elements that it can store before it must allocate more memory. Don't confuse capacity with size. The size of a vector is the number of elements that it currently holds. Capacity is how many it can hold before a reallocation must occur.

You can reserve memory for a vector by using **reserve( )**.

The **reserve( )** function reserves memory for the number of elements specified by *num*. In other words, its sets the capacity of the invoking vector to *num*. Since a call to **reserve( )** may cause a memory reallocation, it might invalidate any pointers or references to elements within the vector.

Here is a short program that illustrates the difference between size and capacity:

```
// Capacity vs size
#include <iostream>
#include <vector>
using namespace std;

int main()
{
  vector<char> v(10);

  cout << "Initial size: " << v.size() << "\n";
  cout << "Initial capacity: " << v.capacity();
  cout << "\n\n";

  v.reserve(20); // reserve more space
  cout << "Size after reserve: " << v.size() << "\n";
  cout << "Capacity after reserve: " << v.capacity();
  cout << "\n\n";

  return 0;
}
```

The output from this program is shown here:

```
Initial size: 10
Initial capacity: 10

Size after reserve: 10
Capacity after reserve: 20
```

When the program begins, **v** is given an initial size of 10. This causes it to also be given an initial capacity of 10. Next, through the use of **reserve( )** the capacity of **v** is increased to 20. As the output shows, increasing the capacity of **v** does not cause its size to increase. Remember, the size of a vector is the number of elements that it currently holds. Its capacity is the number of elements it can ultimately hold before a memory reallocation must occur.

The difference between the size of a vector and its capacity is irrelevant in cases in which you know in advance precisely how many elements you will be storing. Of course, if you know this information then you are probably

4

better off using an array rather than a vector anyway. Where the difference matters is when you will be inserting elements into the vector. In order to maximize performance you will want to minimize the number of reallocations that need to be performed. Also, insertions to the end of a vector take place in amortized constant time and the time being amortized is the time it takes to perform a reallocation. By setting aside a reasonable amount of capacity in advance, you can minimize (or prevent) memory allocations from taking place.

For example, consider a situation in which your program will receive irregularly sized packets of data from some external source in real time, such as data via an A/D converter. If you are storing this information in a vector, you may need to ensure that a reallocation does not take place while data is being received. Since a reallocation takes time, it could cause a unit of data to be missed, resulting in a time-consuming resend request. To avoid this potential problem, you could reserve sufficient capacity for each packet before each transmission begins. The following program emulates the preceding scenario.

```cpp
// Use reserve() to avoid reallocation.
#include <iostream>
#include <vector>
#include <cstdlib>
using namespace std;

const int getsize = 0;
const int getbytes = 1;
const int reset = 2;

int producer(int what);
void consumer(vector<int> &v);

int main()
{
  char more;
  vector<int> v;

  do {
    consumer(v);

    cout << "Current contents of v:\n";
    for(int i=0; i<v.size(); i++) {
      cout << v[i] << " ";
```

```
      if(!((i+1)%16)) cout << "\n";
    }

    cout << "\nMore? (Y/N): ";
    cin >> more;
  } while(more == 'y');

  return 0;
}

// Produce data.
int producer(int what)
{
  static int howmany = rand() % 20 + 1;

  switch(what) {
    case getsize: return howmany;
      break;
    case getbytes: return howmany--;
      break;
    case reset:
      howmany = rand() % 20 + 1;
      return howmany;
  }

  return 0; // error
}

// Read data and put on the end of v.
void consumer(vector<int> &v)
{
  int packet_size = producer(getsize);

  cout << "Producer sending " << packet_size << " units.\n";

  v.reserve(packet_size + v.size());
  do {
    v.push_back(producer(getbytes));
    packet_size--;
  } while(packet_size);

  producer(reset);
}
```

4

The output produced by this program is shown here:

```
Producer sending 2 units.
Current contents of v:
2 1
More? (Y/N): y

Producer sending 8 units.
Current contents of v:
2 1 8 7 6 5 4 3 2 1
More? (Y/N): y

Producer sending 15 units.
Current contents of v:
2 1 8 7 6 5 4 3 2 1 15 14 13 12 11 10
9 8 7 6 5 4 3 2 1
More? (Y/N): n
```

In the program, the **producer( )** function produces irregularly sized packets of data. The **consumer( )** function receives those packets. When **consumer( )** begins, it requests the size of the next packet. It then reserves for **v** a sufficient number of elements to hold whatever the vector currently contains and the elements that it will be receiving. The function then reads the elements, puts them on the end of the vector, resets the producer, and then returns. By setting the capacity, **consumer( )** ensures that a reallocation will not occur during the receipt of the data.

Although the preceding program is simply an illustration of a general principle, it still may have raised this question: Instead of reserving the needed capacity, why not just increase the size of the vector using **resize( )**? The answer is straightforward, even though not immediately obvious. Setting the capacity of a vector *does not* alter its current contents or size in any way. Setting the size of a vector *does* because elements might be added or removed. In general, reserving capacity is the least intrusive way to ensure that a reallocation will not take place.

A call to **reserve( )** does not alter the contents of a vector in any way.

Normally, **vector** is implemented in such a way that it will automatically help reduce the number of reallocations by allocating more memory than required when a reallocation takes place. Typically, when a reallocation occurs, twice as much memory as the vector currently has is allocated. For example, consider the following program.

```
/* A vector may allocate more memory than it
   currently needs. */
#include <iostream>
```

```
#include <vector>
using namespace std;

int main()
{
  vector<char> v(10);

  cout << "Initial size: " << v.size() << "\n";
  cout << "Initial capacity: " << v.capacity();
  cout << "\n\n";

  v.push_back('X'); // push another element onto v

  cout << "Size after push_back: " << v.size() << "\n";
  cout << "New capacity: " << v.capacity();
  cout << "\n\n";

  v.resize(100); // resize up to 100

  cout << "Size after resize: " << v.size() << "\n";
  cout << "Capacity after resize: " << v.capacity();
  cout << "\n\n";

  v.push_back('Y'); // push another element onto v

  cout << "Size after push_back: " << v.size() << "\n";
  cout << "New capacity: " << v.capacity();
  cout << "\n\n";

  return 0;
}
```

4

This program produces the following output when run using the Microsoft Visual C++ implementation of the STL:

```
Initial size: 10
Initial capacity: 10

Size after push_back: 11
New capacity: 20

Size after resize: 100
Capacity after resize: 100

Size after push_back: 101
New capacity: 200
```

As you can see, each time a reallocation is forced when an element is pushed onto the end of **v**, twice as much memory is allocated. Notice, however, that a call to **resize( )** simply sets the capacity equal to the requested size. Additional memory is obtained only as a result of a reallocation.

Reserving extra capacity will be most valuable to those applications in which it is important either to prevent a reallocation because it would invalidate iterators or references, or to prevent a loss of performance due to an excessive amount of reallocations. It is not something that you will have to do each time you use a vector.

Subscripting vs. at( )

The **vector** class provides two ways to index an element. First, and most common, is through the use of the **[ ]** subscripting operator. The other is by calling the **at( )** function. Here are the prototypes for their non-**const** versions:

    reference at(size_type *i*);

    reference operator[ ](size_type *i*);

The **at( )** function returns a reference to the element at location *i*. The **operator[ ]( )** function also returns a reference to the element at location *i*. Given that the **[ ]** is more convenient to use, one might reasonably ask why the **at( )** function is defined by **vector**.

The *at( ) function throws an exception when an attempt is made to access an out-of-bounds element.*

The answer is that **at( )** and **[ ]** act differently when an attempt is made to access an out-of-bounds element. In the case of **at( )**, attempting to access an element that is outside the current bounds of the vector will result in an **out_of_range** exception being thrown. If an attempt is made to index an out-of-bounds element using **[ ]**, the behavior of **vector** is undefined. Here is a program that illustrates the difference:

```
// [] vs at()
#include <iostream>
#include <vector>
using namespace std;

int main()
{
  vector<int> v(10);
  int i;
```

```
    try {
      for(i=0; i<100; i++) v.at(i) = 100;
    } catch(out_of_range excpt) {
      cout << "Out-of-bounds access attempted ";
      cout << "at location " << i << "\n";
    }

    // this will cause a program crash
    // for(i=0; i<100; i++)  v[i] = 100;

    return 0;
}
```

4

The output from the program is shown here:

```
Out-of-bounds access attempted at location 10
```

As you can see, the exception handler was invoked when an attempt was made to access location 10. Since **v** was created with only 10 elements (0 through 9), location 10 is out of bounds. As an experiment, remove the comment symbol from the start of the subscripted line and observe the results. For many environments, doing so will result in a program crash.

One last point: the difference between **at( )** and **[ ]** as just described also applies to **deque**.

Swapping Vectors

Similar to **deque**, the STL provides two ways to exchange the contents of two **vector** containers. First, you can use the **swap( )** member function, which is shown here:

  void vector::swap(vector<T, Allocator> &*ob*);

This function exchanges the contents of *ob* with those of the invoking object.

Second, you can use the **swap( )** algorithm, which has a specialization defined expressly for **vector** objects. The prototype for this specialization is shown here:

  void swap(vector<T, Allocator> &*a*, vector<T, Allocator> &*b*);

This algorithm exchanges the contents of *a* and *b*.

Using clear( )

The meaning of the **clear( )** function as it relates to **vector**s is sometimes misunderstood. Supported by all of the containers, **clear( )** erases all elements from the invoking container. After a call to **clear( )**, the container is empty and has a size of zero, and this is precisely what it does when called on a vector. The trouble is that since **vector**s are dynamic arrays, newcomers to the STL sometimes assume that **clear( )** zeros the elements of a vector, but leaves its size alone (in other words, that in some sense, **clear( )** reinitializes a vector). This is, of course, false. For all containers, **clear( )** removes all elements in the invoking container and reduces its size to zero. In fact, **clear( )** is functionally equivalent to the following:

    erase(v.begin( ), v.end( ))

To understand the operation of **clear( )**, consider the following program:

```
// Using clear()
#include <iostream>
#include <vector>
using namespace std;

int main()
{
  vector<int> v;
  int i;

  for(i=0; i<10; i++) v.push_back(i);

  cout << "Initial contents of v: ";
  for(i=0; i<v.size(); i++)
    cout << v[i] << " ";
  cout << "\n";

  cout << "Initial size of v: ";
  cout << v.size() << "\n";

  cout << "Initial capacity of v: ";
  cout << v.capacity() << "\n\n";

  v.clear();

  cout << "Size of v after clear(): ";
  cout << v.size() << "\n";
```

```
cout << "Capacity of v after clear(): ";
cout << v.capacity() << "\n\n";

// put new values in v
for(i=0; i<10; i++) v.push_back(i*10);

cout << "New contents of v: ";
for(i=0; i<v.size(); i++)
  cout << v[i] << " ";
cout << "\n";

cout << "Size of v after adding new elements: ";
cout << v.size() << "\n";

cout << "Capacity of v after adding new elements: ";
cout << v.capacity() << "\n\n";

return 0;
}
```

4

The program's output is shown here:

```
Initial contents of v: 0 1 2 3 4 5 6 7 8 9
Initial size of v: 10
Initial capacity of v: 16

Size of v after clear(): 0
Capacity of v after clear(): 16

New contents of v: 0 10 20 30 40 50 60 70 80 90
Size of v after adding new elements: 10
Capacity of v after adding new elements: 16
```

Notice that after calling **clear( )**, the size of **v** is zero, but its capacity is still 16. The reason for this is that removing elements from a container does not alter its capacity, only its size. When new elements are added to **vector** after **clear( )** has been called, its size once again increases to 10.

One other point: The reason that the capacity of **v** is 16 is because (in most implementations) the size of the **vector** is doubled with each reallocation. Here, **v** starts off with a size of 0 and is increased to 2 with the first insertion, then 4, then 8, and finally to 16.

vector vs. deque

Since **vector** and **deque** have much in common (for example, both support random-access iterators and the array subscript operator), it might seem that it doesn't really matter which you use for any given situation. But this is not true. There are two factors that help you decide whether you should use a vector or a deque. The first is the speed of access to an element. Although both **vector** and **deque** provide constant time access to any arbitrary element, **vector**'s access time is usually a bit shorter. Thus, if your application will be repeatedly accessing many elements, a vector might be a better choice. The second factor is the number of insertions that will occur at the ends vs. how many will occur in the middle. If a large number of elements will be added at the boundaries—especially to the start—**deque** is a better choice. If few such additions will be made, then **vector**'s enhanced performance makes it the container of choice. As a general rule, **vector**'s ability to quickly access any element makes it the most often used container when an array-like object is needed.

Use a vector when a fast-access dynamic array is needed. Use a deque when many insertions or deletions will occur at the ends.

The following program illustrates a good use for a vector. It computes the average and the standard deviation for a set of values entered by the user. Recall that the standard deviation of a set of values is the average distance that the elements are from the average. It is found by summing of the squares of the differences between each element and the average, and then computing the square root of that sum divided by the number of values.

```
/* Compute average and standard deviation
   of a set of data. */
#include <iostream>
#include <vector>
#include <cmath>
using namespace std;

int main()
{
  vector<double> v;
  int i;
  double sum, avg, std_dev;

  cout << "Enter numbers (0 to stop).\n";
```

```
do {
  cout << ": ";
  cin >> i;
  if(i) v.push_back(i);
} while(i);
cout << "\n";

// find average
for(i=0; i<v.size(); i++)
  sum += v[i];
avg = sum / v.size();
cout << "Average is: " << avg << "\n\n";


// compute standard deviation
sum = 0.0;
for(i=0; i<v.size(); i++)
  sum += (v[i]-avg) * (v[i]-avg);
std_dev = sqrt(sum/v.size());
cout << "Standard deviation is: " << std_dev;
cout << "\n";

  return 0;
}
```

4

A sample run is shown here:

```
Enter numbers (0 to stop).
: 1
: 2
: 3
: 4
: 5
: 0

Average is: 3

Standard deviation is: 1.41421
```

While either a vector or a deque could have been used by the program, the choice of a vector to hold the list of values is an easy one. Once the values have been entered, the size of the vector remains unchanged. No insertions or deletions of any kind are performed. Indeed, if it were not for the fact that the number of values to be processed is not known at compile time, a normal array could have been used. After the values have been entered, the entire contents of the vector are accessed twice, once to compute the average and again to compute the standard deviation. Although the entry of the values by the user does cause several insertions to occur at the end of the vector, this activity is I/O-bound and has no effect on performace. But the computation of the average and standard deviation is compute-bound and **vector**'s optimal access time does positively enhance performance, and is the deciding factor in its favor.

IN DEPTH

Implementation Details

In books and articles about the STL it is not uncommon to find descriptions of the containers that also include implementation details—for example, that a **list** is usually implemented as a linked list. This book is no exception. While most of these details accurately reflect current implementations and are helpful in understanding the structure of the STL, it is important to understand that Standard C++ does not actually state precisely how the STL components will be implemented. It only states the constraints, such as complexity, to which each implementation must adhere. Thus, it is inherently risky to make assumptions about the underlying implementation of the various STL components. It is better to base your programs on the STL's performance guarantees rather than any idiosyncrasies of a specific implementation.

Storing Class Objects in a Vector

A vector can store any type of object, including one of a class that you create. Here is an example that uses a vector to store objects that hold the daily production run for an assembly line. Notice that **DailyOutput** defines the default constructor and provides overloaded versions of the < and == operators. The comparison operators are required by various STL algorithms. Remember, depending upon how your compiler implements the STL and what algorithms you use, other comparison operators may need to be defined.

```
/// Store a class object in a vector.
#include <iostream>
#include <vector>
#include <algorithm>
#include <cstdlib>
using namespace std;

class DailyOutput {
  int units;
public:
  DailyOutput() { units = 0; }
  DailyOutput(int x) { units = x; }

  double get_units() { return units; }
};

bool operator<(DailyOutput a, DailyOutput b)
{
  return a.get_units() < b.get_units();
}

bool operator==(DailyOutput a, DailyOutput b)
{
  return a.get_units() == b.get_units();
}

int main()
{
  vector<DailyOutput> v;
  vector<DailyOutput>::iterator p;
  int i;

  for(i=0; i<14; i++)
    v.push_back(DailyOutput(60 + rand()%10));

  cout << "Daily production:\n";
  for(i=0; i<v.size(); i++)
    cout << v[i].get_units() << " ";
  cout << "\n\n";

  p = min_element(v.begin(), v.end());
  cout << "Minimum units: " << p->get_units();
  cout << "\n";

  p = max_element(v.begin(), v.end());
```

4

```
cout << "Maximum units: " << p->get_units();
cout << "\n\n";

// look for consecutive days with the same production
p = v.begin();
do {
  p = adjacent_find(p, v.end());
  if(p != v.end()) {
    cout << "Two consecutive days with ";
    cout << p->get_units() << " units.\n";
    p++; // move on to next element
  }
} while(p != v.end());

return 0;
}
```

The output from this program is shown here:

```
Daily production:
61 67 64 60 69 64 68 68 62 64 65 65 61 67

Minimum units: 60
Maximum units: 69

Two consecutive days with 68 units.
Two consecutive days with 65 units.
```

In the program, a vector is used to store the number of units produced over a period of 14 days. The algorithms **min_element( )** and **max_element( )** are employed to determine the minimum and maximum daily production. These algorithms use the overloaded < operator to determine when one **DailyOutput** object is less than another. Their prototypes are shown here:

   template <class ForIter>
      ForIter min_element(ForIter *start*, ForIter *last*);

   template <class ForIter>
      ForIter max_element(ForIter *start*, ForIter *last*);

The **min_element( )** algorithm returns an iterator to the minimum element within the range *start* and *last*. The **max_element( )** algorithm returns an iterator to the maximum element within the range *start* and *last*. The specified range need not be ordered.

The program uses the **adjacent_find( )** algorithm to look for consecutive days in which the number of units produced was the same. It has this prototype:

```
template <class ForIter>
    ForIter adjacent_find(ForIter start, ForIter end);
```

The **adjacent_find( )** algorithm searches for adjacent matching elements within a sequence specified by *start* and *end* and returns an iterator to the first element. If no adjacent pair is found, *end* is returned. By continuing the search one element past the element pointed to by the return value, you can find each subsequent pair of equal consecutive elements. In the program, the **adjacent_find( )** algorithm uses the overloaded = = to determine when one **DailyOutput** object is equal to another.

4

The bool Specialization

The STL also contains a specialization of **vector** for Boolean values: **vector<bool>**. It includes all of the functionality of **vector** and adds these two members:

void flip( );	Reverses all bits in the vector.
static void swap (reference *i*, reference *j*);	Exchanges the bits specified by *i* and *j*.

By specializing for **bool**, **vector** can pack true/false values into individual bits. The **vector<bool>** specialization defines a class called **reference** that is used to emulate a reference to a bit.

The next chapter examines another sequence container: **list**. As you will see, **list** offers a useful alternative to **deque** and **vector** for certain applications.

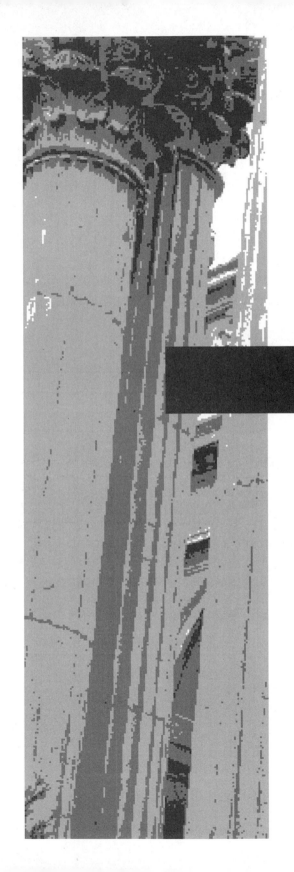

CHAPTER 5

The list Container

The **list** class was briefly introduced in Chapter 2. Here, it is examined in detail. The **list** class implements a bidirectional, sequential container and is most often implemented as a doubly linked list. It is particularly useful when elements will be frequently added to or removed from the middle of the container and random access to elements is not required.

list Fundamentals

The template specification for **list** is

> template <class T, class Allocator = allocator<T> > class list

Here, **T** is the type of data being stored and **Allocator** specifies the allocator, which defaults to the standard allocator. **list** has the following constructors:

> explicit list(const Allocator &*a* = Allocator( ));

> explicit list(size_type *num*, const T &*val* = T ( ),
>   const Allocator &*a* = Allocator( ));

> list(const list<T, Allocator> &*ob*);

> template <class InIter> list(InIter *start*, InIter *end*,
>   const Allocator &*a* = Allocator( ));

The first form constructs an empty list. The second form constructs a list that has *num* elements with the value *val*. The third form is **list**'s copy constructor. The fourth form constructs a list that contains the elements in the range specified by *start* and *end*.

The **list** class overloads the assignment operator. In addition, the following comparison operators are defined for **list**:

> ==, <, <=, !=, >, >=

The **list** class supports bidirectional iterators. Thus, the container can be accessed through an iterator in both the forward and reverse direction. However, random access operations are not supported. Thus, the **at( )** function is not provided and the **[ ]** operator is not overloaded.

The **list** class defines the following concrete types:

size_type	Some type of integer.
difference_type	Some type of integer that can hold the difference between two addresses.
reference	A reference to an element (i.e., **T** &).
const_reference	A **const** reference to an element (i.e., **const T** &).
iterator	An iterator.
const_iterator	A **const** iterator.
reverse_iterator	A reverse iterator.
const_reverse_iterator	A **const** reverse iterator.
value_type	The type of a value stored in a container; same as **T**.
allocator_type	The type of the allocator.
pointer	A pointer to an element (i.e., **T** *).
const_pointer	A **const** pointer to an element (i.e., **const T** *).

5

The **list** class contains the member functions shown in Table 5-1. Notice the functions **merge( )**, **reverse( )**, **unique( )**, **remove( )**, and **remove_if( )**. As you will learn later in this book, these functions duplicate the functionality provided by the standard algorithms of the same names. These **list** member functions have been specially optimized for operation on objects of type **list** and offer a high-performance alternative to their generic counterparts.

Performance Characteristics

Insertion or deletion in a list takes constant time.

Inserting or deleting elements in a list takes place in constant time. It doesn't matter where in the **list** the insertion or deletion will occur. Since **list** is usually implemented as a linked list, an insertion or deletion involves only the rearrangement of the links and not a shifting of elements or the reallocation of memory.

Insertion invalidates no iterators or references.

Deletion invalidates only iterators or references to the deleted elements.

Unlike **vector** and **deque**, insertion into a list invalidates no iterators or references to elements. A deletion invalidates only iterators or references to the deleted elements. The fact that these operations do not affect the validity of iterators or references to existing elements makes the **list** class especially useful for those applications in which nonvolatile iterators and/or references are desired.

Member	Description
template <class InIter> void assign(InIter *start*, InIter *end*);	Assigns the list the sequence defined by *start* and *end*.
void assign(size_type *num*, const T &*val*);	Assigns the list *num* elements of value *val*.
reference back( ); const_reference back( ) const;	Returns a reference to the last element in the list.
iterator begin( ); const_iterator begin( ) const;	Returns an iterator to the first element in the list.
void clear( );	Removes all elements from the list.
bool empty( ) const;	Returns **true** if the invoking list is empty and **false** otherwise.
iterator end( ); const_iterator end( ) const;	Returns an iterator to the end of the list.
iterator erase(iterator *i*);	Removes the element pointed to by *i*. Returns an iterator to the element after the one removed.
iterator erase(iterator *start*, iterator *end*);	Removes the elements in the range *start* to *end*. Returns an iterator to the element after the last element removed.
reference front( ); const_reference front( ) const;	Returns a reference to the first element in the list.
allocator_type get_allocator( ) const;	Returns list's allocator.
iterator insert(iterator *i*, const T &*val* = T( ));	Inserts *val* immediately before the element specified by *i*. An iterator to the element is returned.
void insert(iterator *i*, size_type *num*, const T & *val*;)	Inserts *num* copies of *val* immediately before the element specified by *i*.

template <class InIter>
    void insert(iterator *i*,
            InIter *start*, InIter *end*);
	Inserts the sequence defined by *start* and *end* immediately before the element specified by *i*.

The **list** Member Functions
Table 5-1.

Member	Description
size_type max_size( ) const;	Returns the maximum number of elements that the list can hold.

void merge(list<T, Allocator> &*ob*);
template <class Comp>
   void merge(<list<T, Allocator> &*ob*,
        Comp *cmpfn*);
	Merges the ordered list contained in *ob* with the ordered invoking list. The result is ordered. After the merge, the list contained in *ob* is empty. In the second form, a comparison function can be specified that determines when one element is less than another.

void pop_back( );	Removes the last element in the list.
void pop_front( );	Removes the first element in the list.
void push_back(const T &*val*);	Adds an element with the value specified by *val* to the end of the list.
void push_front(const T &*val*);	Adds an element with the value specified by *val* to the front of the list.
reverse_iterator rbegin( ); const_reverse_iterator rbegin( ) const;	Returns a reverse iterator to the end of the list.
void remove(const T &*val*);	Removes elements with the value *val* from the list.
template <class UnPred> void remove_if(UnPred *pr*);	Removes elements for which the unary predicate *pr* is true.
reverse_iterator rend( ); const_reverse_iterator rend( ) const;	Returns a reverse iterator to the start of the list.
void resize(size_type *num*, T *val* = T ( ));	Changes the size of the list to that specified by *num*. If the list must be lengthened, elements with the value specified by *val* are added to the end.
void reverse( );	Reverses the invoking list.
size_type size( ) const;	Returns the number of elements currently in the list.

5

The **list**
Member
Functions
(continued)
Table 5-1.

Member	Description

void sort( );
template <class Comp>
   void sort(Comp *cmpfn*);
	Sorts the list. The second form sorts the list using the comparison function *cmpfn* to determine when one element is less than another.

void splice(iterator *i*, list<T, Allocator> &*ob*);	The contents of *ob* are inserted into the invoking list at the location pointed to by *i*. After the operation, *ob* is empty.

void splice(iterator *i*,
       list<T, Allocator> &*ob*,
       iterator *el*);
	The element pointed to by *el* is removed from the list *ob* and stored in the invoking list at the location pointed to by *i*.

void splice(iterator *i*,
       list<T, Allocator> &*ob*,
       iterator *start*, iterator *end*);
	The range defined by *start* and *end* is removed from *ob* and stored in the invoking list beginning at the location pointed to by *i*.

void swap(list<T, Allocator> &*ob*)	Exchanges the elements stored in the invoking list with those in *ob*.

void unique( );
template <class BinPred>
   void unique(BinPred *pr*);
	Removes consecutive duplicate elements from the invoking list. The second form uses *pr* to determine when two elements are duplicates.

The **list** Member Functions *(continued)*
Table 5-1.

Exploring list

The **list** class provides many of the same member functions as **deque** and **vector**. However, since **list** was designed with high-performance list operations in mind, it includes a number of functions, such as **splice( )** and **merge( )**, not found in the other sequence containers. It also defines several member functions that are optimized alternatives to the standard algorithms. In this section, we will examine those features of **list** that make it different from the other sequence containers.

We will begin our exploration of **list** with a detailed examination of merging and splicing. Briefly introduced in Chapter 2, these two operations perform two of the most fundamental list manipulations.

Merging

One of the most common list operations is merging. Merging is the process of integrating the elements from one ordered list into another. During a merge, each element of the source list is inserted into its proper location in the target list. Thus, the result is an ordered list that contains all of the elements of the two original lists. Lists are merged using the **merge( )** member function.

The **merge( )** function has the two forms shown here:

```
void merge(list<T, Allocator> &ob);
template <class Comp>  void merge(list<T,  Allocator> &ob,
                                    Comp cmpfn);
```

The first form merges the ordered list contained in *ob* with the ordered invoking list. After the merge, the list contained in *ob* is empty. The lists must be sorted in ascending order. In the second form, a comparison function can be specified that determines when one element is less than another. For both functions, the invoking list is expanded as needed to accommodate the new elements.

The only iterators or references invalidated by a merge are those that point to the affected elements (that is, the ones that are moved to the resultant list). Iterators and references to all other elements, including those in the invoking list, remain unchanged.

Here is a simple example of **merge( )**:

```
// Demonstrate merge().
#include <iostream>
#include <list>
using namespace std;

int main()
{
  list<int> lst1, lst2;
  int i;

  for(i=0; i<10; i+=2)
    lst1.push_back(i);

  for(i=1; i<11; i+=2)
    lst2.push_back(i);
```

5

```
  cout << "Original size of lst1: ";
  cout << lst1.size() << "\n";
  cout << "Original contents of lst1:\n";
  list<int>::iterator p = lst1.begin();
  while(p != lst1.end())
    cout << *p++ << " ";
  cout << "\n\n";

  cout << "Original size of lst2: ";
  cout << lst2.size() << "\n";
  cout << "Original contents of lst2:\n";
  p = lst2.begin();
  while(p != lst2.end())
    cout << *p++ << " ";
  cout << "\n\n";

  // merge the two lists
  lst1.merge(lst2);

  cout << "Size of lst1 after merge: ";
  cout << lst1.size() << "\n";
  cout << "Merged contents of lst1:\n";
  p = lst1.begin();
  while(p != lst1.end())
    cout << *p++ << " ";
  cout << "\n\n";

  cout << "lst2 is now empty, its size is ";
  cout << lst2.size() << "\n";

  return 0;
}
```

Here is the output produced by the program:

```
Original size of lst1: 5
Original contents of lst1:
0 2 4 6 8

Original size of lst2: 5
Original contents of lst2:
1 3 5 7 9

Size of lst1 after merge: 10
Merged contents of lst1:
```

```
0  1  2  3  4  5  6  7  8  9

lst2 is now empty, its size is 0
```

Merging
empties the
merged list.

As you can see, after **lst2** is merged into **lst1**, the size of **lst1** is 10 and the size of **lst2** is zero. When one list is merged into another, the merged list is emptied.

Only ordered
lists can
be merged.

It is important to remember that only ordered (i.e., sorted) lists can be merged. Merging means that the elements of one list are inserted into their proper order in the other list. This requires the use of ordered lists. If you try to merge a list that is not ordered, the merge will be performed incorrectly. The following program illustrates this fact.

5

```cpp
// Merging won't work if the lists aren't ordered.
#include <iostream>
#include <list>
using namespace std;

int main()
{
  list<int> lst1, lst2;
  int i;

  lst1.push_back(2);
  lst1.push_back(0);
  lst1.push_back(8);
  lst1.push_back(4);
  lst1.push_back(6);

  for(i=1; i<11; i+=2)
    lst2.push_back(i);

  cout << "Original contents of lst1:\n";
  list<int>::iterator p = lst1.begin();
  while(p != lst1.end())
    cout << *p++ << " ";
  cout << "\n\n";

  cout << "Original contents of lst2:\n";
  p = lst2.begin();
  while(p != lst2.end())
    cout << *p++ << " ";
  cout << "\n\n";
```

```
  // this merge will fail
  lst1.merge(lst2);

  cout << "Contents of lst1 after failed merge:\n";
  p = lst1.begin();
  while(p != lst1.end())
    cout << *p++ << " ";
  cout << "\n\n";

  return 0;
}
```

The output from the program is shown here:

```
Original contents of lst1:
2 0 8 4 6

Original contents of lst2:
1 3 5 7 9

Contents of lst1 after failed merge:
1 2 0 3 5 7 8 4 6 9
```

As you can see, the elements from **lst2** are not properly merged into **lst1** because **lst1** was not sorted.

By default, **merge( )** uses the **<** operator to compare elements from the two lists. This is why the lists must be sorted in ascending order. You can alter this behavior by using the second form of **merge( )**, which allows you to specify how you want comparisons to be made. For example, the following example shows how to merge two lists that are sorted into descending order.

```
// Merge into descending order.
#include <iostream>
#include <list>
using namespace std;

int main()
{
  list<int> lst1, lst2;
  int i;

  for(i=10; i>=0; i-=2)
    lst1.push_back(i);

  for(i=11; i>=1; i-=2)
```

```
   lst2.push_back(i);

cout << "Original contents of lst1:\n";
list<int>::iterator p = lst1.begin();
while(p != lst1.end())
  cout << *p++ << " ";
cout << "\n\n";

cout << "Original contents of lst2:\n";
p = lst2.begin();
while(p != lst2.end())
  cout << *p++ << " ";
cout << "\n\n";

// merge using greater than, not less than
lst1.merge(lst2, greater<int>());

cout << "Merged contents of lst1:\n";
p = lst1.begin();
while(p != lst1.end())
  cout << *p++ << " ";
cout << "\n\n";

return 0;
}
```

The output from this program is shown here:

```
Original contents of lst1:
10 8 6 4 2 0

Original contents of lst2:
11 9 7 5 3 1

Merged contents of lst1:
11 10 9 8 7 6 5 4 3 2 1 0
```

As you can see, both **lst1** and **lst2** are in descending order. However, they can be successfully merged by **merge( )** when the **greater** function object is used for comparisons.

Splicing

An operation related to merging is splicing. When a splice occurs, the source list is inserted as a unit into the target list. No element-by-element integration of the two lists takes place. A splice is essentially just a "cut-and-paste" operation.

Splicing is accomplished using **splice( )**. It has these forms:

```
void splice(iterator i, list<T, Allocator> &ob);
void splice(iterator i, list<T, Allocator> &ob, iterator el);
void splice(iterator i, list<T, Allocator> &ob,
            iterator start, iterator end);
```

Splicing is essentially a "cut-and-paste" operation.

In the first form, the contents of *ob* are inserted into the invoking list at the location pointed to by *i*. After the operation, *ob* is empty. In the second form, the element pointed to by *el* is removed from the list *ob* and stored in the invoking list at the location pointed to by *i*. The third form splices the range defined by *start* and *end* from *ob* into the invoking list at the location pointed to by *i*. In the process, the range is removed from *ob*. When splicing, neither list need be ordered.

Although a splicing operation could be performed manually using repeated insert and erase operations, **splice( )** is much more efficient. In fact, the first two forms of **splice( )** operate in constant time. The third operates in linear time unless it is splicing elements from the invoking list, in which case it also operates in constant time.

Splicing invalidates only those iterators or references that point to the affected elements (that is, the ones that are moved to the resultant list). Iterators and references to all other elements, including those in the invoking list, remain unchanged.

A splice can take place at any point in the target sequence: at the front, the middle, or the end. When a splice is at the front of a list, the spliced sequence is inserted before **begin( )**. When a splice occurs at the end, the spliced sequence is inserted before **end( )**. Here is an example that illustrates the various ways a splice can occur. It constructs a sentence one phrase at a time.

```cpp
// A splicing example.
#include <iostream>
#include <list>
#include <string>
#include <algorithm>
using namespace std;

int main()
{
```

```
list<string> sentence;
list<string> phrase;
list<string>::iterator p;
string s1[] = {
  "occur", "at", ""
};
string s2[] = {
  "Splicing", "can", ""
};
string s3[] = {
  "or", "the", "end.", ""
};
string s4[] = {
  "the", "front,", "the", "middle,", ""
};
int i;

// construct initial sentence
for(i=0; s1[i]!=""; i++)
  sentence.push_back(s1[i]);

// construct 1st phrase to add
for(i=0; s2[i]!=""; i++)
  phrase.push_back(s2[i]);

cout << "Original sentence:\n";
p = sentence.begin();
while(p != sentence.end())
  cout << *p++ << " ";
cout << "\n\n";

// splice at the front
sentence.splice(sentence.begin(), phrase);

cout << "Sentence after splicing at the front:\n";
p = sentence.begin();
while(p != sentence.end())
  cout << *p++ << " ";
cout << "\n\n";

// construct next phrase
for(i=0; s3[i]!=""; i++)
  phrase.push_back(s3[i]);

// splice at end
```

```
      sentence.splice(sentence.end(), phrase);

      cout << "Sentence after splicing at the end:\n";
      p = sentence.begin();
      while(p != sentence.end())
        cout << *p++ << " ";
      cout << "\n\n";

      // construct final phrase
      for(i=0; s4[i]!=""; i++)
        phrase.push_back(s4[i]);

      // splice in the phrase before the "or"
      p = find(sentence.begin(), sentence.end(), "or");
      sentence.splice(p, phrase);

      cout << "Sentence after splicing in the middle:\n";
      p = sentence.begin();
      while(p != sentence.end())
        cout << *p++ << " ";

      return 0;
    }
```

The output from the program is shown here:

```
Original sentence:
occur at

Sentence after splicing at the front:
Splicing can occur at

Sentence after splicing at the end:
Splicing can occur at or the end.

Sentence after splicing in the middle:
Splicing can occur at the front, the middle, or the end.
```

Notice that this example uses the **find( )** algorithm to find the location at which to insert a phrase into the middle of the list. It has this prototype:

```
template <class InIter, class T>
    InIter find(InIter start, InIter end, const T &val);
```

The **find( )** algorithm searches the range *start* to *end* for the value specified by *val*. It returns an iterator to the first occurrence of the element or to *end* if the value is not in the sequence.

Sorting a List

A list may be sorted by calling the **sort( )** member function. It has the following forms:

```
void sort( );
template <class Comp> void sort(Comp cmpfn);
```

The first form sorts the list into ascending order. The second form sorts the list using the comparison function *cmpfn* to determine when one element is less than another.

The following program creates a list of random integers and then puts the list into sorted order.

```
// Sort a list.
#include <iostream>
#include <list>
#include <cstdlib>
using namespace std;

int main()
{
  list<int> lst;
  int i;

  // create a list of random integers
  for(i=0; i<10; i++)
    lst.push_back(rand());

  cout << "Original contents:\n";
  list<int>::iterator p = lst.begin();
  while(p != lst.end()) {
    cout << *p << " ";
    p++;
  }
  cout << "\n\n";

  // sort the list
  lst.sort();
```

```
cout << "Sorted contents:\n";
p = lst.begin();
while(p != lst.end()) {
  cout << *p << " ";
  p++;
}

return 0;
}
```

Here is sample output produced by the program:

```
Original contents:
41 18467 6334 26500 19169 15724 11478 29358 26962 24464

Sorted contents:
41 6334 11478 15724 18467 19169 24464 26500 26962 29358
```

By default, lists are sorted into ascending order. You can sort a list into reverse (i.e., descending) order by using the predicate form of **sort( )** and using the **greater** function object. For example, try substituting this line into the preceding program.

```
lst.sort(greater<int>());
```

The list will now be in descending order.

IN DEPTH

Why list Must Define Its Own Sort

Several of the **list** member functions—**reverse( )**, **remove( )**, **merge( )**, etc.—duplicate functionality provided by the STL algorithms. Although they are defined by **list** in order to provide higher performance, it is still possible to use the standard algorithms if you so desire. However, this is not the case with sorting.

Although the STL defines the standard algorithm **sort( )**, objects of the **list** class can't use it! Instead, a list must be sorted using the member

IN DEPTH

CONTINUED

function **list::sort( )**. Since sorting is one of the most fundamental algorithms, at first glance this seems to be a serious design flaw in the STL—or, at least, an odd inconsistency! Fortunately, closer examination reveals that this is not the case.

To understand why an object of class **list** cannot be sorted using the **sort( )** algorithm, begin by examining one of its prototypes:

template<class RandIter> void sort(RandIter *start*, RandIter *end*);

The range of elements to be sorted is specified by *start* and *end*. Notice, however, that these must be random-access iterators. The trouble is that **list** supports only bidirectional iterators. Thus, the **sort( )** algorithm cannot be used.

Restricting the **sort( )** algorithm to only those containers that support random-access iterators allows it to be implemented efficiently for **vector** and **deque**. As you probably know, the optimal techniques used for sorting a data structure that supports random access are different from those used for sorting a sequential one. So, instead of degrading the overall efficiency of the **sort( )** algorithm, the STL simply provides a **list** member function that is engineered specifically for sorting lists.

Removing Elements from a List

You can remove an element from a list using **remove( )**. Its prototype is shown here:

void remove(const T &*val*);

This function removes elements with the value *val* from the invoking list. If no element matches *val*, then the list is unchanged.

At first glance, **remove( )** may seem redundant because **list** also defines the **erase( )** function. However, this is not the case. The difference lies in the fact that **erase( )** requires iterators to the element(s) to be deleted. On the other hand, **remove( )** automatically searches the list for the specified element. Here is a short example:

```
// Demonstrate remove().
#include <iostream>
#include <list>
using namespace std;

int main()
{
  list<int> lst;
  list<int>::iterator p;
  int i;

  for(i=0; i<20; i++) lst.push_back(i%3);

  cout << "Original list: ";
  for(p=lst.begin(); p!=lst.end(); p++)
    cout << *p << " ";
  cout << "\n\n";

  lst.remove(1); // remove all 1's

  cout << "Modified list: ";
  for(p=lst.begin(); p!=lst.end(); p++)
    cout << *p << " ";
  cout << "\n\n";

  return 0;
}
```

The output from the program is shown here:

```
Original list: 0 1 2 0 1 2 0 1 2 0 1 2 0 1 2 0 1 2 0 1

Modified list: 0 2 0 2 0 2 0 2 0 2 0 2 0
```

As the evidence shows, the call to **lst.remove(1)** deletes all occurrences of the value 1 from the invoking list.

You can also remove elements that satisfy a certain condition by using **remove_if( )**, whose prototype is shown here:

```
template <class UnPred>  void remove_if(UnPred pr);
```

This function removes elements for which the unary predicate *pr* is true. If no
element satisfies the predicate, then the list is unchanged.

Removing Duplicate Elements

Another way to remove elements from a list is through the use of the
unique( ) member function, which deletes duplicate consecutive elements.
Its prototypes are shown here:

```
void unique( );
template <class BinPred> void unique(BinPred pr);
```

5

The **unique( )**
function
removes
consecutive
duplicate
elements.

The first form removes duplicate elements from the invoking list. The
second form uses *pr* to determine when one element is the same as another.
Thus, **unique( )** creates a list in which no consecutive duplicates are present.
If the initial list is ordered, then after applying **unique( )**, each element
will be unique.

Here is an example that demonstrates **unique( )**:

```cpp
// Demonstrate unique().
#include <iostream>
#include <list>
using namespace std;

int main()
{
  list<int> lst;
  list<int>::iterator p;

  for(int i=0; i<5; i++)
    for(int j=0; j<3; j++) lst.push_back(i);

  cout << "Original list: ";
  for(p=lst.begin(); p!=lst.end(); p++)
    cout << *p << " ";
  cout << "\n\n";

  lst.unique(); // remove consecutive duplicates

  cout << "Modified list: ";
  for(p=lst.begin(); p!=lst.end(); p++)
```

```
    cout << *p << " ";
  cout << "\n\n";

  return 0;
}
```

The output from the program is shown here:

```
Original list: 0 0 0 1 1 1 2 2 2 3 3 3 4 4 4

Modified list: 0 1 2 3 4
```

Reversing a List

To reverse a list, use the **reverse( )** member function. Its prototype is shown here:

   void reverse( );

It reverses the entire contents of the invoking list.

Here is an interesting use of **reverse( )**. It is used to create a palindrome tester. As you may recall, a palindrome is a phrase that, ignoring punctuation, reads forward the same as it reads backward. The following program allows you to easily test a phrase for "palindromeness." It first removes all punctuation, displays the phrase, reverses the characters, and, finally, displays the phrase backward. If the forward and backward lists read the same, a palindrome has been found.

```
// Using reverse() to create a palindrome tester.
#include <iostream>
#include <list>
using namespace std;

char phrases[][80] = {
  "Madam, I'm Adam.",
  "Able was I ere I saw Elba.",
  "A man, a plan, a canal: Panama!",
  "This is not one.",
  ""
};

int main()
{
```

```
list<char> pal;
int i, j;
list<char>::iterator p;

for(i=0; *phrases[i]; i++) {
  for(j=0; phrases[i][j]; j++)
    pal.push_back(phrases[i][j]);

  cout << "Phrase # " << i << " forward: ";
  p = pal.begin();
  while(p != pal.end()) cout << *p++;
  cout << "\n";

  // remove extraneous characters
  pal.remove(',');
  pal.remove('.');
  pal.remove('!');
  pal.remove(':');
  pal.remove('\'');
  pal.remove(' ');

  cout << "Phrase # " << i << " after deletions: ";
  p = pal.begin();
  while(p != pal.end()) cout << *p++;
  cout << "\n";

  pal.reverse(); // reverse the list

  cout << "Phrase # " << i << " backward:          ";
  p = pal.begin();
  while(p != pal.end()) cout << *p++;
  cout << "\n\n";

  pal.clear(); // get ready to try next phrase
  }

  return 0;
}
```

Here is the output produced:

```
Phrase # 0 forward: Madam, I'm Adam.
Phrase # 0 after deletions: MadamImAdam
Phrase # 0 backward:        madAmImadaM
```

```
Phrase # 1 forward: Able was I ere I saw Elba.
Phrase # 1 after deletions: AblewasIereIsawElba
Phrase # 1 backward:        ablEwasIereIsawelbA

Phrase # 2 forward: A man, a plan, a canal: Panama!
Phrase # 2 after deletions: AmanaplanacanalPanama
Phrase # 2 backward:        amanaPlanacanalpanamA

Phrase # 3 forward: This is not one.
Phrase # 3 after deletions: Thisisnotone
Phrase # 3 backward:        enotonsisihT
```

Swapping Lists

As with the other two sequence containers, the STL provides two ways to exchange the contents of two lists. First, you can use the **swap( )** member function, which is shown here:

> void list::swap(list<T, Allocator> &*ob*);

This function exchanges the contents of *ob* with those of the invoking object.

Second, you can use the **swap( )** algorithm, which has a specialization defined expressly for **list** objects. The prototype for this specialization is shown here:

> void swap(list<T, Allocator> &*a*, list<T, Allocator> &*b*);

This algorithm exchanges the contents of *a* and *b*.

Storing Class Objects in a List

To store objects of classes that you create in a list, you will usually need to overload at least the < and = = operators and provide a default constructor. The operators are used to determine the ordering and equality of objects when a list is sorted, merged, etc. Depending upon what you do with your list, other operators may be required.

To illustrate the power of the **list** class a simple mailing list program is shown. In the program, a class called **maillist**, which holds mailing addresses, is defined and two separate mailing lists are created. These lists are then sorted by name and merged. After the merge, the duplicate elements are removed from the resulting list. Notice how little code is required to accomplish these tasks. If you were to write an equivalent, non-STL version of the program, it would be several times longer.

```cpp
// Using a list to store mailing addresses.
#include <iostream>
#include <list>
#include <string>
using namespace std;

class maillist {
  string name;
  string street;
  string city;
  string state;
  string zip;
public:
  maillist() {
    name = street = city = state = zip = "";
  }
  maillist(string n, string s, string c,
           string st, string z) {
    name = n;
    street = s;
    city = c;
    state = st;
    zip = z;
  }

  string getname() { return name; }
  string getcity() { return city; }
  string getstreet() { return street; }
  string getstate() { return state; }
  string getzip() { return zip; }
};

// List sorted by name.
bool operator<(maillist &a, maillist &b)
{
  return a.getname() < b.getname();
}

// List searched by name.
bool operator==(maillist &a, maillist &b)
{
  return a.getname() == b.getname();
}

// Display list on screen.
```

```
void display(list<maillist> &lst)
{
  list<maillist>::iterator p;

  for(p=lst.begin(); p!=lst.end(); p++) {
    cout << p->getname() << ": ";
    cout << p->getstreet() << ", ";
    cout << p->getcity() << ", ";
    cout << p->getstate() << " ";
    cout << p->getzip() << "\n";
  }
}

int main()
{
  list<maillist> mlstA, mlstB;

  mlstA.push_back(maillist("James, Tom",
                  "1102 W. Henry St",
                  "Mission", "TX", "78572"));
  mlstA.push_back(maillist("Newton, Sid",
                  "55 Oscar Blvd",
                  "Kirksville", "MO", "63501"));
  mlstA.push_back(maillist("Henson, Erick",
                  "908 Trunk Ave",
                  "Peoria", "IL", "61615"));
  mlstA.push_back(maillist("Ewen, Heidi",
                  "43645 N. Broadway #4",
                  "Idaho Falls", "ID", "83401"));
  mlstA.push_back(maillist("Mount, W. C.",
                  "78A Wothington Rd",
                  "Berkeley", "CA", "94710"));

  mlstB.push_back(maillist("Williams, Don",
                  "197 NorthRidge Dr",
                  "Walworth", "WI", "53184"));
  mlstB.push_back(maillist("Newton, Sid",
                  "55 Oscar Blvd",
                  "Kirksville", "MO", "63501"));
  mlstB.push_back(maillist("Ewen, Heidi",
                  "43645 N. Broadway #4",
                  "Idaho Falls", "ID", "83401"));
  mlstB.push_back(maillist("Weston, George",
                  "5464 Woodbury Ct",
                  "Baker", "LA", "70714"));

  mlstA.sort();
```

```
    mlstB.sort();

    // merge mailings lists
    mlstA.merge(mlstB);
    cout << "List A after sorting and merging.\n";
    display(mlstA);
    cout << "List A now has " << mlstA.size();
    cout << " entries.\n\n";

    // remove duplicates
    mlstA.unique();
    cout << "List A after removing duplicates.\n";
    display(mlstA);
    cout << "List A now has " << mlstA.size();
    cout << " entries.\n\n";

    return 0;
}
```

The output from the program is shown here:

```
List A after sorting and merging.
Ewen, Heidi: 43645 N. Broadway #4, Idaho Falls, ID 83401
Ewen, Heidi: 43645 N. Broadway #4, Idaho Falls, ID 83401
Henson, Erick: 908 Trunk Ave, Peoria, IL 61615
James, Tom: 1102 W. Henry St, Mission, TX 78572
Mount, W. C.: 78A Wothington Rd, Berkeley, CA 94710
Newton, Sid: 55 Oscar Blvd, Kirksville, MO 63501
Newton, Sid: 55 Oscar Blvd, Kirksville, MO 63501
Weston, George: 5464 Woodbury Ct, Baker, LA 70714
Williams, Don: 197 NorthRidge Dr, Walworth, WI 53184
List A now has 9 entries.

List A after removing duplicates.
Ewen, Heidi: 43645 N. Broadway #4, Idaho Falls, ID 83401
Henson, Erick: 908 Trunk Ave, Peoria, IL 61615
James, Tom: 1102 W. Henry St, Mission, TX 78572
Mount, W. C.: 78A Wothington Rd, Berkeley, CA 94710
Newton, Sid: 55 Oscar Blvd, Kirksville, MO 63501
Weston, George: 5464 Woodbury Ct, Baker, LA 70714
Williams, Don: 197 NorthRidge Dr, Walworth, WI 53184
List A now has 7 entries.
```

The next chapter examines the three sequence container adaptors: **stack**, **queue**, and **priority_queue**.

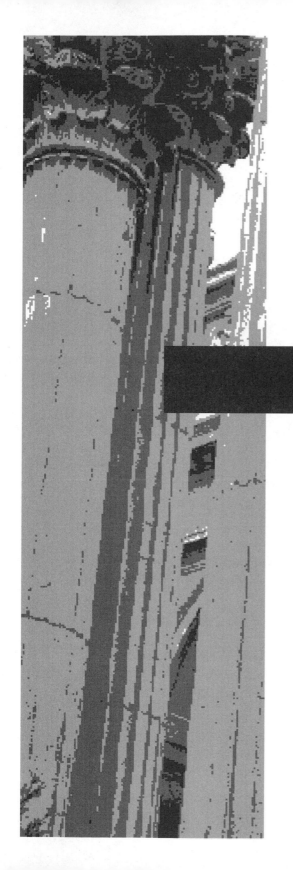

CHAPTER 6

The Container
Adaptors

This chapter examines the container adaptors defined by the STL. These are **queue**, **priority_queue**, and **stack**. They utilize one of the sequence containers as the underlying container, adapting it to their own special purposes. In essence, a container adaptor is simply a tightly controlled interface to another container. Although the container adaptors are built on one of the sequence containers, they are themselves also containers, and you use them much like you use the other containers. It's just that access to their elements is restricted.

Container Restrictions

The container adaptors do not support iterators.

The container adaptors do not support all of the functionality of their underlying containers. The manipulations allowed by an adaptor are a highly restricted subset of what the base container supports. While the precise restrictions differ from adaptor to adaptor, there is one difference that is shared by all: iterators are not supported. If the adaptors supported iterators, then it would be a trivial matter to circumvent the data structure defined by the adaptor and access its elements out of order.

queue

The **queue** class supports a normal, first-in, first-out (FIFO) queue. Elements are inserted into a queue on one end and removed from the other. Elements cannot be accessed in any other fashion. The **queue** template specification is shown here:

    template <class T, class Container = deque<T> > class queue

Here, **T** is the type of data being stored and **Container** is the type of container used to hold the queue, which by default is **deque**. The underlying container is held in a protected object called **c** of type **Container**.

The **queue** adaptor has the following constructor:

    explicit queue(const Container &cnt = Container( ));

The **queue( )** constructor creates an empty queue. To use a queue, include the **<queue>** header.

In general, **queue** can adapt any container that supports the following operations:

> back( )
>
> front( )
>
> pop_front( )
>
> push_back( )

The **queue** class implements a standard first-in, first-out queue.

Thus, you can also use **list** as a container for a queue. However, you cannot use **vector** because **vector** does not provide the **pop_front( )** function. The **queue** class defines the following concrete types.

container_type	The container being adapted.
size_type	Some type of integer.
value_type	The type of a value stored in a container; same as **T**.

6

The following comparison operators are defined for **queue**:

> ==, <, <=, !=, >, >=

The **queue** adaptor contains the member functions shown in Table 6-1. As you can see, **queue** can only be accessed in a first-in, first-out manner.

The **queue** Member Functions **Table 6-1.**

Member	Description
value_type &back( ); const value_type &back( ) const;	Returns a reference to the last element in the queue.
bool empty( ) const;	Returns **true** if the invoking queue is empty and **false** otherwise.
value_type &front( ); const value_type &front( ) const;	Returns a reference to the first element in the queue.

The **queue**
Member
Functions
(continued)
Table 6-1.

Member	Description
void pop( );	Removes the first element in the queue.
void push(const T &*val*);	Adds an element with the value specified by *val* to the end of the queue.
size_type size( ) const;	Returns the number of elements currently in the queue.

Here is a simple example of a **queue**:

```
// Demonstrate the queue class.
#include <iostream>
#include <queue>
#include <string>
using namespace std;

int main()
{
  queue<string> q;

  cout << "Pushing one two three four\n\n";
  q.push("one");
  q.push("two");
  q.push("three");
  q.push("four");

  while(!q.empty()) {
    cout << "Popping ";
    cout << q.front() << "\n";
    q.pop();
  }

  return 0;
}
```

Here is the output from the program:

```
Pushing one two three four

Popping one
Popping two
Popping three
Popping four
```

Somewhat counterintuitively, the **pop( )** function does not return the element at the front of the queue. It simply removes it. As the program illustrates, to obtain the element at the front of the queue, you must use **front( )**.

Because a queue is a controlled sequence, you cannot obtain an iterator to a queue. Nor can you access the queue via the **[ ]** operator. The only way to access a queue is to use **front( )**, **back( )**, **push( )**, and **pop( )**. This enforces the queue's first-in, first-out mechanism. Although you cannot cycle through the contents of a queue via an iterator or access its elements out of sequence, it is possible to enumerate the contents of a queue by repeatedly removing the front element and pushing it onto the rear of the queue until all elements have been examined. Since the size of a queue is readily obtained through a call to **size( )**, this procedure is easy to implement. The following program shows an example.

```
// Cycling through a queue.
#include <iostream>
#include <queue>
#include <string>
using namespace std;

int main()
{
  queue<string> q;

  q.push("one");
  q.push("two");
  q.push("three");
  q.push("four");

  cout << "Contents of queue: ";
  for(int i=0; i<q.size(); i++) {
    cout << q.front() << " ";

    // remove front and push on back
    q.push(q.front());
    q.pop();
  }
  cout << "\n\n";

  cout << "Now, remove elements:\n";
  while(!q.empty()) {
    cout << "Popping ";
    cout << q.front() << "\n";
```

6

```
    q.pop();
  }

  return 0;
}
```

The program's output is shown here:

```
Contents of queue: one two three four

Now, remove elements:
Popping one
Popping two
Popping three
Popping four
```

IN DEPTH

Specifying an Alternative Container

As long as the container meets the requirements specified by the adaptor, any container can be used as the underlying container. To use a different container, simply specify its class name when creating an instance of the adaptor. For example, the following creates a queue that adapts **list** rather than **deque**:

```
queue<char, list<char> > q;
```

Since **q** uses a **list** as its basis, it will be subject to all of **list**'s benefits and disadvantages. Usually, the default container is your best choice, but you *do* have a choice. You could even use your own, custom containers as the basis for a queue. The same general principle applies to the other container adaptors, too.

One other point: Notice that there is a space between the two closing angle brackets that end **queue**'s template specification. Because of a quirk in the C++ syntax, this space is necessary. Without it, the compiler will mistake two closing angle brackets as a right shift (**>>**) and not as nested template terminators. Forgetting this space is a common error that can be hard to find since your program looks correct.

priority_queue

A priority queue orders its contents according to some priority.

The **priority_queue** class supports a single-ended priority queue. A priority queue arranges its contents in order of their priority. The **priority_queue** template specification is shown here:

    template <class T, class Container = vector<T>,
            class Comp = less<Container::value_type> >
            class priority_queue

Here, **T** is the type of data being stored. **Container** is the type of container used to hold the priority queue, which by default is **vector**. The underlying container is held in a protected object called **c** of type **Container**. **Comp** specifies the comparison function object that determines when one member is lower in priority than another. This object is held in a protected member called **comp** of type **Compare**.

The **priority_queue** adaptor has the following constructors:

    explicit priority_queue(const Comp &*cmpfn* = Comp( ),
            Container &*cnt* = Container( ));

    template <class InIter> priority_queue(InIter *start*, InIter *end*,
            const Comp &*cmpfn* = Comp( ),
            Container &*cnt* = Container( ));

The **priority_queue( )** constructor creates an empty priority queue. The second creates a priority queue that contains the elements specified by the range *start* and *end*. To use a priority queue, include the **<queue>** header.

In general, **priority_queue** can adapt any container that supports the following operations:

    front( )

    pop_back( )

    push_back( )

The container must also support random-access iterators. Thus, you can also use **deque** as a container for a queue. However, you cannot use **list** because **list** does not support random-access iterators.

6

The **priority_queue** class defines the following concrete types:

container_type	The container being adapted.
size_type	Some type of integer.
value_type	The type of a value stored in a container; same as **T**.

No operators are defined for **priority_queue**.

The **priority_queue** class contains the member functions shown in Table 6-2. Elements in a priority queue can be accessed only in the order of their priority.

Here is a simple example of **priority_queue**. It stores integers, prioritizing each element based upon its value.

```
// Demonstrate a priority_queue.
#include <iostream>
#include <queue>
using namespace std;

int main()
{
  priority_queue<int> q;

  q.push(1);
  q.push(3);
  q.push(4);
  q.push(2);

  while(!q.empty()) {
    cout << "Popping ";
    cout << q.top() << "\n";
    q.pop();
  }

  return 0;
}
```

Here is the output produced:

```
Popping 4
Popping 3
Popping 2
Popping 1
```

Member	Description
bool empty( ) const;	Returns **true** if the invoking priority queue is empty and **false** otherwise.
void pop( );	Removes the first element in the priority queue.
void push(const T &*val*);	Adds an element to the priority queue.
size_type size( ) const;	Returns the number of elements currently in the priority queue.
const value_type &top( ) const;	Returns a reference to the element with the highest priority. The element is not removed.

The
priority_queue
Member
Functions
Table 6-2.

6

By default,
priority queues
are in order
from highest to
lowest.

By default, the comparison function object is **less**, which orders the priority queue from highest to lowest. You can change the ordering of the elements by specifying a different comparison function object when a **priority_queue** object is created. For example, here is the preceding program recoded so that the elements in the priority queue are in reverse order. To accomplish this, **greater** is used as the comparison function object.

```
// Using a different comparison function.
#include <iostream>
#include <queue>
#include <functional>
using namespace std;

int main()
{
  priority_queue<int, vector<int>, greater<int> > q;

  q.push(1);
  q.push(3);
  q.push(4);
  q.push(2);

  while(!q.empty()) {
    cout << "Popping ";
    cout << q.top() << "\n";
```

```
    q.pop();
  }

  return 0;
}
```

The output, shown here, verifies the reversal of priorities:

```
Popping 1
Popping 2
Popping 3
Popping 4
```

In the program, notice this line:

```
priority_queue<int, vector<int>, greater<int> > q;
```

Since the comparison function object is the last of three parameters to the template specification, all three parameters must be explicitly specified. Even though the container also defaults, it must still be specified, too. In this case, we simply use the default container, **vector**, for the second parameter, but you could also use **deque**.

Of course, you will seldom need to prioritize a list of integers, or any other built-in type. (Actually, prioritizing a sequence of built-in types is simply another means of sorting!) Most often, you will be using **priority_queue** to prioritize a list of class objects. Here is an example that creates a simple event organizer. It prioritizes a list of events in the order in which you should respond to them.

```
// Storing class objects in a priority_queue.
#include <iostream>
#include <queue>
#include <string>
using namespace std;

// A simple event organizer.
class event {
  int priority;
  string name;
public:
  event() { name = ""; priority = 0; }
  event(string n, int p) { name = n; priority = p; }
```

```
     string getname() const { return name; }
     int getpriority() const { return priority; }
};

// Determine priority.
bool operator<(const event &a, const event &b)
{
  return a.getpriority() < b.getpriority();
}

int main()
{
  priority_queue<event> q;

  q.push(event("Fire!", 10));
  q.push(event("Mail Arrives", 2));
  q.push(event("Phone rings", 3));
  q.push(event("Knock on Door", 4));

  // show priority
  cout << "Priorities: ";
  while(!q.empty()) {
    cout << q.top().getname() << "\n";
    cout << "              ";
    q.pop();
  }

  return 0;
}
```

Here is the program's output:

```
Priorities: Fire!
            Knock on Door
            Phone rings
            Mail Arrives
```

When creating classes whose objects will be stored in a priority queue, you must overload the < operator. It is also a good idea to provide a default constructor so that you can control precisely the priority of any default objects that might get created. In general, when storing a class object in an adaptor, the class must implement any operators required by the underlying container.

stack

The **stack** class supports a last-in, first-out (LIFO) stack. Its template specification is shown here:

template <class T, class Container = deque<T> > class stack

Here, **T** is the type of data being stored and **Container** is the type of container used to hold the stack, which by default is **deque**. The underlying container is held in a protected object called **c** of type **Container**.

The **stack** adaptor has the following constructor:

explicit stack(const Container &*cnt* = Container( ));

The **stack( )** constructor creates an empty stack. To use a stack, include the **<stack>** header.

In general, **stack** can adapt any container that supports the following operations:

back( )

pop_back( )

push_back( )

The **stack** adaptor implements a standard, last-in, first-out stack.

Thus, you can also use a list or a vector as a container for a stack.

The **stack** class defines the following concrete types:

container_type	The container being adapted.
size_type	Some type of integer.
value_type	The type of a value stored in a container; same as **T**.

The following comparison operators are defined for **stack**:

==, <, <=, !=, >, >=

The **stack** class contains the member functions shown in Table 6-3. Notice that elements in a stack can be accessed only in last-in, first-out order.

Member	Description
bool empty( ) const;	Returns **true** if the invoking stack is empty and **false** otherwise.
void pop( );	Removes the top of the stack, which is technically the last element in the container.
void push(const T &*val*);	Pushes an element onto the end of the stack. The last element in the container represents the top of the stack.
size_type size( ) const;	Returns the number of elements currently in the stack.
value_type &top( ); cont value_type &top( ) const;	Returns a reference to the top of the stack, which is the last element in the container. The element is not removed.

The **stack**
Member
Functions
Table 6-3.

6

Here is a simple example of **stack**:

```cpp
// A simple stack example.
include <iostream>
#include <stack>
using namespace std;

int main()
{
  stack<char> stck;

  stck.push('A');
  stck.push('B');
  stck.push('C');
  stck.push('D');

  while(!stck.empty()) {
    cout << "Popping: ";
    cout << stck.top() << "\n";
    stck.pop();
  }

  return 0;
}
```

The output from the program is shown here:

```
Popping:  D
Popping:  C
Popping:  B
Popping:  A
```

As you can see, elements are popped from the stack in the reverse order of their insertion. The last element pushed onto the stack is the first one removed.

Stacks are one of computing's most useful data structures. At the machine level, they provide the basic mechanism by which a subroutine can be called. At the program level, stacks are often used to solve several common problems. For example, many AI-based searching routines rely upon stacks. One interesting use of a stack is in a postfix-style calculator. When using this type of calculator, you first enter the operands and then the operation that you want applied. For example, to add 10 to 12, you first enter **10**, then **12**, then **+**. As each operand is entered, it is pushed onto the stack. When an operator is entered, the top two elements are popped, the operation is performed, and the result is pushed onto the stack. The following program uses the **stack** class to implement such a calculator.

```cpp
// A four-function postfix calculator.
#include <iostream>
#include <stack>
#include <string>
#include <cmath>
using namespace std;

int main()
{
  stack<double> stck;
  double a, b;
  string s;

  do {
    cout << ": ";
    cin >> s;
    switch(s[0]) {
      case 'q': // quit the calculator
        break;
      case '.': // show top-of-stack
        cout << stck.top() << "\n";
        break;
      case '+': // add
```

```
      if(stck.size() < 2) {
        cout << "Operand Missing\n";
        break;
      }

      a = stck.top();
      stck.pop();
      b = stck.top();
      stck.pop();
      cout << a+b << "\n";
      stck.push(a+b);
      break;
    case '-': // subtract
      // see if user entering a negative number
      if(s.size() != 1) {
        // push value onto the stack
        stck.push(atof(s.c_str()));
        break;
      }

      // otherwise, is a subtraction
      if(stck.size() < 2) {
        cout << "Operand Missing\n";
        break;
      }

      a = stck.top();
      stck.pop();
      b = stck.top();
      stck.pop();
      cout << b-a << "\n";
      stck.push(b-a);
      break;
    case '*': // multiply
      if(stck.size() < 2) {
        cout << "Operand Missing\n";
        break;
      }

      a = stck.top();
      stck.pop();
      b = stck.top();
      stck.pop();
      cout << a*b << "\n";
      stck.push(a*b);
      break;
    case '/': // divide
```

```
        if(stck.size() < 2) {
          cout << "Operand Missing\n";
          break;
        }

        a = stck.top();
        stck.pop();
        b = stck.top();
        stck.pop();
        cout << b/a << "\n";
        stck.push(b/a);
        break;
      default:
        // push value onto the stack
        stck.push(atof(s.c_str()));
        break;
    }
  } while(s != "q");

  return 0;
}
```

A sample run is shown here:

```
: 10
: 2
: /
5
: -1
: *
-5
: 2.2
: +
-2.8
: 4
: 5
: 6
: +
11
: +
15
: q
```

For the most part, the operation of the calculator is intuitive, but there are a couple of points. First, to see the value on the top of the stack, enter a period. This means that you will need to precede values that are less than 1 with a leading zero. For example, 0.12. Second, notice that when an entry begins with a minus sign, if its length is longer than 1, then it is assumed that the user is entering a negative number and not requesting a subtraction.

The next chapter begins our examination of the associative containers.

6

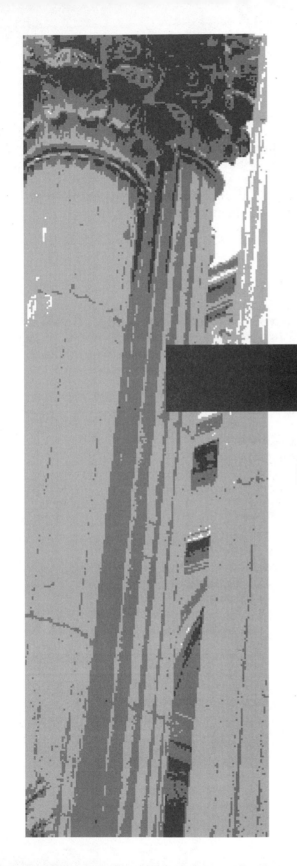

CHAPTER 7

map and multimap

This begins our examination of the STL's associative containers. The associative containers link a key with a value, allowing the value to be found given its key. The most powerful of the associative containers are **map** and **multimap**. These allow both the key and value to be of differing and arbitrary data types. For example, you might use a map to store a parts list in which the key is a string containing a part's name and the value is an integer indicating the number on hand. The difference between **map** and **multimap** is that **map** requires unique keys and **multimap** does not.

map

The **map** class stores key/value pairs in which each key is unique.

The **map** class supports an associative container in which unique keys are mapped with values. In essence, a key is simply a name that you give to a value. Once a value has been stored, you can retrieve it by using its key. Thus, in its most general sense a map is a list of key/value pairs. The power of a map is that you can look up a value given its key. For example, you could define a map that uses a person's name as its key and stores that person's telephone number as its value.

The template specification for **map** is shown here:

```
template <class Key, class T, class Comp = less<Key>,
        class Allocator = allocator<T> > class map
```

Here, **Key** is the data type of the keys, **T** is the data type of the values being stored (mapped), and **Comp** is a function that compares two keys. **map** has the following constructors.

```
explicit map(const Comp &cmpfn = Comp( ),
        const Allocator &a = Allocator( ) );

map(const map<Key, T, Comp, Allocator> &ob);

template <class InIter> map(InIter start, InIter end,
        const Comp &cmpfn = Comp( ),
        const Allocator &a = Allocator( ));
```

The first form constructs an empty map. The second form constructs a map that contains the same elements as *ob* and is **map**'s copy constructor. The third form constructs a map that contains the elements in the range specified by *start* and *end*. The function specified by *cmpfn,* if present, determines the ordering of the map. To use a map, you must include **<map>**.

The **map** class overloads the assignment operator. In addition, the following comparison operators are defined for **map**:

==, <, <=, !=, >, >=

The **map** class supports bidirectional iterators. Thus, the container can be accessed through an iterator in both the forward and reverse directions, but random-access operations are not supported. It does, however, support the **[ ]** operator, but not in its traditional usage.

The **map** class defines the following concrete types:

size_type	Some type of integer.
difference_type	Some type of integer that can hold the difference between two addresses.
reference	A reference to an element.
const_reference	A **const** reference to an element.
iterator	An iterator.
const_iterator	A **const** iterator.
reverse_iterator	A reverse iterator.
const_reverse_iterator	A **const** reverse iterator.
value_type	The type **pair<const Key, T>**.
mapped_type	The type of the value stored in a container; same as **T**.
key_type	The type of the key; same as **Key**.
key_compare	Same as **Comp**.
allocator_type	The type of the allocator.
pointer	A pointer to an element.
const_pointer	A **const** pointer to an element.

Key/value pairs are stored in a map as objects of type **pair**, which has this template specification:

```
template <class Ktype, class Vtype> struct pair {
  typedef Ktype first_type; // type of key
  typedef Vtype second_type; // type of value
```

7

```
Ktype first; // contains the key
Vtype second; // contains the value

// constructors
pair();
pair(const Ktype &k, const Vtype &v);
template<class A, class B> pair(const<A, B> &ob);
}
```

As the comments suggest, the value in **first** contains the key and the value in **second** contains the value associated with that key. The **pair** class requires the **<utility>** header, which is automatically included by **<map>**.

The **pair** class
links two values.

You can construct a pair using either one of **pair**'s constructors or by using **make_pair( )**, which constructs a **pair** object based upon the types of the data used as parameters. **make_pair( )** is a generic function that has this prototype:

> template <class *Ktype*, class *Vtype*>
>   pair<*Ktype*, *Vtype*> make_pair(const *Ktype* &k, const *Vtype* &v);

As you can see, it returns a **pair** object consisting of values of the types specified by *Ktype* and *Vtype*. The advantage of **make_pair( )** is that the types of the objects being stored are determined automatically by the compiler rather than being explicitly specified by you.

The iterator type defined by **map** points to objects of type **pair<Key, T>**. Thus, when a map member function returns an iterator, the key is available through the **first** member of **pair** and the value is obtained through **pair**'s **second** field.

The member functions contained by **map** are shown in Table 7-1. In the descriptions, remember that **key_type** is the type of the key, and **value_type** represents **pair<Key, T>**. A specialization of the standard **swap( )** algorithm is also defined for **map**.

Member	Description
iterator begin( ); const_iterator begin( ) const;	Returns an iterator to the first element in the map.
void clear( );	Removes all elements from the map.
size_type count(const key_type &k) const;	Returns the number of times *k* occurs in the map (1 or zero).

The **map** Member Functions **Table 7-1.**

Member	Description
bool empty( ) const;	Returns **true** if the invoking map is empty and **false** otherwise.
iterator end( ); const_iterator end( ) const;	Returns an iterator to the end of the map.

pair<iterator, iterator>
   equal_range(const key_type &*k*);
 pair<const_iterator, const_iterator>
   equal_range(const key_type &*k*) const;
	Returns a pair of iterators that point to the upper bound and the lower bound in the map for the specified key.

void erase(iterator *i*);	Removes the element pointed to by *i*.
void erase(iterator *start*, iterator *end*);	Removes the elements in the range *start* to *end*.
size_type erase(const key_type &*k*)	Removes from the map elements that have keys with the value *k*.
iterator find(const key_type &*k*); const_iterator find(const key_type &*k*) const;	Returns an iterator to the specified key. If the key is not found, then an iterator to the end of the map is returned.
allocator_type get_allocator( ) const;	Returns the map's allocator.
iterator insert(iterator *i*, const value_type &*val*);	Inserts *val* at or after the element specified by *i*. An iterator to the element is returned.
template <class InIter> void insert(InIter *start*, InIter *end*)	Inserts a range of elements.
pair<iterator, bool> insert(const value_type &*val*);	Inserts *val* into the invoking map. The element is inserted only if it does not already exist. If the element is inserted, **pair<iterator, true>** is returned. Otherwise, **pair<iterator, false>** is returned.

The **map**
Member
Functions
(continued)
Table 7-1.

7

Member	Description
key_compare key_comp( ) const;	Returns the function object that compares keys.

iterator lower_bound(const key_type &k);
const_iterator
    lower_bound(const key_type &k) const;
	Returns an iterator to the first element in the map with the key equal to or greater than *k*.

size_type max_size( ) const;	Returns the maximum number of elements that a map can hold.
reference operator[ ](const key_type &k)	Returns a reference to the value associated with the key specified by *k*. If this element does not exist, it is inserted.
reverse_iterator rbegin( ); const_reverse_iterator rbegin( ) const;	Returns a reverse iterator to the end of the map.
reverse_iterator rend( ); const_reverse_iterator rend( ) const;	Returns a reverse iterator to the start of the map.
size_type size( ) const;	Returns the number of elements currently in the map.
void swap(map<Key, T, Comp, Allocator> &ob)	Exchanges the elements stored in the invoking map with those in *ob*.

iterator upper_bound(const key_type &k);
const_iterator
    upper_bound(const key_type &k) const;
	Returns an iterator to the first element in the map with the key greater than *k*.

value_compare value_comp( ) const;	Returns the function object that compares values.

The **map** Member Functions *(continued)*
Table 7-1.

A Simple Map Example

The following program illustrates the basics of using a map. It stores key/value pairs that show the mapping between the uppercase letters and their ASCII character codes. Thus, the key is a character and the value is an integer. The key/value pairs stored are

A   65

B   66

C   67

and so on. Once the pairs have been stored, you are prompted for a key (i.e., a letter between A and Z) and the ASCII code for that letter is displayed.

```cpp
// A simple map demonstration.
#include <iostream>
#include <map>
using namespace std;

int main()
{
  map<char, int> m;
  int i;

  // put pairs into map
  for(i=0; i<26; i++)
    m.insert(pair<char, int>('A'+i, 65+i));

  char ch;
  cout << "Enter key: ";
  cin >> ch;

  map<char, int>::iterator p;

  // find value given key
  p = m.find(ch);
  if(p != m.end())
    cout << "Its ASCII value is  " << p->second;
  else
    cout << "Key not in map.\n";

  return 0;
}
```

7

Notice the use of the **pair** template class to construct the key/value pairs. The data types specified by **pair** must match those of the **map** into which the pairs are being inserted.

Once the map has been initialized with keys and values, you can search for a value given its key by using the **find( )** function. **find( )** returns an iterator to the matching element or to the end of the map if the key is not found. It is important to remember that the iterator returned by **find( )** is to a **pair** object. It is not an iterator to the value associated with the search key. Thus, when a match is found, the value linked with the key is contained in the **second** member of **pair**.

In the preceding example, key/value pairs were constructed explicitly, using **pair<char, int>**. While there is nothing wrong with this approach, it is often easier to use **make_pair( )**, which constructs a **pair** object based upon the types of the data used as parameters. For example, assuming the previous program, this line of code will also insert key/value pairs into **m**.

```
m.insert(make_pair((char)('A'+i), 65+i));
```

Here, the cast to **char** is needed to override the automatic conversion to **int** when **i** is added to 'A'. Otherwise, the type determination is automatic.

Performance Characteristics

Most insertions or deletions in a map take logarithmic time.

Maps are designed for the efficient storage of key/value pairs. In general, inserting or deleting elements in a map takes place in logarithmic time. There are two exceptions. First, if an element is inserted at a given location, amortized constant time is required. Amortized constant time is also consumed when a specific element is deleted given an iterator to that element.

Insertion invalidates no iterators or references.

Insertion into a map invalidates no iterators or references to elements. A deletion invalidates only iterators or references to the deleted elements.

Deletion invalidates only iterators or references to the deleted elements

Cycling Through a Map Using an Iterator

Maps are stored in ascending order sorted by key.

Even though maps are associative rather than sequence containers, their elements can still be accessed via an iterator. Maps store their elements in ascending order according to the keys. Thus, incrementing an iterator causes it to point to the element with the next greater key. A decrement causes it to point to the previous element. The standard container functions such as **begin( )** and **end( )** are, of course, available.

Here is an example that cycles through a map using an iterator. It is a variation on the preceding program that displays all of the letter/ASCII code pairs.

```cpp
// Cycle through a map using an iterator.
#include <iostream>
#include <map>
using namespace std;

int main()
{
  map<char, int> m;
  int i;

  // put pairs into map
  for(i=0; i<26; i++)
    m.insert(pair<char, int>('A'+i, 65+i));

  map<char, int>::iterator p;

  // Display contents of map
  for(p = m.begin(); p != m.end(); p++) {
    cout << p->first << " has ASCII value of ";
    cout << p->second << endl;
  }

  return 0;
}
```

7

The output from the program is shown here:

```
A has ASCII value of 65
B has ASCII value of 66
C has ASCII value of 67
D has ASCII value of 68
E has ASCII value of 69
F has ASCII value of 70
G has ASCII value of 71
H has ASCII value of 72
I has ASCII value of 73
J has ASCII value of 74
K has ASCII value of 75
```

```
L has ASCII value of 76
M has ASCII value of 77
N has ASCII value of 78
O has ASCII value of 79
P has ASCII value of 80
Q has ASCII value of 81
R has ASCII value of 82
S has ASCII value of 83
T has ASCII value of 84
U has ASCII value of 85
V has ASCII value of 86
W has ASCII value of 87
X has ASCII value of 88
Y has ASCII value of 89
Z has ASCII value of 90
```

The **map** class also supports reverse iterators. For example, here is the preceding program recoded to display the ASCII codes in their reverse order.

```cpp
// Cycle through a map in reverse.
#include <iostream>
#include <map>
using namespace std;

int main()
{
  map<char, int> m;
  int i;

  // put pairs into map
  for(i=0; i<26; i++)
    m.insert(pair<char, int>('A'+i, 65+i));

  map<char, int>::reverse_iterator p;

  // Display contents of map
  for(p = m.rbegin(); p != m.rend(); p++) {
    cout << p->first << " has ASCII value of ";
    cout << p->second << endl;
  }

  return 0;
}
```

Understanding the [ ] Operator

The **map** class supports the [ ] operator, but its operation will probably surprise you. First, the [ ] operator does not take an index but, rather, a key as its operand. Second, it returns a reference to the value associated with the key, not a key/value pair. For example, consider the following variation on the ASCII program.

```
// Using []
#include <iostream>
#include <map>
using namespace std;

int main()
{
  map<char, int> m;
  int i;

  // put pairs into map
  for(i=0; i<26; i++)
    m.insert(pair<char, int>('A'+i, 65+i));

  char ch;
  cout << "Enter key: ";
  cin >> ch;

  // find value given key
  cout << "Its ASCII value is  " << m[ch];

  return 0;
}
```

7

In the program, notice that there is no mechanism that determines whether the key entered by the user actually exists in the map. The program simply assumes that the key will be found and displays its value. This is not an error in the program. Because of the way that the [ ] is implemented, *it will always succeed*. If the key you are looking for is not in the map, it is automatically inserted, with its value being that of the type's default constructor (which is zero for the built-in types). Thus, any key that you search for will always be found! For example, try this version of the preceding program.

```
// [] automatically inserts elements.
#include <iostream>
#include <map>
using namespace std;
```

```
int main()
{
  map<char, int> m;

  cout << "Initial size of map: " << m.size() << endl;

  // find value given key
  cout << "The value associated with A is " << m['A'];
  cout << endl;

  cout << "Size of map is now: " << m.size() << endl;

  return 0;
}
```

The output from this program is shown here:

```
Initial size of map: 0
The value associated with A is 0
Size of map is now: 1
```

Accessing a nonexisting element via the [ ] operator causes that element to be inserted into the map.

As you can see, the map **m** is initially empty, but the attempt to access the nonexistent 'A' key causes it to be added to the map (with an initial value of zero).

The fact that the **[ ]** automatically inserts nonexistent elements into a map may at first seem a bit disconcerting. However, it is actually quite valuable. As mentioned, the value returned by the **[ ]** operator is a reference to the value associated with the key used as the index. Thus, you can use the **[ ]** operator on the left side of an assignment to give an element a new value. For example, assuming some map, *m*, then

$$m[key] = 99;$$

assigns the value linked with *key* the value 99. If the element is not currently in the map, it will first be automatically added (with an initial value of zero), and then assigned the value 99.

Here is another way to rewrite the ASCII program that uses the **[ ]** to insert elements into the map:

```
// Using [] to insert elements
#include <iostream>
#include <map>
using namespace std;
```

```
int main()
{
  map<char, int> m;
  int i;

  // put pairs into map using [ ]
  for(i=0; i<26; i++) m['A'+i] = 65+i;

  char ch;
  cout << "Enter key: ";
  cin >> ch;

  // find value given key
  cout << "Its ASCII value is  " << m[ch];

  return 0;
}
```

In this example, the map is initialized by assigning values to elements through the **[ ]** operator using this **for** loop:

```
for(i=0; i<26; i++) m['A'+i] = 65+i;
```

Since the map is initially empty, none of the values referred to by the **[ ]** operator will be found. This means that they will be first added to the map (using zero for their values) and then assigned the proper value when the assignment takes place. The "automatic insert" capability of **[ ]** adds convenience to many map operations.

Maps Require Unique Keys

Maps do not allow duplicate keys. Thus, each key will be associated with one and only one value. In other words, a map creates a one-to-one mapping of keys and values. Any attempt to store a duplicate key will fail, as the following example shows.

```
// Maps can store only unique keys.
#include <iostream>
#include <map>
using namespace std;
```

7

```
int main()
{
  map<char, int> m;
  pair<map<char,int>::iterator, bool> res;

  // insert A
  res = m.insert(pair<char, int>('A', 65));
  if(res.second) cout << "Insertion occurred.\n";

  // try to insert A again
  res = m.insert(pair<char, int>('A', 99));
  if(!res.second) cout << "Duplicate not allowed.\n";

  map<char, int>::iterator p;

  // find value given key
  p = m.find('A');
  cout << "Its ASCII value is " << p->second;

  return 0;
}
```

The following output is produced:

```
Insertion occurred.
Duplicate not allowed.
Its ASCII value is 65
```

As you can see, the attempt to store 'A' a second time fails and the original value associated with 'A' is unchanged.

As the program illustrates, the success or failure of an insertion can be determined by checking the value returned by **insert( )**, which is a pair of values. If the element was inserted, then **pair<iterator, true>** is returned. Otherwise, **pair<iterator, false>** is returned. By checking the value of the **second** member, you can determine the outcome.

It is important to note that only the **insert(value_type)** version of **insert( )** returns an indication of whether the element was inserted or not. The other versions of **insert( )** simply insert the element (or elements) if it is not already in the list.

Storing Class Objects in a Map

Like all of the containers, you can use a map to store objects of types that you create. For example, the next program creates a simple phone directory. That is, it creates a map of names with their numbers. To do this, it creates two classes called **name** and **number**. Since a map maintains a sorted list of keys, the program also defines the < operator for objects of type **name**. In general, you must define the < operator for any class that you will use as a key. (Some compilers may require that additional comparison operators be defined.) You will need to define the default constructor for any class used as a value associated with a key.

```cpp
// Use a map to create a phone directory.
#include <iostream>
#include <map>
#include <string>
using namespace std;

// This is the key class.
class name {
  string str;
public:
  name() { str = ""; }
  name(string s) { str = s; }
  string get() { return str; }

};

// Must define less than relative to name objects.
bool operator<(name a, name b)
{
    return a.get() < b.get();
}

// This is the value class.
class phoneNum {
  string str;
```

7

```cpp
public:
  phoneNum() { str = ""; }
  phoneNum(string s) { str = s; }
  string get() { return str; }
};

int main()
{
  map<name, phoneNum> directory;

 // put names and numbers into map
  directory.insert(pair<name, phoneNum>(name("Tom"),
                  phoneNum("555-4533")));
  directory.insert(pair<name, phoneNum>(name("Chris"),
                  phoneNum("555-9678")));
  directory.insert(pair<name, phoneNum>(name("John"),
                  phoneNum("555-8195")));
  directory.insert(pair<name, phoneNum>(name("Rachel"),
                  phoneNum("555-0809")));

  // given a name, find number
  string str;
  cout << "Enter name: ";
  cin >> str;

  map<name, phoneNum>::iterator p;

  p = directory.find(name(str));
  if(p != directory.end())
    cout << "Phone number: " <<  p->second.get();
  else
    cout << "Name not in directory.\n";

  return 0;
}
```

Here is a sample run:

```
Enter name: Rachel
Phone number: 555-0809.
```

Specifying a Comparison Object

As the template specification for **map** shows, it is possible to specify a function object that will be used to perform comparisons on the keys stored in a map. By default, the **less** function object is used and most of the time you will not want to change this. But, in the cases in which the default behavior is not acceptable, it is quite easy to do. Simply specify a different function object. For example, here is a map declaration that uses the **greater** function object for its comparison function:

```
map<string, integer, greater<string> > m;
```

Using **greater** causes the keys in the map to be stored in reverse order. If you want to confirm this, try the following program.

```cpp
// Use the greater function object.
#include <iostream>
#include <map>
#include <functional>
#include <string>
using namespace std;

int main()
{
  map<string, int, greater<string> > m;

  m["Alpha"] = 20;
  m["Beta"] = 19;
  m["Gamma"] = 10;

  map<string, int, greater<string> >::iterator p;

  // Display contents of map
  for(p = m.begin(); p != m.end(); p++) {
    cout << p->first << " has value of ";
    cout << p->second << endl;
  }

  return 0;
}
```

7

IN DEPTH

CONTINUED

Here is the output:

```
Gamma has value of 10
Beta has value of 19
Alpha has value of 20
```

As you can see, the keys are stored in reverse order.

multimap

The **multimap** class is similar to **map** except that it allows nonunique keys. Thus, one key can be used for more than one value. A multimap is especially useful when storing key/value pairs in which there is a one-to-many mapping of keys to values. For example, you might use a multimap to store a list of clients indexed by the city in which they reside.

The **multimap** template specification is shown here:

```
template <class Key, class T, class Comp = less<Key>,
         class Allocator = allocator<T> > class multimap
```

Here, **Key** is the data of the keys, **T** is the data type of the values being stored (mapped), and **Comp** is a function that compares two keys. It has the following constructors:

```
explicit multimap(const Comp &cmpfn = Comp( ),
         const Allocator &a = Allocator( ) );

multimap(const multimap<Key, T, Comp, Allocator> &ob);

template <class InIter> multimap(InIter start, InIter end,
         const Comp &cmpfn = Comp( ),
         const Allocator &a = Allocator( ));
```

The **multimap** class stores key/value pairs in which duplicate keys are allowed.

The first form constructs an empty multimap. The second form is **multimap**'s copy constructor. The third form constructs a multimap that contains the elements in the range specified by *start* and *end*. The function specified by *cmpfn*, if present, determines the ordering of the multimap. To utilize **multimap**, you must include **<map>**.

The **multimap** class overloads the assignment operator. In addition, the following comparison operators are defined by **multimap**:

   ==, <, <=, !=, >, >=

The **multimap** class supports bidirectional iterators. Thus, the container can be accessed through an iterator in both the forward and reverse direction. Unlike **map**, **multimap** does not support the **[ ]** operator. (Since there is not a one-to-one mapping of keys to values, it is not possible to index a multimap using a key.)

The **map** class defines the following concrete types:

size_type	Some type of integer.
difference_type	Some type of integer that can hold the difference between two addresses.
reference	A reference to an element.
const_reference	A **const** reference to an element.
iterator	An iterator.
const_iterator	A **const** iterator.
reverse_iterator	A reverse iterator.
const_reverse_iterator	A **const** reverse iterator.
value_type	The type **pair<const Key, T>**.
mapped_type	The type of the value stored in a container; same as **T**.
key_type	The type of the key; same as **Key**.
key_compare	Same as **Comp**.
allocator_type	The type of the allocator.
pointer	A pointer to an element.
const_pointer	A **const** pointer to an element.

7

The member functions contained by **multimap** are shown in Table 7-2. In the descriptions, remember that **key_type** is the type of the key, **T** is the value, and **value_type** represents **pair<Key, T>**. A specialization of the standard **swap( )** algorithm is also defined for **multimap**.

Member	Description
iterator begin( ); const_iterator begin( ) const;	Returns an iterator to the first element in the multimap.
void clear( );	Removes all elements from the multimap.
size_type count(const key_type &k) const;	Returns the number of times *k* occurs in the multimap.
bool empty( ) const;	Returns **true** if the invoking multimap is empty and **false** otherwise.
iterator end( ); const_iterator end( ) const;	Returns an iterator to the end of the multimap.

pair<iterator, iterator>
   equal_range(const key_type &k);
pair<const_iterator, const_iterator>
   equal_range(const key_type &k) const;
	Returns a pair of iterators that point to the upper bound and the lower bound in the multimap for the specified key.

void erase(iterator *i*);	Removes the element pointed to by *i*.
void erase(iterator *start*, iterator *end*);	Removes the elements in the range *start* to *end*.
size_type erase(const key_type &k)	Removes from the multimap elements that have keys with the value *k*.
iterator find(const key_type &k); const_iterator find(const key_type &k) const;	Returns an iterator to the specified key. If the key is not found, then an iterator to the end of the multimap is returned.
allocator_type get_allocator( ) const;	Returns multimap's allocator.

The **multimap** Member Functions

Table 7-2.

Member	Description
iterator insert(iterator *i*, 　　　　　const value_type &*val*);	Inserts *val* at or after the element specified by *i*. An iterator to the element is returned.
template <class InIter> 　void insert(InIter *start*, InIter *end*)	Inserts a range of elements.
iterator insert(const value_type &*val*);	Inserts *val* into the invoking multimap.
key_compare key_comp( ) const;	Returns the function object that compares keys.

iterator lower_bound(const key_type &*k*);
const_iterator
　lower_bound(const key_type &*k*) const;
	Returns an iterator to the first element in the multimap with the key equal to or greater than *k*.

size_type max_size( ) const;	Returns the maximum number of elements that the multimap can hold.
reverse_iterator rbegin( ); const_reverse_iterator rbegin( ) const;	Returns a reverse iterator to the end of the multimap.
reverse_iterator rend( ); const_reverse_iterator rend( ) const;	Returns a reverse iterator to the start of the multimap.
size_type size( ) const;	Returns the number of elements currently in the multimap.
void swap(multimap<Key, T, Comp, 　　　　　Allocator> &*ob*)	Exchanges the elements stored in the invoking multimap with those in *ob*.

iterator upper_bound(const key_type &*k*);
const_iterator
　upper_bound(const key_type &*k*) const;
	Returns an iterator to the first element in the multimap with the key greater than *k*.

value_compare value_comp( ) const;	Returns the function object that compares values.

The **multimap** Member Functions *(continued)*
Table 7-2.

7

Performance Characteristics

Multimaps have the same performance characteristics as maps. In general, inserting or deleting elements in a multimap takes place in logarithmic time. The two exceptions are when an element is inserted at a given location and when a specific element is deleted given an iterator to that element. In these cases, amortized constant time is required.

Insertion into a multimap invalidates no iterators or references to elements. A deletion invalidates only those iterators or references to the deleted elements.

Accessing All Values Associated with a Key

find( ) always returns the first matching element.

Since the defining characteristic of **multimap** is its ability to store more than one value for any given key, this raises the obvious question: How do I find all values associated with a key? The answer is a bit more complicated than you might expect because you cannot use the **find( )** member function to find multiple matches. This function always returns an iterator to the *first matching key*. There is no way to make it move on to the next one. Instead, to obtain the next matching key, you must increment the iterator returned by **find( )**. You stop the process when the last matching key has been found. The end point is easily obtained through the use of the **upper_bound( )** member function. Its non-**const** prototype is shown here:

To find a range of equal keys, use functions such as **upper_bound( )**, **lower_bound( )**, *and* **equal_range( )**.

```
iterator upper_bound(const key_type &k);
```

The **upper_bound( )** function returns an iterator to the first element in the multimap with the key greater than *k*. In other words, it returns an iterator to the element that comes after the ones with the key you specify. Thus, to find all matches for a given key, you will use a sequence like this:

```
p = m.find(key);
if(p != end()) {
  do {
    // ...
    p++;
  } while(p != m.upper_bound(key));
}
```

In this method, an iterator to the first key is found. If this value is not equal to **end( )**, then the match is processed and the iterator is incremented. (The **find( )** function returns **end( )** if the key is not found.) This process continues until **p** points to the upper bound. The following program demonstrates this technique. It creates a multimap that stores the names of family members. The key is a last name and the value is the first name.

```cpp
// Demonstrating a multimap.
#include <iostream>
#include <map>
#include <string>
using namespace std;

int main()
{
  multimap<string, string> names;
  string n;

  names.insert(pair<string, string>("Jones", "Fred"));
  names.insert(pair<string, string>("Jones", "Alice"));

  names.insert(pair<string, string>("Smith", "Tom"));
  names.insert(pair<string, string>("Smith", "Alicia"));
  names.insert(pair<string, string>("Smith", "Jon"));

  names.insert(pair<string, string>("Doe", "Harvey"));
  names.insert(pair<string, string>("Doe", "Wilma"));
  names.insert(pair<string, string>("Doe", "Rachel"));

  names.insert(pair<string, string>("Johnson", "J.T."));

  multimap<string, string>::iterator p;

  cout << "Enter last name: ";
  cin >> n;

  // get iterator to first occurrence
  p = names.find(n);
  if(p != names.end()) { // found a name
    do {
      cout << n << ", " << p->second;
      cout << endl;
      p++;
    } while (p != names.upper_bound(n));
  }
  else
    cout << "Name not found.\n";

  return 0;
}
```

7

Here is a sample run:

```
Enter last name: Smith
Smith, Tom
Smith, Alicia
Smith, Jon
```

As the output shows, each member of the Smith family is found and their names are displayed.

Other functions that are useful when working with multiple matching keys are **lower_bound( )**, which returns an iterator to the first matching key, and **equal_range( )**, which returns a pair of iterators that contain the lower and upper bounds of the specified key.

Storing Class Objects in a Multimap

You follow the same rules for storing class objects in a multimap as you do for **map**. Define at least the **<** operator for the key and the parameterless constructor for the value. Here is an improved version of the telephone number program that uses a multimap. This version allows more than one phone number to be associated with a single name. Since many people have more than one telephone number, a multimap is a better choice for this application.

```cpp
// Use a multimap to improve the phone directory.
#include <iostream>
#include <map>
#include <string>
using namespace std;

// This is the key class.
class name {
  string str;
public:
  name() { str = ""; }
  name(string s) { str = s; }
  string get() { return str; }

};
```

```
// Must define less than relative to name objects.
bool operator<(name a, name b)
{
    return a.get() < b.get();
}

// This is the value class.
class phoneNum {
  string str;
public:
  phoneNum() { str = ""; }
  phoneNum(string s) { str = s; }
  string get() { return str; }
};


int main()
{
  multimap<name, phoneNum> directory;

 // put names and numbers into map
  directory.insert(pair<name, phoneNum>(name("Tom"),
                     phoneNum("555-4533")));
  directory.insert(pair<name, phoneNum>(name("Tom"),
                     phoneNum("555-9999")));
  directory.insert(pair<name, phoneNum>(name("Chris"),
                     phoneNum("555-9678")));
  directory.insert(pair<name, phoneNum>(name("John"),
                     phoneNum("555-8195")));
  directory.insert(pair<name, phoneNum>(name("Rachel"),
                     phoneNum("555-0809")));
  directory.insert(pair<name, phoneNum>(name("Rachel"),
                     phoneNum("555-3434")));
  directory.insert(pair<name, phoneNum>(name("Rachel"),
                     phoneNum("555-7776")));

  // given a name, find number
  string str;
  cout << "Enter name: ";
  cin >> str;

  multimap<name, phoneNum>::iterator p;
```

7

```
p = directory.find(str);
if(p != directory.end()) {
  do {
    cout << "Phone number: " <<  p->second.get();
    cout << endl;
    p++;
  } while(p != directory.upper_bound(str));
}
else
  cout << "Name not in directory.\n";

return 0;
}
```

Notice that the program now stores two numbers for Tom and three for Rachel. Here is a sample run.

```
Enter name: Tom
Phone number: 555-4533
Phone number: 555-9999
```

As you can see, both of Tom's numbers have been found.

The next chapter examines the **set** and **multiset** containers, which are used to support set operations.

CHAPTER 8

set and multiset

This chapter continues our look at the associative containers by examining **set** and **multiset**. The set containers are similar to maps except that the key and the value are not separated from each other. That is, sets store objects in which the key is part of the value. In fact, if you use a set to store one of the built-in types, such as an integer, the key and value are one and the same. Sets provide very efficient containers when there is no need to separate the key from the data.

Since sets are similar to maps, this chapter focuses on their unique attributes and will not repeat the material covered in Chapter 7.

set

The **set** class supports a set in which unique keys are stored. The keys are stored in ascending order. Its template specification is shown here:

> template <class Key, class Comp = less<Key>,
>   class Allocator = allocator<Key> > class set

Here, **Key** is the data of the keys (which also contain the data) and **Comp** is a function that compares two keys. It has the following constructors:

> explicit set(const Comp &*cmpfn* = Comp( ),
>   const Allocator &*a* = Allocator( ));
>
> set(const set<Key, Comp, Allocator> &*ob*);
>
> template <class InIter> set(InIter *start*, InIter *end*,
>   const Comp &*cmpfn* = Comp( ),
>   const Allocator &*a* = Allocator( ));

The first form constructs an empty set. The second form is **set**'s copy constructor. The third form constructs a set that contains the elements in the range specified by *start* and *end*. The function specified by *cmpfn,* if present, determines the ordering of the set. By default, **less** is used. To use a set, you must include **<set>**.

The **set** class
stores unique
keys.

The **set** class overloads the assignment operator. In addition, the following comparison operators are defined for **set**:

> ==, <, <=, !=, >, >=

The **set** class supports bidirectional iterators. Thus, the container can be accessed through an iterator in both the forward and reverse directions, but random access operations are not supported.

The **set** class defines the following concrete types:

size_type	Some type of integer.
difference_type	Some type of integer that can hold the difference between two addresses.
reference	A reference to an element.
const_reference	A **const** reference to an element.
iterator	An iterator.
const_iterator	A **const** iterator.
reverse_iterator	A reverse iterator.
const_reverse_iterator	A **const** reverse iterator.
value_type	Same as **key_type**.
key_type	The type of the key; same as **Key**.
key_compare	Same as **Comp**.
value_compare	Same as **Comp**.
allocator_type	The type of the allocator.
pointer	A pointer to an element.
const_pointer	A **const** pointer to an element.

8

The member functions defined by **set** are shown Table 8-1. In the descriptions, both **key_type** and **value_type** are **typedef**s for **Key**. A specialization of the standard **swap( )** algorithm is also defined for **set**.

Member	Description
iterator begin( ); const_iterator begin( ) const;	Returns an iterator to the first element in the set.
void clear( );	Removes all elements from the set.

Member	Description
size_type count(const key_type &k) const;	Returns the number of times *k* occurs in the set.
bool empty( ) const;	Returns **true** if the invoking set is empty and **false** otherwise.
const_iterator end( ) const; iterator end( );	Returns an iterator to the end of the list.
pair<iterator, iterator> equal_range(const key_type &k) const;	Returns a pair of iterators that point to the upper bound and the lower bound in the set for the specified key.
void erase(iterator *i*);	Removes the element pointed to by *i*.
void erase(iterator *start*, iterator *end*);	Removes the elements in the range *start* to *end*.
size_type erase(const key_type &k)	Removes from the set elements that have keys with the value *k*. The number of elements removed is returned.
iterator find(const key_type &k) const;	Returns an iterator to the specified key. If the key is not found, then an iterator to the end of the set is returned.
allocator_type get_allocator( ) const;	Returns set's allocator.
iterator insert(iterator *i*, const value_type &*val*);	Inserts *val* at or after the element specified by *i*. Duplicate elements are not inserted. An iterator to the element is returned.
template <class InIter> void insert(InIter *start*, InIter *end*);	Inserts a range of elements. Duplicate elements are not inserted.

The **set** Member Functions *(continued)*

Table 8-1.

Member	Description
pair<iterator, bool> insert(const value_type &*val*);	Inserts *val* into the invoking set. An iterator to the element is returned. The element is inserted only if it does not already exist. If the element is inserted, **pair<iterator, true>** is returned. Otherwise, **pair<iterator, false>** is returned.
iterator lower_bound(const key_type &*k*) const;	Returns an iterator to the first element in the set with the key equal to or greater than *k*.
key_compare key_comp( ) const;	Returns the function object that compares keys.
size_type max_size( ) const;	Returns the maximum number of elements that a set can hold.
reverse_iterator rbegin( ); const_reverse_iterator rbegin( ) const;	Returns a reverse iterator to the end of the set.
reverse_iterator rend( ); const_reverse_iterator rend( ) const;	Returns a reverse iterator to the start of the set.
size_type size( ) const;	Returns the number of elements currently in the set.
void swap(set<Key, Comp,Allocator> &*ob*);	Exchanges the elements stored in the invoking set with those in *ob*.
iterator upper_bound(const key_type &*k*) const;	Returns an iterator to the first element in the set with the key greater than *k*.
value_compare value_comp( ) const;	Returns the function object that compares values.

The **set** Member Functions *(continued)*
Table 8-1.

8

Here is a simple example that uses **set**. The program stores a set of strings. In this case, the value being stored is a string, which is also its key.

```cpp
// A simple example that uses a set.
#include <iostream>
#include <set>
#include <string>
using namespace std;

int main()
{
  set<string> s;

  // create a set of strings
  s.insert("Telescope");
  s.insert("House");
  s.insert("Computer");
  s.insert("Mouse");

  set<string>::iterator p = s.begin();

  do {
    cout << *p << " ";
    p++;
  } while(p != s.end());
  cout << endl;

  p = s.find("Telescope");
  if(p != s.end())
    cout << "Found Telescope\n";

  return 0;
}
```

Here is the output produced by the program:

```
Computer House Mouse Telescope
Found Telescope
```

Notice that the strings are automatically stored in ascending order.

Performance Characteristics

Most insertions or deletions in a set take logarithmic time.

Sets are designed for the efficient storage of keys. In general, inserting or deleting elements in a set takes place in logarithmic time. There are two exceptions. First, if an element is inserted at a given location, amortized constant time is required. Amortized constant time is also consumed when a specific element is deleted given an iterator to that element.

Insertion invalidates no iterators or references.

Insertion into a set invalidates no iterators or references to elements. A deletion invalidates only iterators or references to the deleted elements.

Deletion invalidates only iterators or references to the deleted elements.

Storing Class Objects in a Set

At first glance, you might think that applications for **set** are quite limited since the key and the value are one and the same. In fact, storing simple types, such as **int**, **char**, etc., in a set simply creates a sorted list. However, the power of sets becomes apparent when class objects are stored.

For an object to be stored in a set, its class must overload the < operator and provide a parameterless constructor. Sets are ordered by using the < operator. It is also used by the **find( )**, **upper_bound( )**, **lower_bound( )**, and **equal_range( )** member functions. Thus, the secret to using sets to store class objects is to correctly overload **operator<( ).** Typically, the < operator is defined in such a way that only one member of the class is compared. This member thus forms the actual key, even though the entire class forms the element.

Here is an example that uses a set to store states and capitals. Each element in the container is an object that contains both the name of the state and the name of its capital. The name of the state is used by **operator<( )** to determine ordering. Thus, a state's name is its key.

```
// Storing class objects in a set.
#include <iostream>
#include <set>
#include <string>
using namespace std;

// This class stores states and their capitals.
class state {
  string name;
  string capital;
public:
  state() { name = capital = ""; }
```

8

```
    // construct temporary object using only state name
    state(string s) { name = s; capital = ""; }

    // construct an entire state object
    state(string n, string c)
    {
      name = n;
      capital = c;
    }

    string get_name() { return name; }

    string get_capital() { return capital; }
};

// Compare objects using name of state.
bool operator<(state a, state b)
{
  return a.get_name() < b.get_name();
}

// Create an inserter for state.
ostream &operator<<(ostream &s, state &o)
{
  s << o.get_name() << "'s capital is ";
  s << o.get_capital() << "." << endl;

  return s;
}

int main()
{
  set<state> states;

  // initialize the set
  states.insert(state("Illinois", "Springfield"));
  states.insert(state("Wisconsin", "Madison"));
  states.insert(state("Missouri", "Jefferson City"));
  states.insert(state("California", "Sacramento"));
  states.insert(state("Nevada", "Carson City"));
  states.insert(state("Arkansas", "Little Rock"));
  states.insert(state("Alaska", "Juneau"));
  states.insert(state("West Virginia", "Charleston"));
```

```
// display contents of set
set<state>::iterator p = states.begin();
do {
  cout << *p;
  p++;
} while(p != states.end());
cout << endl;

// find a specific state
cout << "Looking for Wisconsin.\n";
p = states.find(state("Wisconsin"));
if(p != states.end()) {
  cout << "Found.\n";
  cout << *p;
}
else
  cout << "State not in list.\n";

return 0;
}
```

The output is shown here:

```
Alaska's capital is Juneau.
Arkansas's capital is Little Rock.
California's capital is Sacramento.
Illinois's capital is Springfield.
Missouri's capital is Jefferson City.
Nevada's capital is Carson City.
West Virginia's capital is Charleston.
Wisconsin's capital is Madison.

Looking for Wisconsin.
Found.
Wisconsin's capital is Madison.
```

There are several interesting things to notice in the program. First, the <
operator is overloaded for objects of type **state**. However, it uses only the
name of the state for the comparison. It ignores the name of the capital.
Thus, when an object of type **state** is stored in a set, the set is ordered
relative to the **name** field and all searches utilize only the state's name.

8

The second thing to notice is the following constructor:

```
// construct temporary object using only state name
state(string s) { name = s; capital = ""; }
```

This constructor creates a **state** object in which only the **name** field actually contains information. This constructor is useful for finding a state given its name. In fact, this is precisely what occurs in the program when these statements execute in **main( )**.

```
// find a specific state
cout << "Looking for Wisconsin.\n";
p = states.find(state("Wisconsin"));
if(p != states.end()) {
  cout << "Found.\n";
  cout << *p;
}
else
  cout << "State not in list.\n";
```

Since only the name is used by the < operator, it is the only piece of information needed to search for a state in the set. If the name is found, the capital is displayed. While it would have been possible to manually construct an object in which the name was specified and the capital was given a null string, defining the preceding constructor adds substantial convenience.

NOTE: Remember, normally you will overload < such that it operates on only one data member of its class. This member is the class' actual key.

multiset

The **multiset** class supports a set in which possibly nonunique keys are stored. Its template specification is shown here:

```
template <class Key, class Comp = less<Key>,
        class Allocator = allocator<Key> > class multiset
```

Here, **Key** is the data of the keys and **Comp** is a function that compares two keys. It has the following constructors:

explicit multiset(const Comp &*cmpfn* = Comp( ),
    const Allocator &*a* = Allocator( ));

multiset(const multiset<Key, Comp, Allocator> &*ob*);

template <class InIter> multiset(InIter *start*, InIter *end*,
    const Comp &*cmpfn* = Comp( ),
    const Allocator &*a* = Allocator( ));

*The **multiset** class stores possibly non-unique keys.*

The first form constructs an empty multiset. The second form constructs a multiset that contains the same elements as *ob*. The third form constructs a multiset from the specified range. The function specified by *cmpfn*, if present, determines the ordering of the set. By default, **less** is the comparison function. To use a multiset, you must include **<set>**.

The **multiset** class overloads the assignment operator. In addition, the following comparison operators are defined for **multiset**:

    ==, <, <=, !=, >, >=

The **multiset** class supports bidirectional iterators. Thus, the container can be accessed through an iterator in both the forward and reverse directions, but random access operations are not supported.

8

The **multiset** class defines the following concrete types:

size_type	Some type of integer.
difference_type	Some type of integer that can hold the difference between two addresses.
reference	A reference to an element (i.e., **Key** &).
const_reference	A **const** reference to an element (i.e., **const Key** &).
iterator	An iterator.
const_iterator	A **const** iterator.
reverse_iterator	A reverse iterator.
const_reverse_iterator	A **const** reverse iterator.

value_type	Same as **key_type**.
key_type	The type of the key; same as **Key**.
key_compare	Same as **Comp**.
value_comparc	Same as **Comp**.
allocator_type	The type of the allocator.
pointer	A pointer to an element (i.e., **Key ***).
const_pointer	A **const** pointer to an element (i.e., **const Key ***).

The member functions defined by **multiset** are shown in Table 8-2. In the descriptions, both **key_type** and **value_type** are **typedef**s for **Key**. A specialization of the standard **swap( )** algorithm is also defined for **multiset**.

Member	Description
iterator begin( ); const_iterator begin( ) const;	Returns an iterator to the first element in the multiset.
void clear( );	Removes all elements from the multiset.
size_type count(const key_type &k) const;	Returns the number of times *k* occurs in the multiset.
bool empty( ) const;	Returns **true** if the invoking multiset is empty and **false** otherwise.
iterator end( ); const_iterator end( ) const;	Returns an iterator to the end of the list.
pair<iterator, iterator> equal_range(const key_type &k) const;	Returns a pair of iterators that point to the upper bound and the lower bound in the multiset for the specified key.

The **multiset**
Member
Functions
Table 8-2.

Member	Description
void erase(iterator *i*);	Removes the element pointed to by *i*.
void erase(iterator *start*, iterator *end*);	Removes the elements in the range *start* to *end*.
size_type erase(const key_type &*k*)	Removes from the multiset elements that have keys with the value *k*.
iterator find(const key_type &*k*) const;	Returns an iterator to the specified key. If the key is not found, then an iterator to the end of the multiset is returned.
allocator_type get_allocator( ) const;	Returns multiset's allocator.
iterator insert(iterator *i*, const value_type &*val*);	Inserts *val* at or after the element specified by *i*. An iterator to the element is returned.
template <class InIter> void insert(InIter *start*, InIter *end*)	Inserts a range of elements.
iterator insert(const value_type &*val*);	Inserts *val* into the invoking multiset. An iterator to the element is returned.
key_compare key_comp( ) const;	Returns the function object that compares keys.
iterator lower_bound(const key_type &*k*) const;	Returns an iterator to the first element in the multiset with the key equal to or greater than *k*.
size_type max_size( ) const;	Returns the maximum number of elements that a multiset can hold.
reverse_iterator rbegin( ); const_reverse_iterator rbegin( ) const;	Returns a reverse iterator to the end of the multiset.
reverse_iterator rend( ); const_reverse_iterator rend( ) const;	Returns a reverse iterator to the start of the multiset.

The **multiset** Member Functions *(continued)*
Table 8-2.

8

Member	Description
size_type size( ) const;	Returns the number of elements currently in the multiset.
void swap(multiset<Key, Comp, Allocator> &*ob*)	Exchanges the elements stored in the invoking multiset with those in *ob*.
iterator upper_bound(const key_type &*k*) const;	Returns an iterator to the first element in the multiset with the key greater than *k*.
value_compare value_comp( ) const;	Returns the function object that compares values.

The **multiset** Member Functions *(continued)* **Table 8-2.**

Performance Characteristics

Multisets have the same performance characteristics as sets. In general, inserting or deleting elements in a multiset takes place in logarithmic time. The two exceptions are when an element is inserted at a given location and when a specific element is deleted given an interator to that element. In these cases, amortized constant time is required.

Insertion into a multiset invalidates no iterators or references to elements. A deletion invalidates only iterators or references to the deleted elements.

Using a Multiset

A multiset is useful when you wish to create a set of objects in which not all keys are necessarily unique. Such sets are actually quite common. For example, consider a set that contains elements that describe a book, such as its author, title, publisher, and copyright date. If the key is the author's name, then each element in the set will not necessarily be unique because many authors write more than one book. The following program shows how **multiset** can be used to store such a list of books:

```
// Storing class objects in a multiset.
#include <iostream>
#include <set>
#include <string>
using namespace std;
```

```
// This class stores info about a book, indexed by author.
class book {
  string author;
  string title;
  string publisher;
  string date;
public:
  book() { title = author = publisher = date = ""; }

  // construct temporary object using only author (i.e., key)
  book(string a) { author = a;
                   title = publisher = date = ""; }

  // construct a complete book object
  book(string t, string a, string p, string d)
  {
    title = t;
    author = a;
    publisher = p;
    date = d;
  }

  // return only author's name
  string get_author() { return author; }

  // obtain all information about a book
  void get_info(string &t, string &a, string &p, string &d)
  {
    t = title;
    a = author;
    p = publisher;
    d = date;
  }

};

// Compare objects using author.
bool operator<(book a, book b)
{
  return a.get_author() < b.get_author();
}

// Create an inserter for book.
ostream &operator<<(ostream &s, book &o)
{
  string t, a, p, d;
```

```
      o.get_info(t, a, p, d);
      s << a << endl;
      s << t << endl;
      s << p << endl;
      s << d << cndl;

      return s;
  }

  int main()
  {
    multiset<book> booklist;
    string a;

    // initialize the set
    booklist.insert(book("C++: The Complete Reference",
                         "Schildt", "Osborne/McGraw-Hill",
                         "1998"));
    booklist.insert(book("C++ From The Ground Up",
                         "Schildt", "Osborne/McGraw-Hill",
                         "1998"));
    booklist.insert(book("Teach Yourself C++",
                         "Schildt", "Osborne/McGraw-Hill",
                         "1997"));
    booklist.insert(book("Executive Orders",
                         "Clancy", "Putnam",
                         "1996"));
    booklist.insert(book("The Hunt for Red October",
                         "Clancy", "Berkeley",
                         "1985"));
    booklist.insert(book("Red Storm Rising",
                         "Clancy", "Berkeley",
                         "1987"));
    booklist.insert(book("Sphere",
                         "Crichton", "Ballantine",
                         "1987"));
    booklist.insert(book("Jurassic Park",
                         "Crichton", "Ballantine",
                         "1990"));
    booklist.insert(book("The Lost World",
                         "Crichton", "Knopf",
                         "1995"));
```

```
// display contents of set
multiset<book>::iterator p = booklist.begin();
do {
  cout << *p << endl;
  p++;
} while(p != booklist.end());
cout << endl;

// find a specific book
cout << "Enter author: ";
cin >> a;
p = booklist.find(book(a));
if(p != booklist.end()) {
  do {
    cout << *p << endl;
    p++;
  } while(p != booklist.upper_bound(a));
}

return 0;
}
```

Here is sample output:

```
Clancy
Executive Orders
Putnam
1996

Clancy
The Hunt for Red October
Berkeley
1985

Clancy
Red Storm Rising
Berkeley
1987

Crichton
Sphere
Ballantine
1987
```

8

```
Crichton
Jurassic Park
Ballantine
1990

Crichton
The Lost World
Knopf
1995

Schildt
C++: The Complete Reference
Osborne/McGraw-Hill
1998

Schildt
C++ From The Ground Up
Osborne/McGraw-Hill
1998

Schildt
Teach Yourself C++
Osborne/McGraw-Hill
1997


Enter author: Clancy

Clancy
Executive Orders
Putnam
1996

Clancy
The Hunt for Red October
Berkeley
1985

Clancy
Red Storm Rising
Berkeley
1987
```

Enumerating Equal Keys

In the multiset example (and in the multimap example in the previous chapter), objects with equal keys are enumerated by storing an iterator to the first object and then incrementing that iterator until it was equal to the value returned by **upper_bound( )**. While this works just fine, there are, of course, other ways to enumerate objects with equal keys. One way uses **count( )**. The **count( )** function returns the number of times that a given key occurs in a set. Thus, another way to obtain all objects with a given key is to store an iterator to the first object and then increment that iterator **count( )** number of times. For example, assuming the book list program, here is another way to display all books in the list that were written by Tom Clancy:

```
p = booklist.find(book("Clancy"));
for(int i=0; i<booklist.count(book("Clancy")); i++) {
  cout << *p << endl;
  p++;
}
```

Another way to enumerate equal keys is to use the **equal_range( )**. This function returns a pair of iterators that point to the lower and upper bounds of the specified key. For example, this fragment uses **equal_range( )** to display all books written by Michael Crichton.

```
pair<multiset<book>::iterator,
       multiset<book>::iterator> range;

range = booklist.equal_range(book("Crichton"));
for(p=range.first; p != range.second; p++)
  cout << *p << endl;
```

One other point. In the **for** loop above, it is not possible to write the expression

```
p != range.second
```

as

```
p < range.second
```

because bidirectional iterators do not support the < operator.

8

Another Multiset Example

Here is another example that demonstrates an interesting use for a multiset. The multiset is used to store responses to a polling question. The respondents can answer one of the following:

◆ Strongly agree

◆ Agree

◆ Disagree

◆ Strongly disagree

◆ No opinion

Each response is added to the set. Once all respondents have answered, the results are displayed. The frequency of each response is determined by the **count( )** function, which counts the number of times a specified element occurs in the set.

```
/* Using a multiset to record responses
   to a polling question. */
#include <iostream>
#include <set>
using namespace std;

enum response { strong_agree, agree, disagree,
                strong_disagree, no_opinion };

int main()
{
  multiset<response> question;

  // create some responses
  question.insert(response(strong_agree));
  question.insert(response(agree));
  question.insert(response(strong_agree));
  question.insert(response(strong_disagree));
  question.insert(response(disagree));
  question.insert(response(disagree));
  question.insert(response(no_opinion));
  question.insert(response(agree));
  question.insert(response(strong_agree));
```

```
    // display results
    cout << "Respondents that strongly agree: ";
    cout << question.count(strong_agree) << endl;

    cout << "Respondents that agree: ";
    cout << question.count(agree) << endl;

    cout << "Respondents that disagree: ";
    cout << question.count(disagree) << endl;

    cout << "Respondents that strongly disagree: ";
    cout << question.count(disagree) << endl;

    cout << "Respondents with no opinion: ";
    cout << question.count(no_opinion) << endl;

    return 0;
}
```

Here is the output:

```
Respondents that strongly agree: 3
Respondents that agree: 2
Respondents that disagree: 2
Respondents that strongly disagree: 2
Respondents with no opinion: 1
```

While both sets and multisets may at first seem to be less valuable than maps and multimaps, they have several uses, and for some applications they might be a bit more efficient.

This chapter concludes our examination of the STL containers. In the next chapter we will begin our exploration of the STL algorithms.

8

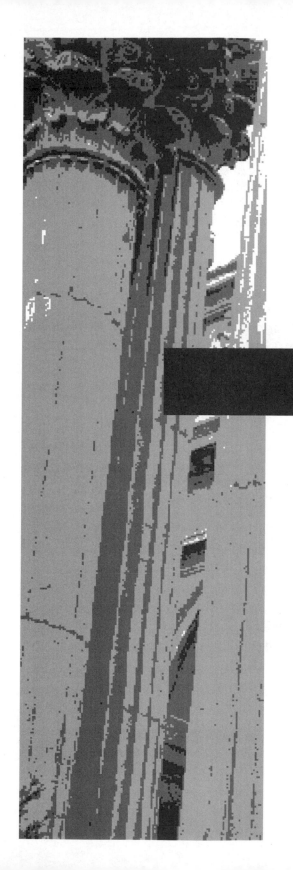

CHAPTER 9

Exploring Algorithms

This chapter explores the STL algorithms. Algorithms act on containers through iterators. Algorithms are one of the three major components of the STL, and they offer functionality not provided by the containers, themselves. This chapter explores algorithms and describes a representative sample. A complete description of all of the algorithms is found in Appendix A.

The Reason for Algorithms

Algorithms allow different types of containers to work together.

As the preceding chapters have shown, all of the container classes include a number of member functions that support a wide variety of operations. This fact gives rise to the following question: Why are separate algorithms needed? The answer to this question has three parts. First, and most importantly, algorithms allow two different types of containers to be operated upon at the same time. Because most algorithms operate through iterators, iterators to different types of containers can be used by the same algorithm. This part of the answer was mentioned in the In Depth box in Chapter 2.

Algorithms support the extensible nature of the STL.

The second part of the answer has to do with the extensibility of the STL. Because an algorithm can operate on any type of container that meets its minimum requirements, it is possible to create your own, custom containers that can be manipulated by the standard algorithms. Although we will look at the details of creating your own containers later, in general, as long as a container supports iterators, it can be used by the STL algorithms. It is also possible to create your own algorithms, as explained at the end of this chapter.

Algorithms provide generalizable operations.

The third reason for algorithms is that they streamline the STL because they provide operations that can be applied to a wide range of containers. The functionality provided by the algorithms need not be duplicated by the member functions of each container.

Algorithms are Template Functions

As explained in Chapter 2, the STL algorithms are template functions. This means that they can be applied to any type of container. With very few exceptions, the algorithms operate through iterators. (The exceptions use reference parameters.) In the algorithm descriptions found throughout this chapter, the following generic iterator type names are used:

Generic Name	Represents
BiIter	Bidirectional iterator
ForIter	Forward iterator
InIter	Input iterator
OutIter	Output iterator
RandIter	Random access iterator

Not all algorithms will work with all types of iterators. For example, the **sort( )** algorithm requires random-access iterators. This means that **sort( )** cannot be used on **list** containers, for example. (This is why **list** provides a member function to sort lists.) When choosing an algorithm, you must make sure that the container upon which it will be operating provides the necessary iterators.

In addition to the iterators, the following generic names are used to represent predicates, comparison functions, etc.:

T	Some type of data
Size	Some type of integer
Func	Some type of function
Generator	A function that generates objects
BinPred	Binary predicate
UnPred	Unary predicate
Comp	Comparison function

To have access to the STL algorithms, you must include **<algorithm>** in your program.

The Algorithm Categories

The STL defines a large number of algorithms, and it is common to group them by category. There are many ways to do this. One way is the categories used by the International Standard for C++, which are shown here:

◆ Nonmodifying sequence operations

◆ Modifying sequence operations

◆ Sorting and related operations

9

Tables 9-1 through 9-3 show the algorithms that comprise each of these categories. The nonmodifying sequence operations do not alter the containers upon which they operate. The modifying operations do. The sorting category includes the various sort algorithms as well as those algorithms that require a sorted sequence, or that in one way or the other order a sequence.

Algorithm	Purpose
adjacent_find	Searches for adjacent matching elements within a sequence and returns an iterator to the first match.
count	Returns the number of elements in the sequence.
count_if	Returns the number of elements in the sequence that satisfy some predicate.
equal	Determines if two ranges are the same.
find	Searches a range for a value and returns an iterator to the first occurrence of the element.
find_end	Searches a range for a subsequence. It returns an iterator to the end of the subsequence within the range.
find_first_of	Finds the first element within a sequence that matches an element within a range.
find_if	Searches a range for an element for which a user-defined unary predicate returns **true**.
for_each	Applies a function to a range of elements.
mismatch	Finds first mismatch between the elements in two sequences. Iterators to the two elements are returned.
search	Searches for subsequence within a sequence.
search_n	Searches for a sequence of a specified number of similar elements.

Nonmodifying
Sequence
Algorithms
Table 9-1.

Algorithm	Purpose
copy	Copies a sequence.
copy_backward	Same as **copy( )** except that it moves the elements from the end of the sequence first.
fill	Fills a range with the specified value.
fill_n	Fills a range with the specified value.
generate	Assigns elements in a range the values returned by a generator function.
generate_n	Assigns elements in a range the values returned by a generator function.
iter_swap	Exchanges the values pointed to by its two iterator arguments.
partition	Arranges a sequence such that all elements for which a predicate returns **true** come before those for which the predicate returns **false**.
random_shuffle	Randomizes a sequence.
replace	Replaces elements in a sequence.
replace_copy	Replaces elements while copying.
replace_copy_if	Replaces, while copying, elements for which a user-defined unary predicate is **true**.
replace_if	Replaces elements for which a user-defined unary predicate is **true**.
remove	Removes elements from a specified range.
remove_copy	Removes and copies elements from a specified range.
remove_copy_if	Removes and copies elements from a specified range for which a user-defined unary predicate is **true**.
remove_if	Removes elements from a specified range for which a user-defined unary predicate is **true**.
reverse	Reverses the order of a range.
reverse_copy	Reverses the order of a range while copying.
rotate	Left-rotates the elements in a range.

9

Modifying
Sequence
Operations
Table 9-2.

Algorithm	Purpose
rotate_copy	Left-rotates the elements in a range while copying.
stable_partition	Arranges a sequence such that all elements for which a predicate returns **true** come before those for which the predicate returns **false**. The partitioning is stable. This means that the relative ordering of the sequence is preserved.
swap	Exchanges two values.
swap_ranges	Exchanges elements in a range.
transform	Applies a function to a range of elements and stores the outcome in a new sequence.
unique	Eliminates duplicate elements from a range.
unique_copy	Eliminates duplicate elements from a range while copying.

Modifying
Sequence
Operations
(continued)
Table 9-2.

Algorithm	Purpose
binary_search	Performs a binary search on an ordered sequence.
equal_range	Returns a range in which an element can be inserted into a sequence without disrupting the ordering of the sequence.
includes	Determines if one sequence includes all of the elements in another sequence.
inplace_merge	Merges a range with another range. Both ranges must be sorted in increasing order. The resulting sequence is sorted.
lexicographical_compare	Alphabetically compares one sequence with another.
lower_bound	Finds the first point in the sequence that is not less than a specified value.
make_heap	Constructs a heap from a sequence.

Sorting and
Related
Algorithms
Table 9-3.

Algorithm	Purpose
max	Returns the maximum of two values.
max_element	Returns an iterator to the maximum element within a range.
merge	Merges two ordered sequences, placing the result into a third sequence.
min	Returns the minimum of two values.
min_element	Returns an iterator to the minimum element within a range.
next_permutation	Constructs the next permutation of a sequence.
nth_element	Arranges a sequence such that all elements less than a specified element E come before that element and all elements greater than E come after it.
partial_sort	Sorts a range.
partial_sort_copy	Sorts a range and then copies as many elements as will fit into a resulting sequence.
pop_heap	Exchanges the first and last −1 elements and then rebuilds the heap.
prev_permutation	Constructs previous permutation of a sequence.
push_heap	Pushes an element onto the end of a heap.
set_difference	Produces a sequence that contains the difference between two ordered sets.
set_intersection	Produces a sequence that contains the intersection of the two ordered sets.
set_symmetric_difference	Produces a sequence that contains the symmetric difference between the two ordered sets.
set_union	Produces a sequence that contains the union of the two ordered sets.
sort	Sorts a range.

9

Sorting and
Related
Algorithms
(continued)

Table 9-3.

Algorithm	Purpose
sort_heap	Sorts a heap within a specified range.
stable_sort	Sorts a range. The sort is stable. This means that equal elements are not rearranged.
upper_bound	Finds the last point in a sequence that is not greater than some value.

While the categories defined by the International Standard for C++ are useful, they each still contain a large number of algorithms. Another way to organize the algorithms is into smaller, functional groupings, such as those shown here:

Copying

copy

copy_backward

iter_swap

fill

fill_n

swap

swap_ranges

Searching Unsorted Sequences

adjacent_find

equal

find

find_end

find_if

find_first_of

mismatch

search

search_n

Replacing and Removing Elements

remove

remove_if

remove_copy

remove_copy_if

replace

replace_if

replace_copy

replace_copy_if

unique

unique_copy

Reordering a Sequence

rotate

rotate_copy

random_shuffle

partition

reverse

reverse_copy

stable_partition

Sorting

nth_element

sort

stable_sort

partial_sort

partial_sort_copy

Sorted Sequence Searching

binary_search

lower_bound

upper_bound

equal_range

Merging Sorted Sequences

merge

inplace_merge

Set Operations

includes

set_difference

set_intersection

set_symmetric_difference

set_union

Heap Operations

make_heap

push_heap

pop_heap

sort_heap

Minimum and Maximum

max

max_element

min

min_element

Permutations

next_permutation

prev_permutation

9

Transforming and Generating a Sequence

generate

generate_n

transform

Miscellaneous

count

count_if

for_each

lexicographical_compare

The remainder of this chapter examines representative algorithms from each of these categories.

Copying

Perhaps the most fundamental algorithms are those that involve copying elements from one sequence to another. Of course, the archetypal algorithm for this is **copy( )**, which copies a range of elements. Other algorithms that copy elements are **copy_backward( )** and the various swapping functions.

The **copy( )** algorithm was briefly mentioned in Chapter 2. We will take a closer look at it now. The prototype for **copy( )** is shown here:

```
template <class InIter, class OutIter>
    OutIter copy(InIter start, InIter end, OutIter result);
```

The **copy( )** algorithm copies a sequence beginning at *start* and ending with *end*, putting the result into the sequence pointed to by *result*. It returns a pointer to the end of the resulting sequence. The range to be copied must not overlap with *result*.

The following program demonstrates **copy( )**:

```
// Using copy()
#include <iostream>
#include <vector>
#include <algorithm>
using namespace std;

int main()
{
  vector<char> v(10);
  vector<char> v2(10);
  int i;

  for(i=0; i<10; i++) v[i] = 'A'+i;
  for(i=0; i<10; i++) v2[i] = 'z';

  // copy all of v into v2
  copy(v.begin(), v.end(), v2.begin());

  cout << "Contents of v2 after complete copy:\n";
  for(i=0; i<10; i++)
    cout << v2[i] << " ";
  cout << "\n\n";

  // re-initialize v2
  for(i=0; i<10; i++) v2[i] = 'z';

  // now copy just part of v into v2
  copy(v.begin()+2, v.end()-2, v2.begin());

  cout << "Contents of v2 after subsequence copy:\n";
  for(i=0; i<10; i++)
    cout << v2[i] << " ";
  cout << "\n\n";

  // re-initialize v2
  for(i=0; i<10; i++) v2[i] = 'z';

  // now copy part of v into middle of v2
  copy(v.begin()+2, v.end()-2, v2.begin()+3);
```

9

```
  cout << "Contents of v2 after copy into middle:\n";
  for(i=0; i<10; i++)
    cout << v2[i] << " ";
  cout << "\n\n";

  return 0;
}
```

The output from the program is shown here:

```
Contents of v2 after complete copy:
A B C D E F G H I J

Contents of v2 after subsequence copy:
C D E F G H z z z

Contents of v2 after copy into middle:
z z z C D E F G H z
```

The target container must be large enough to hold the elements that it receives.

The program illustrates three key capabilities of **copy( )**. First, it can copy the entire contents of one container to another. This is done in the program when the first call to **copy( )** takes place. Second, it can copy part of a container. Since **copy( )** operates on a range of iterators, there is no requirement that the range include the entire container. The second call to **copy( )** demonstrates this capability. Third, since the target of the copy operation is determined by an iterator, **copy( )** can be used to copy into the middle of the target container. It need not start at the beginning. The third call to **copy( )** shows this ability.

There is an important point that needs to be stressed about **copy( )** that also applies to many of the other algorithms, too. The recipient container must be large enough to hold the sequence that it is given. As a general rule, an algorithm will not automatically increase the size of the target container when copying elements to it. The algorithms simply assume that the target container is large enough. For example, the following code fragment will produce an error:

```
vector<char> v(100);
vector<char> v2(10);

// error!  v2 is not large enough to hold all of v
copy(v.begin(), v.end(), v2.begin());
```

Since **v2** is only 10 elements large, it cannot be used to hold **v**, which contains 100 elements.

Sometimes you will want to exchange the contents of one range with another. You can most efficiently accomplish this type of copy operation by using **swap_ranges( )**, shown here:

```
template <class ForIter1, class ForIter2>
    ForIter2 swap_ranges(ForIter1 start1, ForIter1 end1, ForIter2 start2);
```

The **swap_ranges( )** algorithm exchanges elements in the range specified by *start1* and *end1* with elements in the sequence beginning at *start2*. It returns a pointer to the end of the sequence specified by *start2*. The ranges being exchanged must not overlap.

Here is a program that demonstrates **swap_ranges( )**:

```cpp
// Using swap_ranges()
#include <iostream>
#include <vector>
#include <algorithm>
using namespace std;

int main()
{
  vector<char> v(10);
  vector<char> v2(10);
  int i;

  for(i=0; i<10; i++) v[i] = 'A'+i;
  for(i=0; i<10; i++) v2[i] = '0' + i;

  cout << "Original contents of v:\n";
  for(i=0; i<10; i++)
    cout << v[i] << " ";
  cout << "\n";
  cout << "Original contents of v2:\n";
  for(i=0; i<10; i++)
    cout << v2[i] << " ";
  cout << "\n\n";

  // swap ranges in v and v2
  swap_ranges(v.begin()+2, v.end()-3, v2.begin()+4);

  cout << "Contents of v after swap:\n";
```

9

```
  for(i=0; i<10; i++)
    cout << v[i] << " ";
  cout << "\n";
  cout << "Contents of v2 after swap:\n";
  for(i=0; i<10; i++)
    cout << v2[i] << " ";
  cout << "\n";

  return 0;
}
```

The output from the program is shown here:

```
Original contents of v:
A B C D E F G H I J
Original contents of v2:
0 1 2 3 4 5 6 7 8 9

Contents of v after swap:
A B 4 5 6 7 8 H I J
Contents of v2 after swap:
0 1 2 3 C D E F G 9
```

As you can see, the letters C, D, E, F, and G in **v** were exchanged with the digits 4, 5, 6, 7, and 8 in **v2**.

Since one of the main benefits of the algorithms is that they can work with two different types of containers at the same time, it is possible to use **swap_ranges( )** to exchange elements in two different types of containers. For example, here is the preceding program recoded so that the ranges from a vector and a deque are exchanged:

```
// Exchange elements from  two different types of containers.
#include <iostream>
#include <vector>
#include <deque>
#include <algorithm>
using namespace std;

int main()
{
  vector<char> v(10);
  deque<char> deq(10);
  int i;
```

```
for(i=0; i<10; i++) v[i] = 'A'+i;
for(i=0; i<10; i++) deq[i] = '0' + i;

cout << "Original contents of v:\n";
for(i=0; i<10; i++)
  cout << v[i] << " ";
cout << "\n";
cout << "Original contents of deq:\n";
for(i=0; i<10; i++)
  cout << deq[i] << " ";
cout << "\n\n";

// swap ranges in v and deq
swap_ranges(v.begin()+2, v.end()-3, deq.begin()+4);

cout << "Contents of v after swap:\n";
for(i=0; i<10; i++)
  cout << v[i] << " ";
cout << "\n";
cout << "Contents of deq after swap:\n";
for(i=0; i<10; i++)
  cout << deq[i] << " ";
cout << "\n";

return 0;
}
```

9

The output from this program is similar to that just shown. The only difference is that the ranges being exchanged come from two different types of containers.

Searching Unsorted Sequences

The STL provides many algorithms that in one way or another enable you to search an unsorted sequence. It is important to understand that these algorithms can be used to search sorted sequences, too. It's just that they do not require sorted sequences. If the sequence is sorted, however, then in many cases faster search algorithms are available.

Perhaps the most widely used search algorithms are **find( )** and its close relative, **find_if( )**. Here is the prototype for **find( )**:

template <class InIter, class T>
    InIter find(InIter *start*, InIter *end*, const T &*val*);

The **find( )** algorithm searches the range *start* to *end* for the value specified by *val*. It returns an iterator to the first occurrence of the element or to *end* if the value is not in the sequence.

Here is the prototype for **find_if( )**:

```
template <class InIter, class UnPred>
  InIter find_if(InIter start, InIter end, UnPred pfn);
```

The **find_if( )** algorithm works just like **find( )** except that it searches the range *start* to *end* for an element for which the unary predicate *pfn* returns **true**.

Here is an example that illustrates **find( )** and **find_if( )**:

```cpp
// Demonstrate find() and find_if().
#include <iostream>
#include <vector>
#include <algorithm>
#include <cstring>
using namespace std;

// Return true if ch is a comma.
bool iscomma(char ch)
{
  if(ch==',') return true;
  return false;
}

int main()
{
  vector<char> v;
  vector<char>::iterator p;
  char str[] = "One, Two, Three";
  int i;

  for(i=0; i<strlen(str); i++)
    v.push_back(str[i]);

  cout << "Contents of v: ";
  for(i=0; i<v.size(); i++)
    cout << v[i];
  cout << endl;

  // find the first T
  p = find(v.begin(), v.end(), 'T');
```

```
cout << "Sequence beginning with T: ";
while(p != v.end())
  cout << *p++;
cout << endl;

// find first comma
p = find_if(v.begin(), v.end(), iscomma);
cout << "After find first comma: ";
while(p != v.end())
  cout << *p++;
cout << endl;

return 0;
}
```

Here is the output produced by the program:

```
Contents of v: One, Two, Three
Sequence beginning with T: Two, Three
After find first comma: , Two, Three
```

This program creates a vector of characters. It then finds the first occurrence of the letter T using the **find( )** algorithm. Next, it uses **find_if( )** to find the first character in the vector that is a comma.

Another useful search algorithm is **search( )**. It looks for a sequence of elements rather than one specific value. Its prototypes are shown here:

9

> template <class ForIter1, class ForIter2>
>   ForIter1 search(ForIter1 *start1*, ForIter1 *end1*,
>   ForIter2 *start2*, ForIter2 *end2*);

> template <class ForIter1, class ForIter2, class BinPred>
>   ForIter1 search(ForIter1 *start1*, ForIter1 *end1*,
>   ForIter2 *start2*, ForIter2 *end2*, BinPred *pfn*);

The **search( )** algorithm searches for a subsequence within a sequence. The sequence being searched is defined by *start1* and *end1*. The subsequence being sought is specified by *start2* and *end2*. If the subsequence is found, an iterator to its beginning is returned. Otherwise, *end1* is returned. The second form allows you to specify a binary predicate that determines when one element is equal to another.

Here is a program that demonstrates **search( )**:

```cpp
// Demonstrate search().
#include <iostream>
#include <vector>
#include <algorithm>
#include <cstring>
using namespace std;

int main()
{
  vector<char> v, v2;
  vector<char>::iterator p;
  char str1[] = "One, Two, Three, Two again";
  char str2[] = "Two";
  int i;

  for(i=0; i<strlen(str1); i++)
    v.push_back(str1[i]);

  for(i=0; i<strlen(str2); i++)
    v2.push_back(str2[i]);

  cout << "Contents of v: ";
  for(i=0; i<v.size(); i++)
    cout << v[i];
  cout << endl;

  // find the first Two
  p = search(v.begin(), v.end(), v2.begin(), v2.end());
  cout << "Sequence beginning with Two: ";
  while(p != v.end())
    cout << *p++;
  cout << endl;

  return 0;
}
```

Here is the output produced:

```
Contents of v: One, Two, Three, Two again
Sequence beginning with Two: Two, Three, Two again
```

The program creates two vectors, **v** and **v2**. In the program, the sequence defined by **v** is searched for the sequence defined by **v2**, which is "Two". Since **v** contains the sequence "Two", the sequence is found and an iterator to the start of the sequence is returned.

An interesting variation on searching is found in the **mismatch( )** algorithm, which allows you to find the first mismatch between two sequences. Its prototypes are shown here:

```
template <class InIter1, class InIter2>
    pair<InIter1, InIter2> mismatch(InIter1 start1, InIter1 end1,
                                    InIter2 start2);

template <class InIter1, class InIter2, class BinPred>
    pair<InIter1, InIter2> mismatch(InIter1 start1, InIter1 end1,
                                    InIter2 start2, BinPred pfn);
```

The **mismatch( )** algorithm finds the first mismatch between the elements in the sequence delineated by *start1* and *end1* and the one beginning with *start2*. Iterators to the two mismatching elements are returned. If no mismatch is found, then the iterators *last1* and *first2* + (*last1*–*first1*) are returned. Thus, it is the length of the first sequence that determines the number of elements tested. The second form allows you to specify a binary predicate that determines when one element is equal to another. The **pair** template class contains two data members called **first** and **second**, which hold the pair of iterators.

Here is an example that uses **mismatch( )**:

```cpp
// Demonstrate mismatch().
#include <iostream>
#include <vector>
#include <algorithm>
#include <cstring>
#include <utility>
using namespace std;

int main()
{
  vector<char> v, v2;
  pair<vector<char>::iterator, vector<char>::iterator> p;
  char str1[] = "One, Two, Three, Two again";
  char str2[] = "One, Two, Four, Five, Nine";
  int i;
```

9

```
for(i=0; i<strlen(str1); i++)
  v.push_back(str1[i]);

for(i=0; i<strlen(str2); i++)
  v2.push_back(str2[i]);

cout << "Contents of v:  ";
for(i=0; i<v.size(); i++)
  cout << v[i];
cout << endl;

cout << "Contents of v2: ";
for(i=0; i<v2.size(); i++)
  cout << v2[i];
cout << endl;

// find the first mismatch
p = mismatch(v.begin(), v.end(), v2.begin());

if(p.first != v.end()) { // mismatch found
  cout << "The character " << *p.first;
  cout << " in v mismatches the character ";
  cout << *p.second << " in v2.\n";
}

  return 0;
}
```

The following output is produced:

```
Contents of v:  One, Two, Three, Two again
Contents of v2: One, Two, Four, Five, Nine
The character T in v mismatches the character F in v2.
```

As you can see, **mismatch( )** finds the point of first disagreement between the two sequences and returns a pair of iterators to the mismatching elements.

Sorting

The STL provides a rich set of sorting algorithms. At the core is **sort( )**, shown here:

```
template <class RandIter>
    void sort(RandIter start, RandIter end);

template <class RandIter, class Comp>
    void sort(RandIter start, RandIter end, Comp cmpfn);
```

The **sort( )** algorithm works only on those containers that support random-access iterators.

The **sort( )** algorithm sorts the range specified by *start* and *end*. The second form allows you to specify a comparison function that determines when one element is less than another. Notice that **sort( )** requires random-access iterators. Only a few containers, such as **vector** and **deque** support random-access iterators. Those containers, such as **list**, which do not, must provide their own sort routines.

It is important to understand that **sort( )** sorts the range specified by its arguments, which need not include the entire contents of the container. Thus, **sort( )** can be used to sort a subset of a container. To sort an entire container, you must specify **begin( )** and **end( )** as the starting and ending points.

The following program demonstrates the various capabilities of **sort( )**:

9

```cpp
// Demonstrating sort().
#include <iostream>
#include <vector>
#include <algorithm>
using namespace std;

void init_v(vector<int> &v)
{
  v[0] = 99;
  v[1] = 5;
  v[2] = 109;
  v[3] = -3;
  v[4] = 44;
  v[5] = 10;
  v[6] = 108;
  v[7] = 7;
  v[8] = 11;
  v[9] = 76;
}
```

```
int main()
{
  vector<int> v(10);
  int i;

  // sort the entire container
  init_v(v); // initialize v

  cout << "Sort an entire container.\n";
  cout << "Original order:\n";
  for(i=0; i<10; i++)
    cout << v[i] << " ";
  cout << "\n";

  sort(v.begin(), v.end());

  cout << "Order after sorting container:\n";
  for(i=0; i<10; i++)
    cout << v[i] << " ";
  cout << "\n\n";

  // sort a subset of the container
  init_v(v); // re-initialize v

  cout << "Sort a subset of a container.\n";
  cout << "Original order:\n";
  for(i=0; i<10; i++)
    cout << v[i] << " ";
  cout << "\n";

  sort(v.begin()+2, v.end()-2);

  cout << "Order after sorting v[2] through v[7]:\n";
  for(i=0; i<10; i++)
    cout << v[i] << " ";
  cout << "\n\n";

  return 0;
}
```

The output from the program is shown here:

```
Sort an entire container.
Original order:
99 5 109 -3 44 10 108 7 11 76
```

```
Order after sorting container:
-3 5 7 10 11 44 76 99 108 109

Sort a subset of a container.
Original order:
99 5 109 -3 44 10 108 7 11 76
Order after sorting v[2] through v[7]:
99 5 -3 7 10 44 108 109 11 76
```

An interesting variation on sorting is found in **partial_sort( )**. Its prototype is shown here:

```
template <class RandIter>
    void partial_sort(RandIter start, RandIter mid, RandIter end);

template <class RandIter, class Comp>
    void partial_sort(RandIter start, RandIter mid, RandIter end, Comp cmpfn);
```

The **partial_sort( )** algorithm sorts elements from the range *start* to *end.* However, after execution, only elements in the range *start* to *mid* will be in sorted order. The remaining elements are in an arbitrary order. Thus, **partial_sort( )** examines all elements from *start* to *end* but orders only *mid-start* elements from the entire range, and these elements are all less than the remaining, unordered elements. The second form allows you to specify a comparison function that determines when one element is less than another.

Here is program that demonstrates **partial_sort( )**:

```cpp
// Demonstrating partial_sort().
#include <iostream>
#include <vector>
#include <algorithm>
using namespace std;

void init_v(vector<int> &v)
{
  v[0] = 99;
  v[1] = 5;
  v[2] = 109;
  v[3] = -3;
  v[4] = 44;
  v[5] = 10;
  v[6] = 108;
```

9

```
    v[7] = 7;
    v[8] = 11;
    v[9] = 76;
}

int main()
{
  vector<int> v(10);
  int i;

  init_v(v); // initialize v

  cout << "Original order:\n";
  for(i=0; i<10; i++)
    cout << v[i] << " ";
  cout << "\n";

  partial_sort(v.begin(), v.begin()+5, v.end());

  cout << "Order after partial sorting:\n";
  for(i=0; i<10; i++)
    cout << v[i] << " ";
  cout << "\n";

  return 0;
}
```

The output is shown here:

```
Original order:
99 5 109 -3 44 10 108 7 11 76
Order after partial sorting:
-3 5 7 10 11 109 108 99 44 76
```

As the output shows, each element in the container was examined, but only the first five elements are ordered.

Partial sorting
is useful when
the order of only
the top few
elements of a
sequence is
required.

The major uses for the **partial_sort( )** algorithm are found when the order of only the first few elements of a larger set is important. For example, consider a cross-country running competition that has 100 competitors. At the end of the race, it is the order of the top five, or so, that is important. In this situation, it is not necessary to know the precise order of all runners, but only of the top few. Thus, it is not necessary to sort the entire list. The advantage of **partial_sort( )** is that it can partially order a large number of elements in less time than it would take to order the entire list. A useful variation on partial sorting is **partial_sort_copy( )**, which puts the sorted elements into another sequence.

Searching Sorted Sequences

If you are operating on a sorted sequence, then you can use a binary search to find a value. As you know, a binary search is much faster than a sequential search. It does, of course, require a sorted sequence. The prototypes for **binary_search( )** are shown here:

```
template <class ForIter, class T>
    bool binary_search(ForIter start, ForIter end, const T &val);

template <class ForIter, class T, class Comp>
    bool binary_search(ForIter start, ForIter end, const T &val, Comp cmpfn);
```

The **binary_search( )** alogrithm performs a binary search on an ordered sequence beginning at *start* and ending with *end* for the value specified by *val*. It returns **true** if *val* is found and **false** otherwise. The first version compares the elements in the specified sequence for equality. The second version allows you to specify your own comparison function. When acting on random-access iterators, **binary_search( )** consumes logarithmic time. For other types of iterators, the number of comparisons is logarithmic even though the time it takes to move between elements is not.

Here is an example that uses **binary_search( )**:

```cpp
// Demonstrate binary_search().
#include <iostream>
#include <vector>
#include <algorithm>
using namespace std;

int main()
{
  vector<char> v;
  bool result;
  int i;

  for(i=0; i<10; i++)
    v.push_back('A' + i);

  cout << "Contents of v: ";
  for(i=0; i<v.size(); i++)
    cout << v[i];
  cout << endl;
```

9

```
// search for F
cout << "Looking for F.\n";
result = binary_search(v.begin(), v.end(), 'F');
if(result)
  cout << "F Found\n";
else
  cout << "F Not Found\n";

// search for X
cout << "Looking for X.\n";
result = binary_search(v.begin(), v.end(), 'X');
if(result)
  cout << "X Found\n";
else
  cout << "X Not Found\n";

return 0;
}
```

The output is shown here:

```
Contents of v: ABCDEFGHIJ
Looking for F.
F Found
Looking for X.
X Not Found
```

You might be surprised by the fact that **binary_search( )** returns a **true/false** result rather than an iterator to the element that it finds. The justification for this approach is based in the argument that a sorted sequence may contain two or more values that match the one being sought. Thus, there is little value in returning the first one found. While the validity of this argument has been a subject of debate, it is nevertheless the way that **binary_search( )** works.

To actually obtain an iterator to an element in a sorted sequence, you will use one of these algorithms: **lower_bound( )**, **upper_bound( )**, or **equal_range( )**. The prototypes for the nonpredicate versions of these algorithms are shown here:

```
template <class ForIter, class T>
   pair<ForIter, ForIter> equal_range(ForIter start, ForIter end,
                                      const T &val);
```

```
template <class ForIter, class T>
    ForIter lower_bound(ForIter start, ForIter end, const T &val);
```

```
template <class ForIter, class T>
    ForIter upper_bound(ForIter start, ForIter end, const T &val);
```

The **lower_bound( )** algorithm returns an iterator to the first element that matches *val*, **upper_bound( )** returns an iterator one beyond the last matching element, and **equal_range( )** returns a pair of iterators that point to the lower and upper bounds. If the sought-after element is not in the sequence, these functions return iterators to **end( )**. All of these algorithms operate in logarithmic time when acting upon random-access iterators because they, too, use a binary search to find their respective values. For other types of iterators, the number of comparisons is logarithmic even though the time it takes to move between elements is not.

In general, if you want to obtain an iterator to the first matching element in a sorted sequence, use **lower_bound( )**. For example, here is another version of the preceding program:

```cpp
// Demonstrate lower_bound().
#include <iostream>
#include <vector>
#include <algorithm>
using namespace std;
int main()
{
  vector<char> v;
  vector<char>::iterator p;
  int i;

  for(i=0; i<10; i++)
    v.push_back('A' + i);

  cout << "Contents of v: ";
  for(i=0; i<v.size(); i++)
    cout << v[i];
  cout << endl;

  // search for F
  cout << "Looking for F.\n";
  p = lower_bound(v.begin(), v.end(), 'F');
  if(p != v.end())
    cout << *p << " Found\n";
  else
    cout << "F Not Found\n";
```

9

```
  // search for X
  cout << "Looking for X.\n";
  p = lower_bound(v.begin(), v.end(), 'X');
  if(p != v.end())
    cout << *p << " Found\n";
  else
    cout << "X Not Found\n";

  return 0;
}
```

This program produces the same output as the previous one.

Replacing and Removing Elements

The foundational algorithms for removing and replacing elements are
remove( ) and **replace( )**, shown here:

> template <class ForIter, class T>
>   ForIter remove(ForIter *start*, ForIter *end*, const T &*val*);

> template <class ForIter, class T>
>   void replace(ForIter *start*, ForIter *end*, const T &*old*, const T &*new*);

The **remove( )** algorithm removes elements from the specified range that are
equal to *val*. It returns an iterator to the end of the remaining elements.
Within the specified range, the **replace( )** algorithm replaces elements with
the value *old* with elements that have the value *new*.

The following program demonstrates **remove( )** and **replace( )**:

```
// Demonstrating remove() and replace().
#include <iostream>
#include <vector>
#include <algorithm>
using namespace std;

int main()
{
  vector<char> v;
  vector<char>::iterator p, p_end;
  int i;

  for(i=0; i<5; i++) {
    v.push_back('A'+i);
```

```
    v.push_back('A'+i);
    v.push_back('A'+i);
}

cout << "Original contents of v:\n";
for(p=v.begin(); p<v.end(); p++)
  cout << *p << " ";
cout << endl;

// remove all C's
p_end = remove(v.begin(), v.end(), 'C');

cout << "Sequence after removing all C's:\n";
for(p=v.begin(); p<p_end; p++)
  cout << *p << " ";
cout << endl;

// replace D's with X's
replace(v.begin(), v.end(), 'D', 'X');

cout << "Sequence after replacement:\n";
for(p=v.begin(); p<p_end; p++)
  cout << *p << " ";
cout << endl;

return 0;
}
```

9

Here is the output produced by the program:

```
Original contents of v:
A A A B B B C C C D D D E E E
Sequence after removing all C's:
A A A B B B D D D E E E
Sequence after replacement:
A A A B B B X X X E E E
```

In the program, notice that the iterator **p_end** is assigned the end point of the sequence after the C's are removed.

There are two variations of **remove( )** and **replace( )** that you will find useful. Often, you will want to create a new sequence in which certain elements are either removed or replaced. To accomplish this, you can use **remove_copy( )** or **replace_copy( )**. (These algorithms were demonstrated in Chapter 2.) To specify your own criteria for removing or replacing elements, you can use **remove_if( )** and **replace_if( )**.

Another variation on element removal is **unique( )**. It removes consecutive, duplicate elements from a range. Its prototype is shown here:

```
template <class ForIter>
    ForIter unique(ForIter start, ForIter end);
```

```
template <class ForIter, class BinPred>
    ForIter unique(ForIter start, ForIter end, BinPred pfn);
```

Consecutive duplicate elements from the range determined by *start* and *end* are removed. The second form allows you to specify a binary predicate that determines when one element is equal to another. **unique( )** returns an iterator to the end of the resulting range.

Here is an example that uses **unique( )**:

```cpp
// Demonstrating unique().
#include <iostream>
#include <vector>
#include <algorithm>
using namespace std;

int main()
{
  vector<char> v;
  vector<char>::iterator p, p_end;
  int i;

  for(i=0; i<5; i++) {
    v.push_back('A'+i);
    v.push_back('A'+i);
    v.push_back('A'+i);
  }

  cout << "Original contents of v:\n";
  for(p=v.begin(); p<v.end(); p++)
    cout << *p << " ";
  cout << endl;

  // remove duplicates
  p_end = unique(v.begin(), v.end());
```

```
cout << "Sequence after removing duplicates:\n";
for(p=v.begin(); p<p_end; p++)
  cout << *p << " ";
cout << endl;

return 0;
}
```

Here is the program's output:

```
Original contents of v:
A A A B B B C C C D D D E E E
Sequence after removing duplicates:
A B C D E
```

A useful alternative to **unique( )** is **unique_copy( )**, which copies the result to another sequence.

Transforming and Generating Sequences

The STL supplies algorithms that transform and generate sequences. These are **transform( )**, **generate( )**, and **generate_n( )**. Each is examined here.

The **transform( )** algorithm has these two forms:

> template <class InIter, class OutIter, class Func)
>   OutIter transform(InIter *start*, InIter *end*, OutIter *result*, Func *unaryfunc*);

> template <class InIter1, class InIter2, class OutIter, class Func)
>   OutIter transform(InIter1 *start1*, InIter1 *end1*, InIter2 *start2*,
>   OutIter *result*, Func *binaryfunc*);

The **transform( )** algorithm applies a function to a range of elements and stores the outcome in *result*. In the first form, the range is specified by *start* and *end*. The function to be applied is specified by *unaryfunc.* This function receives the value of an element in its parameter and it must return its transformation. In the second form of **transform( )**, the transformation is applied using a binary operator function that receives the value of an element from the sequence to be transformed (*start1* to *end1*) in its first parameter and an element from the second sequence (beginning at *start2*) as its second parameter. Both versions of **transform( )** return an iterator to the end of the resulting sequence.

9

An example that uses a unary transformation function was presented in Chapter 2. Here is an example that uses a binary function to transform a sequence. It computes the midpoints between corresponding elements in two numeric sequences.

```
// Transforming a sequence.
#include <iostream>
#include <vector>
#include <algorithm>
using namespace std;

double midpoint(double a, double b)
{
  return ((a-b) / 2) + b;
}

int main()
{
  vector<double> v1(5), v2(5), v3(5);
  int i;

  v1[0] = 10.0;
  v1[1] = 98.6;
  v1[2] = 12.23;
  v1[3] = 88.8;
  v1[4] = -212.01;

  v2[0] = 2.0;
  v2[1] = 3.3;
  v2[2] = 4.19;
  v2[3] = 155.0;
  v2[4] = -2.0;

  cout << "Values in v1: ";
  for(i=0; i<v1.size(); i++)
    cout << v1[i] << " ";
  cout << endl;

  cout << "Values in v2: ";
  for(i=0; i<v2.size(); i++)
    cout << v2[i] << " ";
  cout << endl;

  // find midpoints between elements in v1 and those in v2
  transform(v1.begin(), v1.end(), v2.begin(),
            v3.begin(), midpoint);
```

```
  // midpoints:
  cout << "Midpoints: ";
  for(i=0; i<v3.size(); i++)
    cout << v3[i] << " ";

  return 0;
}
```

The output is shown here:

```
Values in v1: 10 98.6 12.23 88.8 -212.01
Values in v2: 2 3.3 4.19 155 -2
Midpoints: 6 50.95 8.21 121.9 -107.005
```

As the program illustrates, the function used by the binary-function version of **transform( )** must have two parameters whose types are compatible with the types of the elements in the sequences. Also, it must return a compatible type. Each time the function is called, a value from the first sequence is passed to its first parameter and a value from the second sequence is passed to its second parameter. The result of the transformation must be returned.

Sometimes you will want to generate a sequence that is not based on any preexisting sequence. To do this, use **generate( )** or **generate_n( )**, shown here:

    template <class ForIter, class Generator>
        void generate(ForIter *start*, ForIter *end*, Generator *fngen*);

    template <class OutIter, class Size, class Generator>
        void generate_n(OutIter *start*, Size *num*, Generator *fngen*);

The algorithms **generate( )** and **generate_n( )** assign values returned by a generator function to elements within a specified range. For **generate( )**, the range being assigned is specified by *start* and *end*. For **generate_n( )**, the range begins at *start* and runs for *num* elements. The generator function is passed in *fngen*. It has no parameters.

The following program uses **generate( )** to create a sequence that contains the following series:

    1, 1/2, 1/4, 1/8 ...

9

```
// Generating a sequence.
#include <iostream>
```

```
#include <vector>
#include <algorithm>
using namespace std;

// A simple generator function.
double f()
{
  static double val = 1.0;
  double t;

  t = 1.0 / val;
  val += val;

  return t;
}

int main()
{
  vector<double> v(5);
  int i;

  // generate a series
  generate(v.begin(), v.end(), f);

  cout << "Series: ";
  for(i=0; i<v.size(); i++)
    cout << v[i] << " ";

  return 0;
}
```

Here is the output from the program:

```
Series: 1 0.5 0.25 0.125 0.0625
```

As the output shows, each element in the sequence, moving from beginning to end, has been assigned the value generated by **f( )**.

Reordering a Sequence

In addition to the various sort algorithms, there are several STL algorithms that alter the order of elements within a sequence. One of the most commonly used is **reverse( )**, which reverses the order of elements. This algorithm was described earlier in this book, in Chapter 2. Other commonly used order-changing algorithms are **rotate( )** and **random_shuffle( )**. They are examined here.

The **rotate( )** algorithm performs a left-rotate. A rotate is a shift in which the value shifted off one end is put onto the other end. The prototype for **rotate( )** is shown here:

```
template <class ForIter>
  void rotate(ForIter start, ForIter mid, ForIter end);
```

The **rotate( )** algorithm left-rotates the elements in the range specified by *start* and *end* so that the element specified by *mid* becomes the new first element.

Here is an example that uses **rotate( )**:

```
// Rotate a sequence.
#include <iostream>
#include <vector>
#include <algorithm>
using namespace std;

int main()
{
  vector<int> v;
  vector<int>::iterator p;
  int i;

  for(i=0; i<10; i++) v.push_back(i);

  cout << "Original ordering: ";
  for(p=v.begin(); p<v.end(); p++)
    cout << *p << " ";
  cout << endl;

  // rotate left one position
  rotate(v.begin(), v.begin()+1, v.end());

  cout << "Order after left rotate: ";
  for(p=v.begin(); p<v.end(); p++)
    cout << *p << " ";
  cout << endl;

  return 0;
}
```

9

The output from the program is shown here:

```
Original ordering: 0 1 2 3 4 5 6 7 8 9
Order after left rotate: 1 2 3 4 5 6 7 8 9 0
```

IN DEPTH

Using Reverse Iterators to Perform a Right-Rotate

Although the STL supplies a left-rotate algorithm, it does not provide
one that right-rotates. At first this might seem like a serious flaw in the
STL's design, or at least a troublesome omission. But neither is the case.
To perform a right-rotate you simply use the **rotate( )** algorithm, but
call it using reverse iterators. Since reverse iterators run backwards, the
net effect of such a call is that a right-rotate is performed on the
sequence! For example, consider the following program:

```cpp
// Right-rotate a sequence.
#include <iostream>
#include <vector>
#include <algorithm>
using namespace std;

int main()
{
  vector<int> v;
  vector<int>::iterator p;
  int i;

  for(i=0; i<10; i++) v.push_back(i);

  cout << "Original ordering: ";
  for(p=v.begin(); p<v.end(); p++)
    cout << *p << " ";
  cout << endl;

  // rotate right two positions using reverse iterators
  rotate(v.rbegin(), v.rbegin()+2, v.rend());
```

IN DEPTH
CONTINUED

```
cout << "Order after two right rotates: ";
 for(p=v.begin(); p<v.end(); p++)
   cout << *p << " ";
 cout << endl;

 return 0;
}
```

Here is the program's output:

```
Original ordering: 0 1 2 3 4 5 6 7 8 9
Order after two right rotates: 8 9 0 1 2 3 4 5 6 7
```

As you can see, the original sequence was rotated right two positions.

As you learn more about the STL, you will see that part of its power and elegance come from the subtleties of its design. By defining reverse iterators, the creators of the STL made it possible to reverse the direction of several algorithms, thus reducing the need to explicitly define a backwards-running complement for each algorithm. While it certainly would have been possible to create a standard template library that did not include such things as reverse iterators, it is these types of constructs that streamline its design.

9

An algorithm that is particularly useful to programmers creating simulations is **random_shuffle( )**. It reorders the elements in a sequence in some random way. Its prototype is shown here:

    template <class RandIter>
        void random_shuffle(RandIter *start*, RandIter *end*);

    template <class RandIter, class Generator>
        void random_shuffle(RandIter *start*, RandIter *end*, Generator *rand_gen*);

The **random_shuffle( )** algorithm randomizes the sequence defined by *start* and *end*. In the second form, *rand_gen* specifies a custom random number generator. This function must have the following general form:

    rand_gen(*num*);

It must return a random number between zero and *num*.

The following program demonstrates **random_shuffle( )**:

```
// Demonstrate random_shuffle().
#include <iostream>
#include <vector>
#include <algorithm>
using namespace std;

int main()
{
  vector<char> v;
  int i;

  for(i=0; i<26; i++) v.push_back('A'+i);

  cout << "Original contents of v:\n";
  for(i=0; i<v.size(); i++)
    cout << v[i];
  cout << "\n\n";

  random_shuffle(v.begin(), v.end());

  cout << "Shuffled contents of v:\n";
  for(i=0; i<v.size(); i++)
    cout << v[i];

  return 0;
}
```

Here is the output produced:

```
Original contents of v:
ABCDEFGHIJKLMNOPQRSTUVWXYZ

Shuffled contents of v:
ETARKMILSYGQHOJXUZWPNBFDVC
```

As is evident, the contents of **v** have been randomized.

Merging

There are two STL algorithms that merge sorted sequences: **merge( )** and **inplace_merge( )**. A merge integrates the elements of one sequence into another and the resulting sequence is in sorted order.

The prototype for **merge( )** is shown here:

```
template <class InIter1, class InIter2, class OutIter>
    OutIter merge(InIter1 start1, InIter1 end1,
                  InIter2 start2, InIter2 end2,
                  OutIter result);

template <class InIter1, class InIter2, class OutIter, class Comp>
    OutIter merge(InIter1 start1, InIter1 end1,
                  InIter2 start2, InIter2 end2,
                  OutIter result, Comp cmpfn);
```

The **merge( )** algorithm merges two ordered sequences, placing the result
into a third sequence. The sequences to be merged are defined by *start1*, *end1*
and *start2*, *end2*. The result is put into the sequence pointed to by *result*. An
iterator to the end of the resulting sequence is returned. The second form
allows you to specify a comparison function that determines when one
element is less than another.

Here is a sample that demonstrates merging:

```cpp
// Merge two sequences.
#include <iostream>
#include <vector>
#include <algorithm>
using namespace std;

int main()
{
  vector<char> v1, v2, v3(26);
  int i;

  for(i=0; i<26; i+=2) v1.push_back('A'+i);
  for(i=0; i<26; i+=2) v2.push_back('B'+i);

  cout << "Original contents of v1:\n";
  for(i=0; i<v1.size(); i++)
    cout << v1[i];
  cout << "\n\n";

  cout << "Original contents of v2:\n";
  for(i=0; i<v2.size(); i++)
    cout << v2[i];
  cout << "\n\n";

  // merge sequences
  merge(v1.begin(), v1.end(),
        v2.begin(), v2.end(),
```

9

```
        v3.begin());

  cout << "Result of merge:\n";
  for(i=0; i<v3.size(); i++)
    cout << v3[i];

  return 0;
}
```

Here is the output:

```
Original contents of v1:
ACEGIKMOQSUWY

Original contents of v2:
BDFHJLNPRTVXZ

Result of merge:
ABCDEFGHIJKLMNOPQRSTUVWXYZ
```

The program merges the ordered sequences in **v1** and **v2**, each of which contains one half of the alphabet. The result is the complete alphabet, in order.

NOTE: As mentioned in Chapter 5, when operating on **list** containers, you will usually want to use **list**'s **merge( )** member function, rather than the **merge( )** algorithm, because it is more efficient.

The **merge( )** algorithm merges two separate ranges, putting the result into a third sequence. However, it is possible to perform a merge in-place on two consecutive ranges within the same container, with the result replacing the original two ranges. To accomplish this, use **inplace_merge( )**, shown here:

template <class BiIter>
    void inplace_merge(BiIter *start*, BiIter *mid*, BiIter *end*);

template <class BiIter, class Comp>
    void inplace_merge(BiIter *start*, BiIter *mid*, BiIter *end,* Comp *cmpfn*);

Within a single sequence, the **inplace_merge( )** algorithm merges the range defined by *start* and *mid* with the range defined by *mid* and *end*. Both ranges must be sorted in increasing order. After executing, the resulting sequence is sorted and is contained in the range *start* to *end*. The second form allows you to specify a comparison function that determines when one element is less than another.

Here is a modified version of the preceding program that performs its merge in-place:

```cpp
// Perform an in-place merge.
#include <iostream>
#include <vector>
#include <algorithm>
using namespace std;

int main()
{
  vector<char> v1;
  int i;

  for(i=0; i<26; i+=2) v1.push_back('A'+i);
  for(i=0; i<26; i+=2) v1.push_back('B'+i);

  cout << "Original contents of v1:\n";
  for(i=0; i<v1.size(); i++)
    cout << v1[i];
  cout << "\n\n";

  // merge two ranges within v1
  inplace_merge(v1.begin(), v1.begin()+13, v1.end());

  cout << "Result of merge:\n";
  for(i=0; i<v1.size(); i++)
    cout << v1[i];

  return 0;
}
```

Here is the output produced:

```
Original contents of v1:
ACEGIKMOQSUWYBDFHJLNPRTVXZ
```

9

```
Result of merge:
ABCDEFGHIJKLMNOPQRSTUVWXYZ
```

As you can see, the first half of **v1** is merged with the second half and the resulting sequence is stored in **v1**.

The Set Algorithms

The STL provides five algorithms that perform set operations. Understand that these algorithms operate on any type of container; they are not for use only with the **set** or **multiset** class. The one requirement is that the contents of the containers must be in sorted order. The set algorithms are **set_union( )**, **set_difference( )**, **set_symmetric_difference( )**, **set_intersection( )**, and **includes( )**. Each is examined here.

To obtain the union of two ordered sets, use **set_union( )**. It has the following prototypes:

*The set algorithms work with any type of container, not just **set** or **multiset**.*

    template <class InIter1, class InIter2, class OutIter>
      OutIter set_union(InIter1 *start1*, InIter1 *end1*,
              InIter2 *start2*, InIter2 *last2*, OutIter *result*);

    template <class InIter1, class InIter2, class OutIter, class Comp>
      OutIter set_union(InIter1 *start1*, InIter1 *end1*,
              InIter2 *start2*, InIter2 *last2*, OutIter *result*, Comp *cmpfn*);

The **set_union( )** algorithm produces a sequence that contains the union of the two sets defined by *start1*, *end1* and *start2*, *end2*. Thus, the resultant set contains those elements that are in both sets. The result is ordered and put into *result*. It returns an iterator to the end of the result. The second form allows you to specify a comparison function that determines when one element is less than another.

To obtain the difference between two ordered sets, use **set_difference( )**. It has the following prototypes:

    template <class InIter1, class InIter2, class OutIter>
      OutIter set_difference(InIter1 *start1*, InIter1 *end1*,
              InIter2 *start2*, InIter2 *last2*, OutIter *result*);

```
template <class InIter1, class InIter2, class OutIter, class Comp>
OutIter set_difference(InIter1 start1, InIter1 end1,
        InIter2 start2, InIter2 last2,
        OutIter result, Comp cmpfn);
```

The **set_difference( )** algorithm produces a sequence that contains the difference between the two sets defined by *start1*, *end1* and *start2*, *end2*. That is, the set defined by *start2*, *end2* is removed from the set defined by *start1*, *end1*. The result is ordered and put into *result*. It returns an iterator to the end of the result. The second form allows you to specify a comparison function that determines when one element is less than another.

The symmetric difference of two ordered sets can be found using the **set_symmetric_difference( )** algorithm. Its prototypes are shown here:

```
template <class InIter1, class InIter2, class OutIter>
OutIter set_symmetric_difference(InIter1 start1, InIter1 end1,
        InIter2 start2, InIter2 last2, OutIter result);
```

```
template <class InIter1, class InIter2, class OutIter, class Comp>
OutIter set_symmetric_difference(InIter1 start1, InIter1 end1,
        InIter2 start2, InIter2 last2, OutIter result, Comp cmpfn);
```

The **set_symmetric_difference( )** algorithm produces a sequence that contains the symmetric difference between the two ordered sets defined by *start1*, *end1* and *start2*, *end2*. The symmetric difference of two sets contains only those elements that are not common to both sets. The result is ordered and put into *result*. It returns an iterator to the end of the result. The second form allows you to specify a comparison function that determines when one element is less than another.

The intersection of two ordered sets can be obtained by calling **set_intersection( )**, shown here:

```
template <class InIter1, class InIter2, class OutIter>
OutIter set_intersection(InIter1 start1, InIter1 end1,
        InIter2 start2, InIter2 last2, OutIter result);
```

```
template <class InIter1, class InIter2, class OutIter, class Comp>
OutIter set_intersection(InIter1 start1, InIter1 end1,
        InIter2 start2, InIter2 last2,
        OutIter result, Comp cmpfn);
```

9

The **set_intersection( )** algorithm produces a sequence that contains the intersection of the two sets defined by *start1*, *end1* and *start2*, *end2*. These are the elements that are common to both sets. The result is ordered and put into *result*. It returns an iterator to the end of the result. The second form allows you to specify a comparison function that determines when one element is less than another.

To see if the entire content of one ordered set is included in another, use **includes( )**, shown here:

```
template <class InIter1, class InIter2>
    bool includes(InIter1 start1, InIter1 end1,
                  InIter2 start2, InIter2 end2);

template <class InIter1, class InIter2, class Comp>
    bool includes(InIter1 start1, InIter1 end1,
                  InIter2 start2, InIter2 end2, Comp cmpfn);
```

The **includes( )** algorithm determines if the sequence defined by *start1* and *end1* includes all of the elements in the sequence defined by *start2* and *end2*. It returns **true** if the elements are all found and **false** otherwise. The second form allows you to specify a comparison function that determines when one element is less than another.

The following program demonstrates the set algorithms:

```
// Demonstrate the set algorithms.
#include <iostream>
#include <vector>
#include <algorithm>
using namespace std;

int main()
{
  vector<char> v1, v2, v_res(26), v3;
  vector<char>::iterator p, pres_end;
  int i;

  for(i=0; i<20; i++) v1.push_back('A'+i);
  for(i=10; i<26; i++) v2.push_back('A'+i);

  cout << "Contents of v1:\n";
  for(i=0; i<v1.size(); i++)
    cout << v1[i];
```

```
cout << "\n";

cout << "Contents of v2:\n";
for(i=0; i<v2.size(); i++)
  cout << v2[i];
cout << "\n\n";

// union
pres_end = set_union(v1.begin(), v1.end(),
                v2.begin(), v2.end(),
                v_res.begin());

cout << "Set union: ";
for(p=v_res.begin(); p!=pres_end; p++)
  cout << *p;
cout << "\n\n";

// difference
pres_end = set_difference(v1.begin(), v1.end(),
                v2.begin(), v2.end(),
                v_res.begin());

cout << "Set difference: ";
for(p=v_res.begin(); p!=pres_end; p++)
  cout << *p;
cout << "\n\n";

// symmetric difference
pres_end = set_symmetric_difference(v1.begin(), v1.end(),
                v2.begin(), v2.end(),
                v_res.begin());

cout << "Set symmetric difference: ";
for(p=v_res.begin(); p!=pres_end; p++)
  cout << *p;
cout << "\n\n";

// intersection
pres_end = set_intersection(v1.begin(), v1.end(),
                v2.begin(), v2.end(),
                v_res.begin());

cout << "Set intersection: ";
for(p=v_res.begin(); p!=pres_end; p++)
  cout << *p;
```

9

```
cout << "\n\n";

// includes
v3.push_back('A');
v3.push_back('C');
v3.push_back('D');

if(includes(v1.begin(), v1.end(),
            v3.begin(), v3.end()))
  cout << "v1 includes all of v3\n";
else
  cout << "v3 contains elements not found in v1\n";

return 0;
}
```

This program generates the following output:

```
Contents of v1:
ABCDEFGHIJKLMNOPQRST
Contents of v2:
KLMNOPQRSTUVWXYZ

Set union: ABCDEFGHIJKLMNOPQRSTUVWXYZ

Set difference: ABCDEFGHIJ

Set symmetric difference: ABCDEFGHIJUVWXYZ

Set intersection: KLMNOPQRST

v1 includes all of v3
```

Permutations

The STL enables you to generate permutations of any sorted list. The algorithms that accomplish this are **next_permutation( )**, which generates the next permutation, and **prev_permutation( )**, which generates the previous permutation. The prototypes for these functions are shown here:

```
template <class BiIter>
    bool next_permutation(BiIter start, BiIter end);

template <class BiIter, class Comp>
    bool next_permutation(BiIter start, BiIter end, Comp cmfn);
```

```
template <class BiIter>
  bool prev_permutation(BiIter start, BiIter end);

template <class BiIter, class Comp>
  bool prev_permutation(BiIter start, BiIter end, Comp cmpfn);
```

The **next_permutation( )** algorithm constructs the next permutation of a
sequence. The permutations are generated assuming a sorted sequence
represents the first permutation. If the next permutation does not exist,
next_permutation( ) sorts the sequence as its first permutation and
returns **false**. Otherwise, it returns **true**. The second form allows you to
specify a comparison function that determines when one element is less than
another.

The **prev_permutation( )** algorithm constructs the previous permutation
of a sequence. The permutations are generated assuming a sorted sequence
represents the first permutation. If the previous permutation does not exist,
prev_permutation( ) sorts the sequence as its final permutation and
returns **false**. Otherwise, it returns **true**. The second form allows you to
specify a comparison function that determines when one element is less than
another.

The following program uses **next_permutation( )** to generate all possible
permutations of three elements:

```
// Create permutations.
#include <iostream>
#include <vector>
#include <algorithm>
using namespace std;

int main()
{
  vector<char> v;
  int i;

  for(i=0; i<3; i++) v.push_back('A'+i);

  cout << "All permutations of 3 characters:\n";

  do {
    for(i=0; i<v.size(); i++)
      cout << v[i];
```

9

```
    cout << "\n";
  } while(next_permutation(v.begin(), v.end()));

  return 0;
}
```

The output from the program is shown here:

```
All permutations of 3 characters:
ABC
ACB
BAC
BCA
CAB
CBA
```

Heap Algorithms

There are four algorithms that support heap operations:

> make_heap( )
>
> pop_heap( )
>
> push_heap( )
>
> sort_heap( )

A heap is a tree-structured sequence in which the root is the first element. The root is also the largest element in the sequence. Each subsequent element is less than its root.

You can construct a heap by using the **make_heap( )** algorithm, shown here:

> template <class RandIter>
>   void make_heap(RandIter *start*, RandIter *end*);
>
> template <class RandIter, class Comp>
>   void make_heap(RandIter *start*, RandIter *end*, Comp *cmpfn*);

The **make_heap( )** algorithm constructs a heap from the sequence defined by *start* and *end*. The second form allows you to specify a comparison function that determines when one element is less than another. Any container that supports random-access iterators can be used to hold a heap. Building a heap takes linear time.

You can push a new element onto the heap using **push_heap( )**, shown here:

```
template <class RandIter>
    void push_heap(RandIter start, RandIter end);

template <class RandIter, class Comp>
    void push_heap(RandIter start, RandIter end, Comp cmpfn);
```

The **push_heap( )** algorithm puts the element at *end*–1 into the heap defined by *start* through *end*–1. That is, the element at *end*–1 is put into the heap that is defined by the range *start* to *end*–1. In other words, the current heap ends at *end*–2 and **push_heap( )** adds the element at *end*–1. The resulting heap will then end at *end*–1. The second form allows you to specify a comparison function that determines when one element is less than another. Pushing an element onto a heap consumes logarithmic time.

You can remove an element using **pop_heap( )**, shown here:

```
template <class RandIter>
    void pop_heap(RandIter start, RandIter end);

template <class RandIter, class Comp>
    void pop_heap(RandIter start, RandIter end, Comp cmpfn);
```

The **pop_heap( )** exchanges the *start* and *end*–1 elements and then rebuilds the heap. The second form allows you to specify a comparison function that determines when one element is less than another. Popping an element from a heap consumes logarithmic time.

You can sort a heap into ascending order using **sort_heap( )**. Its prototypes are shown here:

```
template <class RandIter>
    void sort_heap(RandIter start, RandIter end);

template <class RandIter, class Comp>
    void sort_heap(RandIter start, RandIter end, Comp cmpfn);
```

9

The **sort_heap( )** algorithm sorts a heap within the range specified by *start* and *end*. The second form allows you to specify a comparison function that determines when one element is less than another. Sorting a heap requires time proportional to *N* log *N*.

Here is program that builds a heap, then adds and removes elements:

```cpp
// Work with heaps.
#include <iostream>
#include <vector>
#include <algorithm>
using namespace std;

int main()
{
  vector<char> v;
  int i;

  for(i=0; i<20; i+=2) v.push_back('A'+i);

  cout << "Sequence before building heap:\n";
  for(i=0; i<v.size(); i++)
    cout << v[i] << " ";
  cout << "\n\n";

  // construct a heap
  make_heap(v.begin(), v.end());

  cout << "Sequence after building heap:\n";
  for(i=0; i<v.size(); i++)
    cout << v[i] << " ";
  cout << "\n\n";

  // push H onto heap
  v.push_back('H'); // first put H into vector
  push_heap(v.begin(), v.end()); // now, push H onto heap

  cout << "Sequence after pushing onto heap:\n";
  for(i=0; i<v.size(); i++)
    cout << v[i] << " ";
  cout << "\n\n";

  // pop value from heap
  pop_heap(v.begin(), v.end());

  cout << "Sequence after popping from heap:\n";
  for(i=0; i<v.size(); i++)
```

```
        cout << v[i] << " ";
    cout << "\n\n";

    return 0;
}
```

Here is the output from the program:

```
Sequence before building heap:
A C E G I K M O Q S

Sequence after building heap:
S Q M O I K E A G C

Sequence after pushing onto heap:
S Q M O I K E A G C H

Sequence after popping from heap:
Q O M H I K E A G C S
```

Popping from a heap does not actually remove the element from the container.

Notice the contents of **v** after calling **pop_heap( )**. The S is still present, but it is now at the end. As described, popping from a heap causes the first element to be moved to the end and then a new heap is constructed on the remaining (*N*–1) elements. Thus, although the popped element (S, in this case) remains in the container, it is not part of the heap.

Finding Minimums and Maximums

9

If you have a sorted sequence, it is a trivial matter to obtain the smallest or the largest element because this will be at the beginning or end of the sequence, respectively. But there will be times when you want to obtain the minimum or maximum element in a sequence that is not sorted. To do this, you will use one of the STL's minimum or maximum algorithms.

To obtain the value of the largest element in a sequence, use **max_element( )**. To obtain the smallest element, use **min_element( )**. Their prototypes are shown here:

```
template <class ForIter>
    ForIter max_element(ForIter start, ForIter last);

template <class ForIter, class Comp>
    ForIter max_element(ForIter start, ForIter last, Comp cmpfn);
```

```
template <class ForIter>
    ForIter min_element(ForIter start, ForIter last);

template <class ForIter, class Comp>
    ForIter min_element(ForIter start, ForIter last, Comp cmpfn);
```

The **max_element( )** algorithm returns an iterator to the maximum element within the range *start* and *last* and the **min_element( )** algorithm returns an iterator to the minimum element within the range *start* and *last*. The second forms of each allow you to specify a comparison function that determines when one element is less than another.

Here is a program that demonstrates **max_element( )** and **min_element( )**:

```cpp
// Find minimum and maximum.
#include <iostream>
#include <vector>
#include <algorithm>
using namespace std;

int main()
{
  vector<int> v(5);
  int i;

  v[0] = 100;
  v[1] = -4;
  v[2] = 55;
  v[3] = 19;
  v[4] = 122;

  cout << "Contents of v: ";
  for(i=0; i<v.size(); i++)
    cout << v[i] << " ";
  cout << "\n\n";

  cout << "Maximum element is: ";
  cout << *max_element(v.begin(), v.end());
  cout << "\n";

  cout << "Minimum element is: ";
  cout << *min_element(v.begin(), v.end());

  return 0;
}
```

The output from the program is shown here:

```
Contents of v: 100 -4 55 19 122

Maximum element is: 122
Minimum element is: -4
```

As you can see, the algorithms find the maximum and minimum elements in the sequence even though the sequence is not sorted.

The STL also includes the **min( )** and **max( )** algorithms, which return the smaller and larger, respectively, of the two values they are passed.

The for_each( ) Algorithm

The last algorithm that we will look at comes from the miscellaneous category: **for_each( )**. Don't let its simplicity fool you; it is one of the STL's most useful functions. Its prototype is shown here:

```
template<class InIter, class Func>
    Func for_each(InIter start, InIter end, Func fn);
```

The **for_each( )** algorithm applies the function *fn* to the range of elements specified by *start* and *end*. It returns *fn*. The function pointed to by *fn* must be defined like this:

```
void fn(type arg)
```

9

Here, *type* is the type of the data that it will be passed, which must be the same as the type of data stored in the container upon which **for_each( )** is being called. The value of the element is received in *arg*. Technically, *fn* could return a value, but if it does, it is ignored by **for_each( )**.

The reason that **for_each( )** is so useful is that it can simplify many tedious operations. For example, consider the following short program:

```
#include <iostream>
#include <vector>
using namespace std;

int main()
{
  vector<int> v;
  int i;

  for(i=0; i<10; i++) v.push_back(i);
```

```
  cout << "Contents of v: ";
  for(i=0; i<v.size(); i++)
    cout << v[i] << " ";
  cout << "\n";

  return 0;
}
```

This program creates a vector, initializes it with the numbers 0 through 9, and then displays the vector's contents. Its output is shown here:

```
Contents of v: 0 1 2 3 4 5 6 7 8 9
```

It is possible to rewrite the preceding program so that the values contained within **v** are displayed by calling **for_each( )** rather than by an explicit loop. Here is the **for_each( )** version of the program:

```
// Use for_each().
#include <iostream>
#include <vector>
#include <algorithm>
using namespace std;

void show(int i)
{
  cout << i << " ";
}

int main()
{
  vector<int> v;
  int i;

  for(i=0; i<10; i++) v.push_back(i);

  cout << "Contents of v: ";
  for_each(v.begin(), v.end(), show);
  cout << "\n";

  return 0;
}
```

This program produces precisely the same output as the previous one. However, in this version, **for_each( )** calls the function **show( )** once for each element in **v**. The **show( )** function simply displays its argument. In a program that outputs the contents of a container frequently, using **for_each( )** as shown provides a significant benefit. As an experiment, you might want to try using **for_each( )** to display output in some of the programs shown earlier.

Creating Your Own Algorithms

The STL is designed to be easily extended, and you can define your own algorithms if you choose. This is actually a very simply matter. Just create a template function that operates through iterators that it is passed as arguments. For example, consider the following program that creates an algorithm called **times2( )**, which doubles the elements in the range with which it is called:

```cpp
// Creating a custom algorithm
#include <iostream>
#include <vector>
#include <list>
#include <algorithm>
using namespace std;

/* An algorithm that doubles the values in
   specified range. */
template<class ForIter>
  void times2(ForIter start, ForIter end)
{
  while(start != end) {
    *start *= 2;
    start++;
  }
}

int main()
{
  int i;

  //**************************************
  // apply times2 to a vector of ints
  vector<int> v;
```

```cpp
  for(i=0; i<10; i++) v.push_back(i);

  cout << "Initial Contents of v: ";
  for(i=0; i<v.size(); i++)
    cout << v[i] << " ";
  cout << "\n";

  times2(v.begin(), v.end());

  cout << "Contents of v doubled: ";
  for(i=0; i<v.size(); i++)
    cout << v[i] << " ";
  cout << "\n\n";

  //****************************************
  // now, apply times2 to a list of floats
  list<float> lst;
  list<float>::iterator p;

  for(i=0; i<5; i++) lst.push_back((float)i*3.1416);

  cout << "Initial Contents of lst: ";
  for(p=lst.begin(); p!=lst.end(); p++)
    cout << *p << " ";
  cout << "\n";

  times2(lst.begin(), lst.end());

  cout << "Contents of lst doubled: ";
  for(p=lst.begin(); p!=lst.end(); p++)
    cout << *p << " ";
  cout << "\n\n";

  return 0;
}
```

Here is the program's output:

```
Initial Contents of v: 0 1 2 3 4 5 6 7 8 9
Contents of v doubled: 0 2 4 6 8 10 12 14 16 18
```

```
Initial Contents of lst: 0 3.1416 6.2832 9.4248 12.5664
Contents of lst doubled: 0 6.2832 12.5664 18.8496 25.1328
```

In the program, the algorithm **times2( )** is applied to a **list** and a **vector** container. In general, **times2( )** can be applied to any type of container that supports forward iterators (this includes those that support bidirectional iterators and random-access iterators, too).

One important point: The generic name you give to an iterator in an algorithm template specification has no effect on the type of iterators that you can use when calling the algorithm. The generic iterator type names are simply conventions that indicate how an algorithm can be used. Thus, using the name **ForIter** in **times2( )** does not enforce that only iterators with at least forward capability be used. Rather, it is how you use the iterator within the algorithm that determines the capabilities that are needed. For example, if you apply + or − to the iterator, then only random-access iterators can be used as arguments.

In the next chapter we will explore a feature of the STL that is often used in conjunction with algorithms: function objects.

9

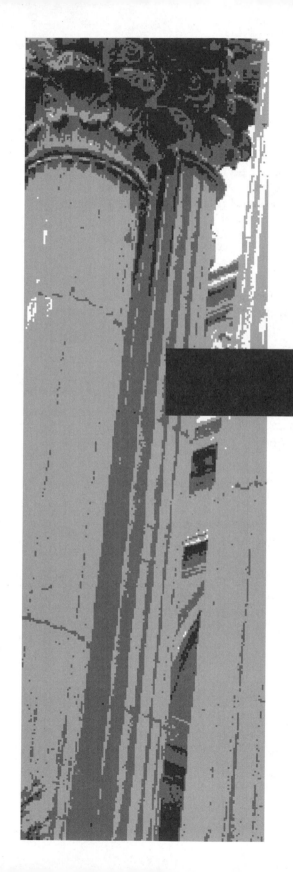

CHAPTER 10

Function Objects, Binders, Negators, and Function Adaptors

This chapter examines function objects, binders, negators, and function adaptors. These elements enhance the efficiency and flexibility of the STL. Function objects provide an alternative to passing function pointers in many situations. Binders, negators, and function adaptors increase the types of situations in which function objects can be employed. Frankly, mastery of function objects and their support elements is crucial to a full utilization of the STL.

Function Objects

Function objects were introduced in Chapter 2, and the built-in ones have been used from time to time in the preceding chapters. Here, we will look at them in detail. Let's begin by reviewing the material covered in Chapter 2.

A Review of Function Object Basics

Function objects are classes that define **operator( )**

Function objects are classes that define **operator( )**. A function object can often be used in place of a function pointer, such as when passing a predicate to an algorithm. Function objects offer more flexibility than do function pointers, and might be more efficient. Many built-in function objects, such as **less**, **minus**, etc. are provided by the STL. You can also define your own.

There are two types of function objects: unary and binary. A unary function object requires one argument; a binary function object requires two. You must use the type of object required. For example, if an algorithm is expecting a binary function object, you must pass it a binary function object.

The built-in binary function objects are shown here:

plus	minus	multiplies	divides	modulus
equal_to	not_equal_to	greater	greater_equal	less
less_equal	logical_and	logical_or		

Here are the unary function objects.

logical_not	negate

All of the built-in function objects are template classes, which means that they can work on any type of data for which their associated operation is defined. The built-in function objects use the header **<functional>**.

Although it is certainly permissible to construct a function object in advance, most often you will construct a function object when it is passed to an algorithm. You do this by explicitly calling its constructor using the following general form:

func_ob<type>( )

For example,

```
less<int>()
```

constructs a **less** object for use on operands of type **int**.

Chapter 2 presented two examples that used the built-in function objects. Here are two more. The following program uses the **transform( )** algorithm and the **logical_not** unary function object to invert the values of a vector containing Boolean values:

```
// Use the logical_not unary function object.
#include <iostream>
#include <vector>
#include <functional>
#include <algorithm>
using namespace std;

int main()
{
  vector<bool> v;
  int i;

  // put values into v
  for(i=1; i<10; i++) v.push_back((bool)(i%2));

  // turn on boolalpha I/O flag
  cout << boolalpha;

  cout << "Original contents of v:\n";
  for(i=0; i<v.size(); i++)
    cout << v[i] << " ";
  cout << endl;

  // use the logical_not function object
  transform(v.begin(), v.end(), v.begin(),
            logical_not<bool>()); // use function object
```

10

```
  cout << "Inverted contents of v:\n";
  for(i=0; i<v.size(); i++)
    cout << v[i] << " ";
  cout << endl;

  return 0;
}
```

This program produces the following output:

```
Original contents of v:
true false true false true false true false true
Inverted contents of v:
false true false true false true false true false
```

In the program, notice how a **logical_not** function object is created when it is passed to **transform( )**. Since **v** is a vector of **bool** values, **logical_not** is constructed by explicitly calling its constructor and specifying **bool** as the data type. The **transform( )** algorithm automatically calls **logical_not::operator( )** for each element in the sequence. Thus, the single parameter defined by **logical_not::operator( )** receives as its argument an element from the sequence. It returns the complement of its argument. The **logical_not** object will go out of scope (and be destroyed) when the call to **transform( )** returns.

NOTE: Remember, function objects are classes that overload **operator( )**. It is this function that returns the result of the specified operation on whatever type of data you select.

The next program demonstrates the use of the binary function object, **greater**. The program sorts a vector into descending order. As you know, by default **sort( )** orders a sequence into ascending order because **sort( )** normally compares elements using the **<** operator. However, if you use the predicate form of **sort( )**, shown here, you can specify your own comparison function:

```
template <class RandIter, class Comp>
    void sort(RandIter start, RandIter end, Comp cmpfn);
```

Specifying the **greater** function object for *cmpfn* reverses the comparison, causing the sequence to be sorted into descending order:

```
// Sorting a vector into descending order.
#include <iostream>
#include <vector>
#include <algorithm>
#include <functional>
using namespace std;

int main()
{
  vector<char> v(26);
  int i;

  for(i=0; i<v.size(); i++) v[i] = 'A'+i;

  cout << "Original ordering of v:\n";
  for(i=0; i<v.size(); i++)
    cout << v[i] << " ";
  cout << "\n\n";

  // sort into descending order
  sort(v.begin(), v.end(), greater<char>());

  cout << "After sorting v using greater():\n";
  for(i=0; i<v.size(); i++)
    cout << v[i] << " ";
  cout << "\n";

  return 0;
}
```

10

The output from this program is shown here:

```
Original ordering of v:
A B C D E F G H I J K L M N O P Q R S T U V W X Y Z

After sorting v using greater():
Z Y X W V U T S R Q P O N M L K J I H G F E D C B A
```

In this case, the binary function object **greater** compares elements in **v** to determine which element is larger, rather than smaller, as **sort( )** would normally do. This causes the sequence to be sorted in reverse order.

In general, binary function objects receive their arguments in this order:

    bin_func(first, second)

where *first* and *second* are relative to the algorithm. Thus, in the preceding example, *first* and *second* receive pairs of elements from the sequence being sorted.

Creating a Function Object

In addition to using the built-in function objects, you can create your own. To do so, you will simply create a class that overloads the **operator( )** function. However, for the greatest flexibility, you will want to use one of the following classes defined by the STL as a base class for your function objects:

```
template <class Argument, class Result> struct unary_function {
  typedef Argument argument_type;
  typedef Result result_type;
};

template <class Argument1, class Argument2, class Result>
struct binary_function {
  typedef Argument1 first_argument_type;
  typedef Argument2 second_argument_type;
  typedef Result result_type;
};
```

Function objects normally inherit either **unary_function** or **binary_function**.

These template classes provide concrete type names for the generic data types used by the function object. Although they are technically a convenience, they are almost always used when creating function objects.

Creating Unary Function Objects

Perhaps the best way to understand how to create a function object is to begin with a program that uses a function pointer, instead. In Chapter 2, you saw this program:

```
// Demonstrate count_if().
#include <iostream>
#include <vector>
#include <algorithm>
using namespace std;
```

```
/* This is a unary predicate that determines
   if number is even. */
bool isEven(int i)
{
  return !(i%2);
}

int main()
{
  vector<int> v;
  int i;

  for(i=1; i < 20; i++) v.push_back(i);

  cout << "Sequence:\n";
  for(i=0; i<v.size(); i++)
    cout << v[i] << " ";
  cout << endl;

  i = count_if(v.begin(), v.end(), isEven);
  cout << i << " numbers are evenly divisible by 2.\n";

  return 0;
}
```

The program creates a vector containing the numbers 1 through 19. It then counts those that are even by calling the **count_if( )** algorithm. Recall that the **count_if( )** algorithm has the following prototype:

> template <class InIter, class UnPred>
>   size_t count_if(InIter *start*, InIter *end*, UnPred *pfn*);

10

The third argument to **count_if( )** is a unary predicate that determines when an element should be counted. In this program, the unary predicate is the function **isEven( )**, which returns **true** if its argument is even. A pointer to **isEven( )** is passed in *pfn* when **count_if( )** is called. The program produces the following output:

```
Sequence:
1 2 3 4 5 6 7 8 9 10 11 12 13 14 15 16 17 18 19
9 numbers are evenly divisible by 2.
```

It is a simple matter to convert **isEven( )** into a function object. Just follow these steps:

1. Create a class called **isEven** that inherits **unary_function**.
2. Overload **operator( )** to perform the test for evenness and return the result.

For a unary function object, **operator( )** will have one parameter, which receives an element, and it must return the result of the operation applied to that element. In the case of **isEven**, the result will be a **true** or **false** value. Of course, other types of unary function objects will return other types of values.

The following program implements this conversion. It produces the same results as the original:

```
// Use a unary function object to determine even/odd.
#include <iostream>
#include <vector>
#include <algorithm>
#include <functional>
using namespace std;

// isEven determines whether a number is even or odd.
class isEven: public unary_function<int, bool> {
public:
  result_type operator()(argument_type i)
  {
    return (result_type) !(i%2);
  }
};

int main()
{
  vector<int> v;
  int i;

  for(i=1; i < 20; i++) v.push_back(i);

  cout << "Sequence:\n";
  for(i=0; i<v.size(); i++)
    cout << v[i] << " ";
  cout << endl;
```

```
    i = count_if(v.begin(), v.end(), isEven());
    cout << i << " numbers are evenly divisible by 2.\n";

    return 0;
}
```

Notice how an **isEven** object is passed to **count_if( )**. The **isEven** object is constructed explicitly by calling its constructor when the call to **count_if( )** takes place. Of course, it would be possible to construct an **isEven** object earlier, passing it to **count_if( )** when the time comes, but usually function objects are simply constructed as needed. The advantage to this is that they will go out of scope (and be destroyed) when the call to the algorithm returns.

Notice that **isEven::operator( )** makes use of **argument_type** and **result_type.** This is an important point. By inheriting **unary_function**, your function object has access to these type names, which gives your function object access to the types of data that it is operating upon and that it must return. The importance of this feature is shown by the next example.

As **isEven** is currently written, it can determine only whether integers are even or odd because the data types to **unary_function** are hardcoded. Of course, this is a simple matter to change. Just make **isEven** into a template class and specify the type of data when an **isEven** object is constructed, as shown in this version of the program:

```
// Use a template unary function object to determine even/odd.
#include <iostream>
#include <vector>
#include <algorithm>
#include <functional>
using namespace std;

// isEven determines whether an number is even or odd.
// Template Version
template <class Arg> class isEven:
  public unary_function<Arg, bool> {
public:
  result_type operator()(argument_type i)
  {
    return (result_type) !(i%2);
  }
```

10

```
};

int main()
{
  vector<int> v;
  int i;

  for(i=1; i < 20; i++) v.push_back(i);

  cout << "Sequence:\n";
  for(i=0; i<v.size(); i++)
    cout << v[i] << " ";
  cout << endl;

  i = count_if(v.begin(), v.end(), isEven<int>());
  cout << i << " numbers are evenly divisible by 2.\n";

  return 0;
}
```

Notice how **isEven** is used in the line

```
i = count_if(v.begin(), v.end(), isEven<int>());
```

The type of data is specified when the object is created in the call to **count_if( )**. Because **isEven** is now templated, it can work with any type of object for which the **%** operator is defined.

Here is another example. It creates a unary function object called **reciprocal** that returns the reciprocal of a value. A version of this program was shown in Chapter 2 that used a function pointer instead of a function object. You might want to compare it with the version shown here:

```
// Create a reciprocal function object.
#include <iostream>
#include <list>
#include <functional>
#include <algorithm>
using namespace std;

// A simple function object.
template <class T> class reciprocal:
```

```
      unary_function<T, T> {
public:
  result_type operator()(argument_type i)
  {
    return (result_type) 1.0/i; // return reciprocal
  }
};

int main()
{
  list<double> vals;
  int i;

  // put values into list
  for(i=1; i<10; i++) vals.push_back((double)i);

  cout << "Original contents of vals:\n";
  list<double>::iterator p = vals.begin();
  while(p != vals.end()) {
    cout << *p << " ";
    p++;
  }
  cout << endl;

  // use reciprocal function object
  p = transform(vals.begin(), vals.end(),
                vals.begin(),
                reciprocal<double>()); // call function object

  cout << "Transformed contents of vals:\n";
  p = vals.begin();
  while(p != vals.end()) {
    cout << *p << " ";
    p++;
  }

  return 0;
}
```

Here is the output from the program:

```
Original contents of vals:
1 2 3 4 5 6 7 8 9
Transformed contents of vals:
1 0.5 0.333333 0.25 0.2 0.166667 0.142857 0.125 0.111111
```

Creating Binary Function Objects

To create a binary function object, you will use a process similar to that shown for unary function objects except that your class will inherit **binary_function** and the **operator( )** function will have two parameters rather than one. Here is an example that creates a binary function object. It converts the midpoint program from Chapter 9 so that it uses a function object rather than a function pointer.

```
// Creating a binary function object.
#include <iostream>
#include <vector>
#include <algorithm>
#include <functional>
using namespace std;

template <class T> class midpoint:
  binary_function<T, T, T>
{
public:
  result_type operator()(first_argument_type a,
                         second_argument_type b)
  {
    return (result_type) ((a-b) / 2) + b;
  }
};

int main()
{
  vector<double> v1(5), v2(5), v3(5);
  int i;

  v1[0] = 10.0;
  v1[1] = 98.6;
  v1[2] = 12.23;
  v1[3] = 88.8;
  v1[4] = -212.01;
```

```
v2[0] = 2.0;
v2[1] = 3.3;
v2[2] = 4.19;
v2[3] = 155.0;
v2[4] = -2.0;

cout << "Values in v1: ";
for(i=0; i<v1.size(); i++)
  cout << v1[i] << " ";
cout << endl;

cout << "Values in v2: ";
for(i=0; i<v2.size(); i++)
  cout << v2[i] << " ";
cout << endl;

// find midpoints between elements in v1 and those in v2
transform(v1.begin(), v1.end(), v2.begin(),
          v3.begin(), midpoint<double>());

// midpoints:
cout << "Midpoints: ";
for(i=0; i<v3.size(); i++)
  cout << v3[i] << " ";

return 0;
}
```

The output from the program is shown here (and is the same as that shown in Chapter 9):

```
Values in v1: 10 98.6 12.23 88.8 -212.01
Values in v2: 2 3.3 4.19 155 -2
Midpoints: 6 50.95 8.21 121.9 -107.005
```

10

IN DEPTH

Why Function Objects Are Important

A few words about why function objects are important will be helpful at this point. At first glance, it may seem that function objects require a bit more work than simply using normal functions and offer no advantages. But this is not the case. Function objects expand the scope and power of the STL in three ways.

First, they can provide a more efficient mechanism by which functions are passed to algorithms. For example, it is possible for the compiler to in-line a function object. Second, using a function object can simplify and better structure the implementation of complicated operations because the class that defines a function object can hold values and provide additional capabilities. Third, a function object defines a type name. A function does not. This enables function objects to be specified as template type arguments.

In the final analysis, while there is nothing wrong with using regular functions where applicable, function objects offer a powerful alternative. Once you begin to think in terms of function objects, many solutions involving the STL algorithms can be simplified. Mastery of function objects is well worth the effort.

Using Binders

As explained, a binary function object takes two parameters. Normally, these parameters receive values from the sequence or sequences upon which the object is operating. For example, when sorting, the binary comparison function receives pairs of elements from the range being ordered. While the default behavior of binary function objects is quite useful, there are times when you will want to alter it. To understand why, consider the following.

Suppose that you want to remove all elements from a sequence that are greater than some value, such as 8. Your first thought, quite naturally, is to use the **greater** function object. However, by default, **greater** receives values from the sequences on which it is operating. Thus, by itself, there is no way to have it compare elements from a sequence with the value 8. To use **greater** for this purpose, you need some way to bind the value 8 to its right-hand operand. That is, you need some way to make **greater** perform the following comparison

val > 8

Binders associate a value with a parameter.

for each element of the sequence. Fortunately, the STL provides a mechanism, called *binders*, that accomplishes this. A binder links a value to one of the arguments of a binary function object.

There are two binders: **bind2nd( )** and **bind1st( )**. They take these general forms:

bind1st(*binfunc_obj, value*)

bind2nd(*binfunc_obj, value*)

bind1st( ) binds the left-hand operand and **bind2nd( )** binds the right-hand operand.

Here, *binfunc_obj* is a binary function object. **bind1st( )** returns a unary function object that has *binfunc_obj*'s left-hand operand bound to *value*. **bind2nd( )** returns a unary function object that has *binfunc_obj*'s right-hand operand bound to *value*. The **bind2nd( )** binder is the most commonly used. In either case, the outcome of a binder is a unary function object that is bound to the value specified.

To demonstrate the use of a binder, we will use the **remove_if( )** algorithm. It removes elements from a sequence based upon the outcome of a predicate. Recall that it has this prototype:

```
template <class ForIter, class UnPred>
    ForIter remove_if(ForIter start, ForIter end, UnPred func);
```

The algorithm removes elements from the sequence defined by *start* and *end* if the unary predicate defined by *func* is **true**. The algorithm returns a pointer to the new end of the sequence that reflects the deletion of the elements.

The following program removes all values from a sequence that are greater than the value 8. Since the predicate required by **remove_if( )** is unary, we cannot simply use the **greater** function object as is because **greater** is a binary object. Instead, we must bind the value 8 to the second argument of **greater** using the **bind2nd( )** binder, as shown in the program:

```
// Demonstrate bind2nd().
#include <iostream>
#include <list>
```

10

```cpp
#include <functional>
#include <algorithm>
using namespace std;

int main()
{
  list<int> lst;
  list<int>::iterator p, endp;

  int i;

  for(i=1; i < 20; i++) lst.push_back(i);

  cout << "Original sequence:\n";
  p = lst.begin();
  while(p != lst.end()) {
    cout << *p << " ";
    p++;
  }
  cout << endl;

  endp = remove_if(lst.begin(), lst.end(),
                   bind2nd(greater<int>(), 8));

  cout << "Resulting sequence:\n";
  p = lst.begin();
  while(p != endp) {
    cout << *p << " ";
    p++;
  }

  return 0;
}
```

The output produced by the program is shown here:

```
Original sequence:
1 2 3 4 5 6 7 8 9 10 11 12 13 14 15 16 17 18 19
Resulting sequence:
1 2 3 4 5 6 7 8
```

As the output shows, the resulting sequence contains the elements 1 through 8. Those elements greater than 8 have been removed. This is the case because **remove_if( )** compares each element in the sequence against the value 8.

The binary function object **greater** receives elements from the sequence in its first parameter and the value 8 in its second, since the second parameter is bound to 8 using **bind2nd( )**. Thus, for each element in the sequence, the comparison

    element > 8

is evaluated.

As explained, the **bind1st( )** binder binds a value to the first parameter. To see the effects of this, try substituting this line into the preceding program:

```
endp = remove_if(lst.begin(), lst.end(),
                 bind1st(greater<int>(), 8));
```

This causes elements from the sequence to be passed to the second parameter of **greater** and the value 8 is bound to the first parameter. Thus, for each element in the sequence, the following comparison is performed:

    8 > element

This causes **greater** to return **true** for elements that are less than 8. The output produced after you have substituted **bind1st( )** is shown here:

```
Original sequence:
1 2 3 4 5 6 7 8 9 10 11 12 13 14 15 16 17 18 19
Resulting sequence:
8 9 10 11 12 13 14 15 16 17 18 19
```

As you can see, those elements that are less than 8 have been removed.

As the preceding discussion illustrates, you will probably not use **bind1st( )** as often as you use **bind2nd( )** because it often leads to results that are not intuitive. For example, if you want to remove elements that are less than 8, it would be better to use this statement:

```
endp = remove_if(lst.begin(), lst.end(),
                 bind2nd(less<int>(), 8));
```

Here, the **less** function object is used and the results reflect what one would normally expect to occur when **less** is employed. Using **bind1st( )** and reversing the comparison achieves the same results, but can lead to confusing code.

10

You might want to experiment on your own with binders, trying different algorithms, function objects, and binding different values. As you will discover, binders expand the power of the STL in very significant ways.

Negators

There is an object related to a binder, called a *negator*. The negators are **not1( )** and **not2( )**. They return the negation (i.e., the complement) of whatever predicate they modify. They have these general forms:

not1(*unary_predicate*)

not2(*binary_predicate*)

Negators reverse the result of the predicate they modify.

The **not1( )** negator is for use with unary predicates and **not2( )** is applied to binary predicates.

Here is an example that demonstrates **not1( )**. It creates a vector that contains the letters of the alphabet. It first counts those that are greater than the letter E. It then counts those that are not greater than E.

```cpp
// Demonstrate not1().
#include <iostream>
#include <vector>
#include <functional>
#include <algorithm>
using namespace std;

int main()
{
  vector<char> v;
  int num;
  int i;

  for(i=0; i<26; i++) v.push_back(i+'A');

  cout << "Sequence contains:\n";
  for(i=0; i<v.size(); i++)
    cout << v[i] << " ";
  cout << endl;

  // first, count those elements greater than E
  num = count_if(v.begin(), v.end(),
                 bind2nd(greater<int>(), 'E'));
```

```
    cout << "There are " << num;
    cout << " elements greater than E.\n";

    // now, count those that are not greater than E
    num = count_if(v.begin(), v.end(),
                   not1(bind2nd(greater<int>(), 'E')));
    cout << "There are " << num;
    cout << " elements not greater than E.\n";

    return 0;
}
```

The output from the program is shown here:

```
Sequence contains:
A B C D E F G H I J K L M N O P Q R S T U V W X Y Z
There are 21 elements greater than E.
There are 5 elements not greater than E.
```

In the program, the **count_if( )** algorithm is used to count the number of elements in **v** for which the specified unary predicate is **true**. The program uses the **greater** function object in conjunction with a binder to perform the comparisons. In the first case, the comparison is used as is. In the second case, it is modified by **not1( )**. One last point: Although **greater** is a binary function object, the binder **bind2nd( )** converts it into a unary object. This is why **not1( )** rather than **not2( )** is used.

Here is an example that uses **not2( )**. It shows another way to sort a sequence into descending order.

10

```
// Another way to sort a sequence into descending order.
#include <iostream>
#include <vector>
#include <algorithm>
#include <functional>
using namespace std;

int main()
{
  vector<char> v(26);
  int i;

  for(i=0; i<v.size(); i++) v[i] = 'A'+i;
```

```
    cout << "Original ordering of v:\n";
    for(i=0; i<v.size(); i++)
      cout << v[i] << " ";
    cout << "\n\n";

    // sort into descending order
    sort(v.begin(), v.end(), not2(less<char>()));

    cout << "After sorting v using not2(less<char>()):\n";
    for(i=0; i<v.size(); i++)
      cout << v[i] << " ";
    cout << "\n";

    return 0;
}
```

It produces the following output:

```
Original ordering of v:
A B C D E F G H I J K L M N O P Q R S T U V W X Y Z

After sorting v using not2(less<char>()):
Z Y X W V U T S R Q P O N M L K J I H G F E D C B A
```

Function Adaptors

Function adaptors allow functions to be fully integrated with the STL.

The header **<functional>** defines several classes called *function adaptors* that allow you to adapt a function pointer to a form that can be used by various STL components. For example, you can use an adaptor to allow a function such as **strcmp( )** to be used with a binder. Adaptors also exist for calling class member functions through pointers or references.

The Pointer-to-Function Adaptors

As you have seen, it is possible to pass a pointer to a function (rather than passing a function object) as a predicate to an algorithm. As long as the function performs the desired operation, there is no trouble in doing this. However, if you wish to bind a value or use a negator with that function, then trouble will occur because it is not possible to apply these modifiers directly to function pointers. To allow functions to be used with binders and negators, you will need to use the pointer-to-function adaptors.

The pointer-to-function adaptors are shown here:

```
template <class Argument, class Result>
    pointer_to_unary_function<Argument, Result>
        ptr_fun(Result (*func)(Argument));
```

```
template <class Argument1, class Argument2, class Result>
    pointer_to_binary_function<Argument1, Argument2, Result>
        ptr_fun(Result (*func)(Argument1, Argument2));
```

Here, **ptr_fun( )** returns either an object of type **pointer_to_unary_function** or an object of type **pointer_to_binary_function**. These classes are shown here:

```
template <class Argument, class Result>
class pointer_to_unary_function:
  public unary_function<Argument, Result>
{
public:
  explicit pointer_to_unary_function(Result (*func)(Argument));
  Result operator()(Argument arg) const;
};

template <class Argument1, class Argument2, class Result>
class pointer_to_binary_function:
  public binary_function<Argument1, Argument2, Result>
{
public:
  explicit pointer_to_binary_function(
           Result (*func)(Argument1, Argument2));
  Result operator()(Argument1 arg1, Argument2 arg2) const;
};
```

10

For unary functions, **operator( )** returns

func(*arg*);

For binary functions, **operator( )** returns

func(*arg1*, *arg2*);

The type of the result of the operation is specified by the **Result** generic type.

Here is an example that uses **ptr_fun( )**. It creates a vector of character pointers that point to character strings. It then uses the standard library function **strcmp( )** to find the pointer that points to "Three". Since **strcmp( )** is not a function object, the adaptor **ptr_fun( )** is used to allow the value "Three" to be bound to **strcmp( )**'s second parameter using **bind2nd( )**. Since **strcmp( )** returns **false** on success, the negator **not1( )** is applied to reverse this condition. Without the use of **ptr_fun( )**, it would not be possible to apply **bind2nd( )** to **strcmp( )**. That is, since **strcmp( )** is a function, it is not possible for it to be used with **bind2nd( )** directly.

```cpp
// Use a function adaptor.
#include <iostream>
#include <vector>
#include <algorithm>
#include <functional>
#include <cstring>
using namespace std;

int main()
{
  vector<char *> v;
  vector<char *>::iterator p;
  int i;

  v.push_back("One");
  v.push_back("Two");
  v.push_back("Three");
  v.push_back("Four");
  v.push_back("Five");

  cout << "Sequence contains:\n";
  for(i=0; i<v.size(); i++)
    cout << v[i] << " ";
  cout << "\n\n";

  cout << "Searching sequence for Three.\n";

  // use a pointer-to-function adaptor
  p = find_if(v.begin(), v.end(),
      not1(bind2nd(ptr_fun(strcmp), "Three")));

  if(p != v.end()) {
    cout << "Found.\n";
    cout << "Sequence from that point is:\n";
    do {
```

```
      cout << *p++ << " ";
   } while (p != v.end());
}

return 0;
}
```

The program's output is shown here:

```
Sequence contains:
One Two Three Four Five

Searching sequence for Three.
Found.
Sequence from that point is:
Three Four Five
```

The Pointer-to-Member Function Adaptors

Assume that you have a sequence that stores elements of some class. Sometimes you will want an algorithm, such as **for_each( )**, to call a member function of that class for each element stored in the sequence. This cannot be done using the **ptr_fun( )** function because it is not designed to operate on members of classes. Instead, you must use either **mem_fun( )** and **mem_fun1( )** or **mem_fun_ref( )** and **mem_fun1_ref( )**. These are collectively called the pointer-to-member function adaptors, and they are examined here.

Calling Member Functions Through Pointers

If you want to be able to call a member function through a pointer to an object of its class, you will use **mem_fun( )** or **mem_fun1( )**, shown here:

```
template<class Result, class T>
    mem_fun_t<Result, T> mem_fun(Result (T::*func)( ));

template<class Result, class T, class Argument>
    mem_fun1_t<Result, T, Argument>
        mem_fun1(Result (T::*func)(Argument));
```

10

Here, **mem_fun( )** returns an object of type **mem_fun_t** and **mem_fun1** returns an object of type **mem_fun1_t**. These classes are shown here:

```
template <class Result, class T> class mem_fun_t:
  public unary_function<T *, Result> {
public:
  explicit mem_fun_t(Result (T::*func)());
  Result operator() (T *func) const;
};

template <class Result, class T,
          class Argument> class mem_fun1_t:
  public binary_function<T *, Argument, Result> {
public:
  explicit mem_fun1_t(Result (T::*func)(Argument));
  Result operator() (T *func, Argument arg) const;
};
```

Here, the **mem_fun_t** constructor calls the member function specified as its parameter. The **mem_fun1_t** constructor calls the member function specified as its first parameter, passing a value of type **Argument** as its second parameter.

Here is an example that demonstrates the **mem_fun( )** and **mem_fun1( )** pointer-to-member function adaptors. The program creates a class called **Test** that stores a value. It uses the **for_each( )** algorithm to display and to alter the values. Notice the syntax used in each call.

```
// Use mem_fun() and mem_fun1() function adaptors.
#include <iostream>
#include <vector>
#include <algorithm>
#include <functional>
using namespace std;

class Test {
  int val;
public:
  Test() { val = 0; }
  Test(int x) { val = x; }

  bool showval() { cout << val << " "; return true; }
  int doubleval() { val += val; return val; }
  int addval(int i) { val += i; return val; }
```

```cpp
};

int main()
{
  vector<Test *> v;

  v.push_back(&Test(1));
  v.push_back(&Test(2));
  v.push_back(&Test(3));
  v.push_back(&Test(4));
  v.push_back(&Test(5));

  cout << "Sequence contains: ";
  // display each value using showval()
  for_each(v.begin(), v.end(),
          mem_fun(&Test::showval));
  cout << endl;

  // double each member using doubleval()
  for_each(v.begin(), v.end(),
          mem_fun(&Test::doubleval));

  cout << "Sequence after doubling: ";
  for_each(v.begin(), v.end(),
          mem_fun(&Test::showval));
  cout << endl;

  // add 10 to each member using addval()
  for_each(v.begin(), v.end(),
          bind2nd(mem_fun1(&Test::addval), 10));

  cout << "Sequence after adding 10: ";
  for_each(v.begin(), v.end(),
          mem_fun(&Test::showval));

  return 0;
}
```

The output from the program is shown here:

```
Sequence contains: 1 2 3 4 5
Sequence after doubling: 2 4 6 8 10
Sequence after adding 10: 12 14 16 18 20
```

10

Notice that all of the member functions called through **for_each( )** return a value of some type other than **void**. This is the case even for **showval( )**, which always returns **true**. The reason all of the functions return a value is that the implementation of the STL (Microsoft Visual C++) used to test the code examples in this book required a non-**void** return value for any function used with **mem_fun( )** or **mem_fun1( )**. Because of the way that the pointer-to-member function adaptors are defined, this will probably be the case with other implementations, too.

Calling Member Functions Through References

If you want an algorithm to be able to call a member function through a reference rather than a pointer, use **mem_fun_ref( )** or **mem_fun1_ref( )**. Their general forms are shown here:

> template<class Result, class T>
>   mem_fun_ref_t<Result, T> mem_fun_ref(Result (T::*func)( ));

> template<class Result, class T, class Argument>
>   mem_fun1_ref_t<Result, T, Argument>
>   mem_fun1_ref(Result (T::*func)(Argument));

The classes **mem_fun_ref_t** and **mem_fun1_ref_t** are shown here:

```
template <class Result, class T> class mem_fun_ref_t:
  public unary_function<T, Result>
{
public:
  explicit mem_fun_ref_t(Result (T::*func)());
  Result operator()(T &func) const;
};

template <class Result, class T, class Argument>
  class mem_fun1_ref_t:
    public binary_function<T, Result, Argument>
{
public:
  explicit mem_fun1_ref_t(Result (T::*func)(Argument));
  Result operator()(T &func, Argument arg) const;
};
```

Here is a program that demonstrates **mem_fun_ref( )**. It creates a class called **Numbers** that stores an integer and defines several member functions that are capable of determining various attributes of that integer. The program creates a vector of **Numbers** and uses **mem_fun_ref( )** to call the member functions for each element in the vector.

```cpp
// Use mem_fun_ref() function adaptor.
#include <iostream>
#include <vector>
#include <algorithm>
#include <functional>
using namespace std;

class Numbers {
  int val;
public:
  Numbers() { val = 0; }
  Numbers(int x) { val = x; }

  bool showval() { cout << val << " "; return true; }

  bool isPrime() {
    for(int i = 2; i<=(val/2); i++)
      if(!(val%i)) return false;
    return true;
  }

  bool isEven() { return (bool) !(val % 2); }
  bool isOdd() { return (bool) (val %2); }
};

int main()
{
  vector<Numbers> v(10);
  vector<Numbers>::iterator end_p;
  int i;

  // initialize sequence
  for(i = 0; i<10; i++)
    v[i] = Numbers(i+1);

  cout << "Sequence contains: ";
  for_each(v.begin(), v.end(),
           mem_fun_ref(&Numbers::showval));
  cout << endl;
```

10

```
  // remove the primes
  end_p = remove_if(v.begin(), v.end(), // primes.begin(),
                    mem_fun_ref(&Numbers::isPrime));

  cout << "Sequence after removing primes: ";
  for_each(v.begin(),  end_p,
           mem_fun_ref(&Numbers::showval));
  cout << endl;

  // restore sequence
  for(i = 0; i<10; i++)
    v[i] = Numbers(i+1);

  // remove even values
  end_p = remove_if(v.begin(), v.end(),
                    mem_fun_ref(&Numbers::isEven));

  cout << "Sequence after removing even values: ";
  for_each(v.begin(), end_p,
           mem_fun_ref(&Numbers::showval));
  cout << endl;

  // restore sequence
  for(i = 0; i<10; i++)
    v[i] = Numbers(i+1);

  // remove odd values
  end_p = remove_if(v.begin(), v.end(),
                    mem_fun_ref(&Numbers::isOdd));

  cout << "Sequence after removing odd values: ";
  for_each(v.begin(), end_p,
           mem_fun_ref(&Numbers::showval));
  cout << endl;

  return 0;
}
```

The output from the program is shown here:

```
Sequence contains: 1 2 3 4 5 6 7 8 9 10
Sequence after removing primes: 4 6 8 9 10
Sequence after removing even values: 1 3 5 7 9
Sequence after removing odd values: 2 4 6 8 10
```

As this chapter has shown, function objects, negators, binders, and function adaptors greatly increase the range of programming problems that can be solved using the STL. Because they help integrate the STL into the rest of the C++ programming environment, you can expect to see programmers integrating STL-based solutions into upgrades to existing applications. The STL is not just for new code. It can be used wherever efficient solutions based on containers are required.

In the next chapter, we will explore the world of iterators.

10

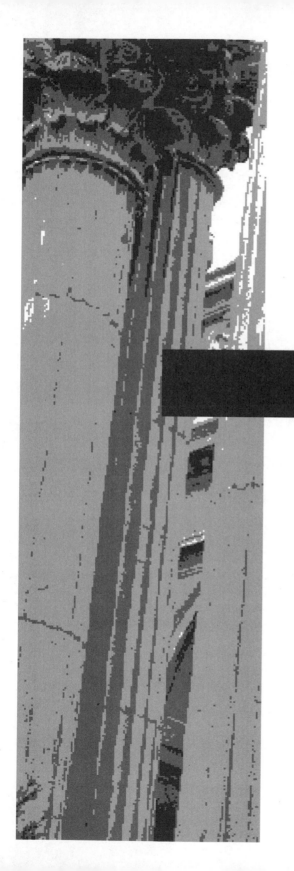

CHAPTER 11

Iterators

As stated several times before, the STL consists of algorithms acting on containers through iterators. Iterators are the conduit through which information flows. They are fundamental to STL programming, and they are required for nearly every use to which it can be put. Since iterators are a generalization (or perhaps more precisely, an abstraction) of a pointer, they are readily used by any experienced C++ programmer. This is why we did not need to spend much time on them prior to this point. In fact, for most uses of the STL, you don't need to know any more about iterators than you already do. However, for sophisticated applications of the STL, a more detailed knowledge of iterators is required.

As you have seen in the preceding chapters, each container provides built-in iterators, and you can make extensive use of the STL using only these standard objects. That said, the STL defines several iterator adaptors and additional classes that expand the capabilities of many algorithms and enable the STL to interface more completely to the rest of the C++ library. As you will see, the classes, adaptors, and techniques described here greatly enhance the STL programming environment. For example, stream-based iterators are available that allow you to operate on streams through iterators. Insert iterator classes are provided that simplify the insertion of elements into a container.

We will begin by reviewing the central concepts associated with iterators.

Iterator Fundamentals

As you already know, iterators are handled in your program in the same way as pointers, and they implement the standard pointer operators. They give you the ability to cycle through the contents of a container in much the same way that you would use a pointer to cycle through an array. Each container defines one or more iterator types that your program can use to declare iterators compatible with that container. Iterators use the header **<iterator>**.

There are five types of iterators:

Iterator	Access Allowed
Random Access	Store and retrieve values. Elements may be accessed randomly.
Bidirectional	Store and retrieve values. Forward and backward moving.
Forward	Store and retrieve values. Forward moving only.
Input	Retrieve, but not store values. Forward moving only.
Output	Store, but not retrieve values. Forward moving only.

In general, an iterator that has greater access capabilities can be used in place of one that has lesser capabilities. For example, a forward iterator can be used in place of an input iterator.

All iterators do not support the same operations.

The STL also supports reverse iterators. Reverse iterators are either bidirectional or random-access iterators that move through a sequence in the reverse direction. Thus, if a reverse iterator points to the end of a sequence, incrementing that iterator will cause it to point one element before the end.

All iterators must support the types of pointer operations allowed by their category. For example, an input iterator class must support –>, ++, *, ==, and !=. Further, the * operator cannot be used to assign a value. By contrast, a random-access iterator must support –>, +, ++, –, – –, *, <, >, <=, >=,–=, +=, ==, !=, and [ ]. Also, the * must allow assignment. The operations that are supported for each type of iterator are shown here.

Iterator	Operations Supported
Random Access	*, –>, =, +, –, ++, – –, [ ], <, >, <=, >=, –=, +=, ==, !=
Bidirectional	*, –>, =, ++, – –, ==, !=
Forward	*, –>, =, ++, ==, !=
Input	*, –>, =, ++, ==, !=
Output	*, =, ++,

11

Each of the STL containers defines its own iterator type, which is **typedef**ed as **iterator**. Containers also define a reverse iterator, **typedef**ed as **reverse_iterator.** To obtain an iterator for a particular container, simply qualify the name of the iterator with the name of the container. For example,

```
vector<double>::iterator p;
```

This declares an iterator variable called **p** for use with vectors containing elements of type **double**. You have seen this type of statement many times in the preceding chapters.

The container classes also define **const** iterators, called **const_iterator** and **const_reverse_iterator**. These are used when dealing with **const** objects.

The Low-Level Iterator Classes

The STL defines a set of classes that provide the underpinning for iterators. For the vast majority of STL-based programming tasks, you will not use these classes directly. Instead, you will use the iterators provided by the various containers or created by the various iterator adaptors. The preceding notwithstanding, it is still valuable to have a general understanding of the iterator base classes and their contents because they define several types that are used by other iterator classes.

The **iterator** class is a base for iterators. It is shown here:

```
template <class Cat, class T, class Diff = ptrdiff_t,
  class Pointer = T *, class Ref = T &>
struct iterator {
  typedef T value_type;
  typedef Diff difference_type;
  typedef Pointer pointer;
  typedef Ref reference;
  typedef Cat iterator_category;
};
```

Here, **difference_type** is a type that can hold the difference between two addresses, **value_type** is the type of value operated upon, **pointer** is the type of a pointer to a value, **reference** is the type of a reference to a value, and **iterator_category** describes the type of the iterator (such as input, random-access, etc.). Several of the iterator classes make use of the **ptrdiff_t** type. This type is capable of representing the difference between two pointers.

The following category classes are provided:

```
struct input_iterator_tag {};
struct output_iterator_tag {};
struct forward_iterator_tag: public input_iterator_tag {};
struct bidirectional_iterator_tag: public forward_iterator_tag {};
struct random_access_iterator_tag: public
        bidirectional_iterator_tag {};
```

The class **iterator_traits** provides a convenient means of exposing the various types defined by an iterator. It is defined like this:

```
template<class Itr> struct iterator_traits {
  typedef Itr::difference_type difference_type;
  typedef Itr::value_type value_type;
  typedef Itr::pointer pointer;
  typedef Itr::reference reference;
  typedef Itr::iterator_category iterator_category;
}
```

We won't be making any direct use of these classes, but they are available to you if needed.

The Iterator Adaptors

The iterator adaptors change the behavior of an iterator.

Standard C++ defines several iterator adaptors that are used to transform an iterator into a more convenient form. These adaptors are shown in Table 11-1. As the table shows, there are two basic types: insert adaptors and reverse adaptors. You are already familiar with reverse iterators. An insert iterator is used to insert, rather than overwrite elements when an assignment takes place. These classes require the header **<iterator>**.

As a point of interest, the insert and reverse iterator adaptors are also referred to as *predefined iterators* by the International Standard for C++. You can expect both terms to be used interchangeably.

11

Using the Insert Iterators

The insert iterator adaptors are quite useful tools. To understand why, consider the following two behaviors associated with iterators. First, when using normal iterators to copy an element into a container, the current contents of the target container are overwritten. That is, the element being copied is not inserted into the container, but replaces (that is, overwrites) the

Class	Description
insert_iterator	An output iterator that inserts anywhere in the container
back_insert_iterator	An output iterator that inserts at the end of a container
front_insert_iterator	An output iterator that inserts at the front of a container
reverse_iterator	A reverse, bidirectional, or random-access iterator

The Iterator
Adaptor
Classes
Table 11-1.

The insert
iterators insert
elements rather
than overwriting
existing
elements.

previous element. Thus, the previous contents of the target container are not preserved. Second, when elements are copied into a container through a normal iterator, it is possible to overrun the end of the container. Recall that a container will not automatically increase its size when it is used as the target of an algorithm; it must be large enough to accommodate the number of elements that it will receive before a copy operation takes place. An insert iterator allows us to alter these two behaviors.

When an element is added to a container through an insert iterator, the element is inserted at the location pointed to by the iterator, with the remaining elements moving down to make room for the new element. Thus, the original contents of the container are preserved. If necessary, the size of the container is increased to accommodate the inserted element. It is not possible to overrun the end of the target container.

insert_iterator

An **insert_
iterator** inserts
elements
anywhere in a
container.

The **insert_iterator** class creates output iterators that insert objects into a container. Its template definition is shown here:

```
template <class Cont> class insert_iterator:
    public iterator<output_iterator_tag, void, void, void, void>
```

Here, **Cont** is the type of container that the iterator operates upon. **insert_iterator** has the following constructor:

```
insert_iterator(Cont &cnt, typename Cont::iterator itr);
```

Here, *cnt* is the container being operated upon and *itr* is an iterator being adapted.

The **insert_iterator** class defines the following operators: =, *, ++. A pointer to the container is stored in a protected variable called **container**. The container's iterator is stored in a protected variable called **iter**.

The function **inserter( )** is also defined, which creates an **insert_iterator**. It is shown here:

> template <class Cont, class OutIter> insert_iterator<Cont>
>   inserter(Cont &*cnt*, OutIter *itr*);

As explained, insert iterators insert into, rather than overwrite, the contents of a container. To fully understand the effects of an insert iterator, consider the following program. It first creates a small vector of integers. It then uses an **insert_iterator** to insert new elements into the vector rather than overwriting existing elements.

```
// Demonstrate insert_iterator.
#include <iostream>
#include <iterator>
#include <vector>
using namespace std;

int main()
{
  vector<int> v;
  vector<int>::iterator itr;
  int i;

  for(i=0; i<5; i++)
    v.push_back(i);

  cout << "Original contents of v: ";
  itr = v.begin();
  while(itr != v.end())
    cout << *itr++ << " ";
  cout << endl;

  itr = v.begin();
  itr += 2; // point to element 2

  // create insert_iterator to element 2
  insert_iterator<vector<int> > i_itr(v, itr);

  // insert rather than overwrite
```

11

```
  *i_itr++ = 100;
  *i_itr = 200;

  cout << "v after insertion: ";
  itr = v.begin();
  while(itr != v.end())
    cout << *itr++ << " ";

  return 0;
}
```

The output from the program is shown here:

```
Original contents of v: 0 1 2 3 4
v after insertion: 0 1 100 200 2 3 4
```

In the program, had the assignments of 100 and 200 been done using a standard iterator, the original elements in the array would have been overwritten. Instead, the new elements are inserted between the existing ones.

While the foregoing program is a valid use of an insert iterator, it does not show its true power. This is best demonstrated by its use in an algorithm. For example, the following program inserts one vector into another using an insert iterator:

```
// Insert one vector into another using an insert iterator.
#include <iostream>
#include <iterator>
#include <vector>
#include <string>
using namespace std;

int main()
{
  vector<string> v, v2;
  vector<string>::iterator itr;

  v.push_back("The");
  v.push_back("STL");
  v.push_back("are");
  v.push_back("powerful.");

  v2.push_back("and");
```

```
v2.push_back("insert");
v2.push_back("iterators");

cout << "Original size of v: " << v.size() << endl;
cout << "Original contents of v:\n";
itr = v.begin();
while(itr != v.end())
  cout << *itr++ << " ";
cout << "\n\n";

// insert v2
copy(v2.begin(), v2.end(), inserter(v, v.begin()+2));

cout << "Size of v after insertion: ";
cout << v.size() << endl;
cout << "Contents of v after insertion:\n";
itr = v.begin();
while(itr != v.end())
  cout << *itr++ << " ";

return 0;
}
```

Here is the output from the program:

```
Original size of v: 4
Original contents of v:
The STL are powerful.

Size of v after insertion: 7
Contents of v after insertion:
The STL and insert iterators are powerful.
```

As you can see, **v2** was inserted into **v1**. In the process, **v1** was automatically increased in size to hold the additional elements. If an insert iterator had not been used, the original contents of **v1** would have been partially overwritten.

back_insert_iterator

A **back_insert_iterator** inserts elements at the end of a container.

The **back_insert_iterator** class adapts output iterators so that they insert objects on the end of a container using **push_back( )**. Its template definition is shown here:

```
template <class Cont> class back_insert_iterator:
    public iterator<output_iterator_tag, void, void, void, void>
```

11

Here, **Cont** is the type of container that the iterator operates upon. **back_insert_iterator** has the following constructor:

    explicit back_insert_iterator(Cont &*cnt*);

Here, *cnt* is the container being operated upon. All insertions will occur at the end. Thus, a back insert iterator adapts *cnt.end( )* for insert operations.

back_insert_iterator defines the following operators: **=**, *****, **++**. A pointer to the container is stored in a protected variable called **container**.

The function **back_inserter( )** is also defined, which creates a **back_insert_iterator**. It is shown here:

    template <class Cont> back_insert_iterator<Cont> back_inserter(Cont &*cnt*);

Here is an example that uses **back_insert_iterator**:

```
// Demonstrate back_insert_iterator.
#include <iostream>
#include <iterator>
#include <vector>
using namespace std;

int main()
{
  vector<int> v, v2;
  vector<int>::iterator itr;
  int i;

  for(i=0; i<5; i++)
    v.push_back(i);

  cout << "Original contents of v: ";
  itr = v.begin();
  while(itr != v.end())
    cout << *itr++ << " ";
  cout << endl;

  // create a back_insert_iterator to v
  back_insert_iterator<vector<int> > bck_i_itr(v);

  // insert rather than overwrite at end
  *bck_i_itr++ = 100;
  *bck_i_itr = 200;
```

```
    cout << "v after insertion: ";
    itr = v.begin();
    while(itr != v.end())
      cout << *itr++ << " ";
    cout << endl;

    cout << "Size of v2 before copy: " << v2.size()
         << endl;

    // copy v to v2 using back inserter
    copy(v.begin(), v.end(), back_inserter(v2));

    cout << "Size of v2 after copy: " << v2.size()
         << endl;

    cout << "Contents of v2 after insertion: ";
    itr = v2.begin();
    while(itr != v2.end())
      cout << *itr++ << " ";

    return 0;
}
```

Here is the program's output:

```
Original contents of v: 0 1 2 3 4
v after insertion: 0 1 2 3 4 100 200
Size of v2 before copy: 0
Size of v2 after copy: 7
Contents of v2 after insertion: 0 1 2 3 4 100 200
```

In the program, the vector **v** is given five initial values, then two more are inserted at its end using a back inserter. Next, **v** is copied into **v2**. Notice that initially **v2** is empty and has a size of zero. After the call to **copy( )**, **v2** contains the same elements as **v** and its size has been increased to seven. The automatic increase takes place only because a **back_insert_iterator** is used to insert elements into **v2**. Had a normal iterator been used, **v2** would have been overrun and a runtime error would have occurred.

11

A **front_insert_iterator** inserts elements at the front of a container.

front_insert_iterator

The **front_insert_iterator** class creates output iterators that insert objects on the front of a container using **push_front( )**. Its template definition is shown here:

template <class Cont> class front_insert_iterator:
    public iterator<output_iterator_tag, void, void, void, void>

Here, **Cont** is the type of container that the iterator operates upon. **front_insert_iterator** has the following constructor:

explicit front_insert_iterator(Cont &*cnt*);

Here, *cnt* is the container being operated upon. All insertions will occur at the front. Thus, it is *cnt.begin( )* that is being adapted.

front_insert_iterator defines the following operators: **=**, *****, **++**. A pointer to the container is stored in a protected variable called **container**.

The function **front_inserter( )** is also defined, which creates a **front_insert_iterator**. It is shown here:

template <class Cont> front_insert_iterator<Cont>
    front_inserter(Cont &*cnt*);

Here is an example that uses a front insert iterator:

```
// Demonstrate front_insert_iterator.
#include <iostream>
#include <iterator>
#include <list>
using namespace std;

int main()
{
  list<int> v, v2;
  list<int>::iterator itr;
  int i;

  for(i=0; i<5; i++)
    v.push_back(i);

  cout << "Original contents of v: ";
  itr = v.begin();
  while(itr != v.end())
    cout << *itr++ << " ";
  cout << endl;

  // create a front_insert_iterator to v
  front_insert_iterator<list<int> > frnt_i_itr(v);
```

```
// insert rather than overwrite at front
*frnt_i_itr++ = 100;
*frnt_i_itr = 200;

cout << "v after insertion: ";
itr = v.begin();
while(itr != v.end())
  cout << *itr++ << " ";
cout << endl;

cout << "Size of v2 before copy: " << v2.size()
     << endl;

// copy v to v2 using front inserter
copy(v.begin(), v.end(), front_inserter(v2));

cout << "Size of v2 after copy: " << v2.size()
     << endl;

cout << "Contents of v2 after insertion: ";
itr = v2.begin();
while(itr != v2.end())
  cout << *itr++ << " ";

return 0;
}
```

Here is the program's output:

```
Original contents of v: 0 1 2 3 4
v after insertion: 200 100 0 1 2 3 4
Size of v2 before copy: 0
Size of v2 after copy: 7
Contents of v2 after insertion: 4 3 2 1 0 100 200
```

As you can see, the elements of **v** are inserted onto the front of **v2**.

Reverse Iterators

The **reverse_iterator** class supports reverse iterator operations. As you know, a reverse iterator operates the opposite of a normal iterator. For example, **++** causes a reverse iterator to back up. Its template definition is shown here:

11

```
.template <class Itr> class reverse_iterator:
     public iterator<iterator_traits<Itr>::iterator_category,
                     iterator_traits<Itr>::value_type,
                     iterator_traits<Itr>::difference_type,
                     iterator_traits<Itr>::pointer,
                     iterator_traits<Itr>::reference>
```

Here, **Itr** is either a random-access iterator or a bidirectional iterator. **reverse_iterator** has the following constructors:

reverse_iterator( );

explicit reverse_iterator(Itr *itr*);

Here, *itr* is an iterator that specifies the starting location.

If **Itr** is a random-access iterator, then the following operators are available: **–>, +, ++, –, – –, *, <, >, <=, >=, – =, +=, ==, !=,** and **[ ]** . If **Itr** is a birectional iterator, then only **–>, ++, – –, *, ==,** and **!=** are available.

The **reverse_iterator** class defines a protected member called **current**, which is an iterator to the current location.

The function **base( )** is also defined by **reverse_iterator**. Its prototype is shown here:

Itr base( ) const;

It returns an iterator to the current location.

For the most part, when you need a reverse iterator, you will simply use the one defined by the container that you are operating upon.

Using the Stream Iterators

The stream iterators allow you to utilize streams as if they were containers.

The STL defines four classes that enable you to obtain iterators to I/O streams. These classes are shown in Table 11-2. The stream iterators are among some of the STL's most interesting objects because they allow the STL to perform I/O operations. Using the stream iterators, it is possible to view an I/O stream as simply another type of container. Frankly, for most I/O operations you will still use the standard I/O operators and functions, but the ability to apply algorithms to streams offers a new dimension in programming. It can also simplify certain I/O situations. Each stream iterator is examined here.

Class	Description
istream_iterator	An input stream iterator
istreambuf_iterator	An input streambuf iterator
ostream_iterator	An output stream iterator
ostreambuf_iterator	An output streambuf iterator

The Stream
Iterator Classes
Table 11-2.

The Formatted Stream Iterators

The STL defines two stream iterators that are designed for use on formatted I/O streams: **istream_iterator** and **ostream_iterator**. These iterators are capable of reading or writing formatted data, which means that they can read or write character, integer, floating point, and string values. This makes them especially useful when operating on files that contain human-readable information.

istream_iterator

istream_iterator
reads data from
a stream.

The **istream_iterator** class supports input iterator operations on a stream. Its template definition is shown here:

    template <class T, class CharType, class Attr = char_traits<CharType>,
        class Diff = ptrdiff_t> class istream_iterator:
      public iterator<input_iterator_tag, T, Diff, const T *, const T &>

Here, **T** is the type of data being transferred and **CharType** is the character type (**char** or **wchar_t**) that the stream is operating upon. **Diff** is a type capable of holding the difference between two addresses. **istream_iterator** has the following constructors:

    istream_iterator( );
    istream_iterator(istream_type &*stream*);
    istream_iterator(const istream_iterator<T, CharType, Attr, Diff> &*ob*);

The first constructor creates an iterator that indicates end-of-stream. This object can be used to check for the end of input. (That is, it will compare equal to end-of-stream.) The second creates an iterator to the stream specified

11

When an
istream_iterator
is constructed
on a stream, it
attempts to
read the first
object from that
stream.

by *stream*. It then reads the first object from the stream. The type **istream_type** is a **typedef** of **basic_istream** that specifies the type of the input stream. The third form is **istream_iterator**'s copy constructor.

The **istream_iterator** class defines the following operators: **->**, *****, **++**. The **->** and the ***** act as expected. The **++** operator requires a bit of explanation. When used in its prefix form, the **++** causes the next value to be read from the input stream. When used in its postfix form, the current value of the stream is stored and then the next value of the stream is read. Often, it doesn't matter which form you use. The operators **==** and **!=** are also defined for objects of type **istream_iterator**.

Here is a short program that demonstrates **istream_iterator**. It reads and displays characters from **cin** until a period is received. Notice how the code is written. Since constructing an **istream_iterator** on a stream causes an initial read operation to take place, the first statement within the loop obtains that first character. Then the iterator is incremented, causing the next read operation to take place.

```
// Use istream_iterator
#include <iostream>
#include <iterator>
using namespace std;

int main()
{
  istream_iterator<char> in_itr(cin);

  do {
    cout << *in_itr;
    ++in_itr;
  } while (*in_itr != '.');

  return 0;
}
```

Of course, you are not restricted to reading only characters from an **istream_iterator**. For example, the following program reads integers, doubles, and strings:

```
// Use istream_iterator to read various data types.
#include <iostream>
#include <iterator>
#include <string>
```

```cpp
#include <vector>
using namespace std;

int main()
{
  int i;
  double d;
  string str;
  vector<int> vi;
  vector<double> vd;
  vector<string> vs;

  cout << "Enter some integers, enter 0 to stop.\n";
  istream_iterator<int> int_itr(cin);
  do {
    i = *int_itr; // read next int
    if(i != 0) {
      vi.push_back(i); // store it
      ++int_itr; // input next int
    }
  } while (i != 0);

  cout << "Enter some doubles, enter 0 to stop.\n";
  istream_iterator<double> double_itr(cin);
  do {
    d = *double_itr; // read next double
    if(d != 0.0) {
      vd.push_back(d); // store it
      ++double_itr; // input next double
    }
  } while (d != 0.0);

  cout << "Enter some strings, enter 'quit' to stop.\n";
  istream_iterator<string> string_itr(cin);
  do {
    str = *string_itr; // read next string
    if(str != "quit") {
      vs.push_back(str); // store it
      ++string_itr;
    }
  } while (str != "quit"); // input next string

  cout << "Here is what you entered:\n";
  for(i=0; i<vi.size(); i++)
    cout << vi[i] << " ";
```

```
  cout << endl;

  for(i=0; i<vd.size(); i++)
    cout << vd[i] << " ";
  cout << endl;

  for(i=0; i<vs.size(); i++)
    cout << vs[i] << " ";

  return 0;
}
```

Here is a sample run:

```
Enter some integers, enter 0 to stop.
1
2
3
0
Enter some doubles, enter 0 to stop.
1.1
2.2
3.3
0.0
Enter some strings, enter 'quit' to stop.
this
is
a
test
quit
Here is what you entered:
1 2 3
1.1 2.2 3.3
this is a test
```

While using stream iterators as just shown is interesting, doing so offers no advantage over C++'s normal I/O operators. The benefit of the stream iterators is found when they are used in conjunction with algorithms. For example, consider the following program that uses the **copy( )** algorithm to read integers from **cin**, putting them into a vector:

```
// Use istream_iterator with the copy algorithm.
#include <iostream>
#include <iterator>
```

```
#include <algorithm>
#include <vector>
using namespace std;

int main()
{
  int i;
  vector<int> v(5);

  cout << "Enter 5 integers: \n";

  istream_iterator<int> int_itr(cin);
  copy(int_itr, istream_iterator<int>(), v.begin());

  cout << "Here are the values you entered: ";
  for(i=0; i<v.size(); i++) cout << v[i] << " ";

  return 0;
}
```

Here is a sample run:

```
Enter 5 integers:
1
2
3
4
5

Here are the values you entered: 1 2 3 4 5
```

There are a couple of important points to mention about the preceding program. First, notice that in the call to **copy( )**, the source range is specified as starting at **in_itr** and ending at **istream_iterator<int>( )**. As explained earlier, the default **istream_iterator** constructor creates an object that will test equal to end-of-stream. Thus, the range of elements to be copied begins with the first element read and ends when the end of the stream is encountered. This will occur when end-of-file is encountered in the underlying stream. (When reading from **cin**, most computers generate an end-of-file character when you press CTRL-Z.) Second, it is trivially easy to overrun the vector **v** by inputting too many integers. As an exercise, you might want to try modifying the program so that it uses an insert iterator to prevent an overrun from occurring.

11

ostream_itera-
tor writes data
to a stream.

ostream_iterator

The **ostream_iterator** class supports output iterator operations on a stream. Its template definition is shown here:

```
template <class T, class CharType, class Attr = char_traits<CharType> >
class ostream_iterator:
    public iterator<output_iterator_tag, void, void, void, void>
```

Here, **T** is the type of data being transferred and **CharType** is the character type (**char** or **wchar_t**) that the stream is operating upon. **ostream_iterator** has the following constructors:

```
ostream_iterator(ostream_type &stream);
ostream_iterator(ostream_type &stream, const CharType *delim);
ostream_iterator(const ostream_iterator<T, CharType, Attr> &ob);
```

The first creates an iterator to the stream specified by *stream*. The type **ostream_type** is a **typedef** that specifies the type of the output stream. The second form creates an iterator to the stream specified by *stream* and uses the delimiters specified by *delim*. The delimiters are written to the stream after every output operation. The third form creates a copy of an **ostream_iterator** object.

The **ostream_iterator** class defines the following operators: **=**, *****, **++**.

Here is a short program that demonstrates **ostream_iterator**:

```
// Use ostream_iterator
#include <iostream>
#include <iterator>
using namespace std;

int main()
{
  ostream_iterator<char> out_it(cout);

  *out_it = 'X';
  out_it++;
  *out_it = 'Y';
  out_it++;
  *out_it = ' ';

  char str[] = "C++ Iterators are powerful.\n";
  char *p = str;

  while(*p) *out_it++ = *p++;
```

```
ostream_iterator<double> out_double_it(cout);
*out_double_it = 187.23;
out_double_it++;
*out_double_it = -102.7;

return 0;
}
```

The output from this program is shown here:

```
XY C++ Iterators are powerful.
187.23-102.7
```

As was the case with **istream_iterator**, the benefits of **ostream_iterator** are most readily apparent when it is used in conjunction with an algorithm. Here is a simple example that uses **copy( )** to copy the contents of a list to **cout**:

```
// Use ostream_iterator
#include <iostream>
#include <list>
#include <iterator>
#include <string>
#include <algorithm>
using namespace std;

int main()
{
  list<string> lst;
  ostream_iterator<string> out_it(cout);

  lst.push_back("Stream ");
  lst.push_back("iterators ");
  lst.push_back("are ");
  lst.push_back("useful.");

  copy(lst.begin(), lst.end(), out_it);

  return 0;
}
```

Here is the output produced:

```
Stream iterators are useful.
```

11

The Low-Level Character Stream Iterators

In addition to the high-level stream iterators just described, the STL provides a set of low-level character stream iterators called **istreambuf_iterator** and **ostreambuf_iterator**. These iterators can work only on streams consisting of either **char** or **wchar_t** characters. While you will want to use the high-level stream iterators for most tasks, the major advantage of the low-level stream iterators is that they give your program access to the raw I/O stream in the form of characters.

istreambuf_iterator

istreambuf_ iterator reads characters from a stream.

The **istreambuf_iterator** class supports low-level character input iterator operations on a stream. Its template definition is shown here:

```
template <class CharType, class Attr = char_traits<CharType> >
class istreambuf_iterator:
    public iterator<input_iterator_tag, CharType, typename Attr::off_type,
            CharType *, CharType &>
```

Here, **CharType** is the character type (**char** or **wchar_t**) that the stream is operating upon. **istreambuf_iterator** has the following constructors:

```
istreambuf_iterator( ) throw( );
istreambuf_iterator(istream_type &stream) throw( );
istreambuf_iterator(streambuf_type *streambuf) throw( );
```

The first constructor creates an iterator that indicates end-of-stream. The second creates an iterator to the stream specified by *stream*. The type **istream_type** is a **typedef** that specifies the type of the input stream. The third form creates an iterator to the stream specified by *streambuf*. The type **streambuf_type** is a **typedef** that specifies the type of the stream buffer.

The **istreambuf_iterator** class defines the following operators: *****, **++**. The operators **==** and **!=** are also defined for objects of type **istreambuf_iterator**.

istreambuf_iterator defines the member function **equal( )**, which is shown here:

```
bool equal(istreambuf_iterator<CharType, Attr> &ob);
```

Its operation is a bit counterintuitive. It returns **true** if the invoking iterator and *ob* both point to the end of the stream. It also returns **true** if both iterators do not point to the end of the stream. There is no requirement that what they point to be the same. It returns **false** otherwise. The **==** and **!=** operators work in the same fashion.

ostream-
buf_iterator
*writes
characters to a
stream.*

ostreambuf_iterator

The **ostreambuf_iterator** class supports low-level character output iterator operations on a stream. Its template definition is shown here:

```
template <class CharType, class Attr = char_traits<CharType> >
class ostreambuf_iterator:
    public iterator<output_iterator_tag, void, void, void, void>
```

Here, **CharType** is the character type (**char** or **wchar_t**) that the stream is operating upon. **ostreambuf_iterator** has the following constructors:

```
ostreambuf_iterator(ostream_type &stream) throw( );
ostreambuf_iterator(streambuf_type *streambuf) throw( );
```

The first creates an iterator to the stream specified by *stream*. The type **ostream_type** is a **typedef** that specifies the type of the input stream. The second form creates an iterator using the stream buffer specified by *streambuf*. The type **streambuf_type** is a **typedef** that specifies the type of the stream buffer.

The **ostreambuf_iterator** class defines the following operators: **=**, *****, **++**. The member function **failed( )** is also defined, as shown here:

```
bool failed( ) const throw( );
```

It returns **false** if no failure has occurred and **true** otherwise.

A Low-Level Stream Iterator Example

The low-level stream iterators are most useful when you want to use STL algorithms to directly manipulate the contents of a character stream, bypassing the buffering and possible character translations that might occur with the high-level stream iterators. One such use is found in the following program. It copies a file and in the process replaces all spaces with vertical bars. To accomplish this, it uses the character stream iterators and the **replace_copy( )** algorithm.

11

```
/* Use istreambuf_iterator, ostreambuf_iterator, and
   replace_copy() to filter a file. */
```

```
#include <iostream>
#include <fstream>
#include <iterator>
#include <algorithm>
using namespace std;

int main(int argc, char *argv[])
{
  if(argc!=3) {
    cout << "Usage: replace in out\n";
    return 1;
  }

  ifstream in(argv[1]);
  ofstream out(argv[2]);

  // make sure files are open
  if(!in) {
    cout << "Cannot open input file.\n";
    return 1;
  }
  if(!out) {
    cout << "Cannot open output file.\n";
    return 1;
  }

  // create stream iterators
  istreambuf_iterator<char> in_itr(in);
  ostreambuf_iterator<char> out_itr(out);

  // copy file, replacing characters in the process
  replace_copy(in_itr, istreambuf_iterator<char>(),
               out_itr, ' ', '|');

  in.close();
  out.close();

  return 0;
}
```

To understand the effects of the program, assume the following input:

```
This is a test of the stream
iterators.  It is replacing spaces
with vertical bars.
```

The program converts the foregoing into this output file:

```
This|is|a|test|of|the|stream
iterators.||It|is|replacing|spaces
with|vertical|bars.
```

IN DEPTH

Are the Stream Iterator Classes Adaptors?

Here is an interesting philosophical question: Are the stream iterators adaptors? As it relates to the STL, the term "adaptor" is used to describe a component that transforms one type of object into another, typically so that it may be used by yet some other, incompatible component. As you know, there are container adaptors, function adaptors, and iterator adaptors, but historically, the term "adaptor" has not been applied to the stream iterators. For example, the International Standard for C++ does not refer to the stream iterators as adaptors. But the question can still be asked: Are the stream iterators adaptors?

It is clear that the stream iterators adapt a stream for use by the STL. This is their entire point, after all. Without the stream iterator classes, it would not be possible to use streams directly within algorithms. From this point of view, the stream iterators deserve the title of adaptor.

On the other hand, the other adaptors defined by the STL usually convert one thing into a slightly different, but related, form. For example, a function adaptor, such as **ptr_fun( )**, allows a non-STL function to be used by a binder, but it does not create a fundamentally different type of object. The same is true for a container adaptor such as **stack**. It transforms a vector or a deque into a stack by providing a restricted interface. In essence, the **stack** adaptor simply creates a specialized form of the component it is adapting. This is not the situation for the stream iterator classes. The stream is not really being transformed into a different form by the stream iterator classes. Instead, the stream is overlaid by an iterator mechanism. Also, streams and iterators are two completely different types of objects. From this point of view, the stream iterator classes can not be called adaptors in the proper sense.

While the issue of whether the stream iterators are also adaptors is of no practical importance, it can make for a lively debate. You might want to toss this question out the next time you're in a group of programmers!

11

Two Iterator Functions

There are two special functions defined for iterators: **advance( )** and **distance( )**. They are shown here:

template <class InIter, class Diff> void advance(InIter &*itr*, Diff *d*);

template <class InIter>
  iterator_traits<InIter>::diference_type distance(InIter *start*, InIter *end*);

The **advance( )** function increments *itr* by the amount specified by *val*. The **distance( )** function returns the number of elements between *start* and *end*.

The reason for these two functions is that only random-access iterators allow a value to be added to or subtracted from an iterator, or allow one iterator to be subtracted from another. The **advance( )** and **distance( )** functions overcome this restriction. It must be noted, however, that some iterators will not be able to implement these functions efficiently.

Here is a program that illustrates **advance( )** and **distance( )**:

```
// Demonstrate advance() and distance().
#include <iostream>
#include <list>
#include <iterator>
using namespace std;

int main()
{
  list<char> lst;
  list<char>::iterator p;
  int i;

  for(i=0; i<10; i++) lst.push_back('A'+i);

  p = lst.begin();
  cout << "Character at p: " << *p << endl;

  // move two characters forward using advance()

//  p += 2; // not allowed for lists!
  advance(p, 2); // this is OK
  cout << "Character at p+2: " << *p << endl;

  // demonstrate distance()
  cout << "Number of elements from lst.begin() ";
```

```
   cout << "to lst.end(): ";

// cout << lst.end()-lst.begin(); // not allowed!
   cout << distance(lst.begin(), lst.end());

   return 0;
}
```

The program's output is shown here:

```
Character at p: A
Character at p+2: C
Number of elements from lst.begin() to lst.end(): 10
```

As you know, the **list** container supports bidirectional iterators, not random-access ones. This means that neither iterator subtraction nor adding or subtracting integer values from a **list** iterator are supported. That is, for a **list** iterator, the following operations are not allowed:

p2 – p2
p2 += n

However, these operations may still be accomplished through the **advance( )** and **distance( )** functions, as the program shows.

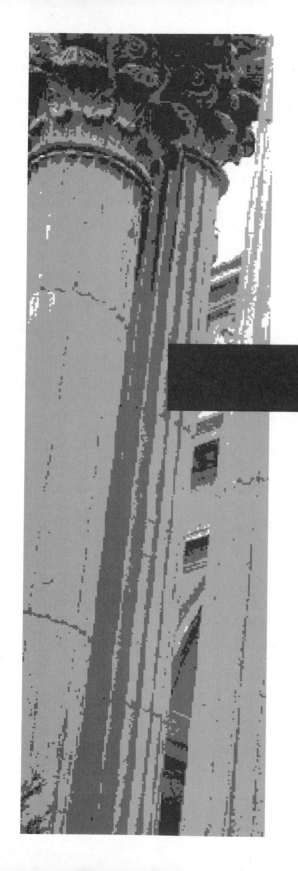

CHAPTER 12

Allocators, Custom Containers, and Other Advanced Topics

This chapter discusses the last of the major STL components: allocators. It also examines the **bitset** class, the raw storage iterator, the relationship between arrays and containers, and the requirements for a container. The chapter concludes by developing a custom container.

Allocators

Allocators are the memory managers of the STL, and one is required by each of the containers. Fortunately, a default allocator is automatically provided and most programmers, rightfully, rely upon it. It is possible, though, to create your own custom allocator. While we won't actually do this, a general understanding of what constitutes an allocator is important for all programmers. With this in mind, a brief discussion of allocators follows.

The Default Allocator

The default allocator is **allocator** and it is defined within the header **<memory>**. Its template specification is shown here:

    template <class T> class allocator

The default
allocator is
allocator.

Here, **T** is the type of objects that **allocator** will be allocating. **allocator** defines the following constructors:

    allocator( ) throw( );

    allocator(const allocator<T> &ob) throw( );

    template <class T2> allocator(const allocator<T2> &ob) throw( );

The first creates new allocator. The second creates a copy of *ob* and is **allocator**'s copy constructor. The third creates an allocator from another allocator.

The operators **==** and **!=** are defined for **allocator**. The member functions defined by **allocator** are shown in Table 12-1. Also, a specialization for **void * ** pointers is defined along with the following structure:

    template <class T2> struct rebind { typedef allocator<T2> ob; }

Function	Description
pointer address(reference *ob*) const; const_pointer address(const_reference *ob*) const;	Returns the address of *ob*.
pointer allocate(size_type *num*, typename allocator<void>::const_pointer *h* = 0);	Returns a pointer to allocated memory that is large enough to hold *num* objects of type T. The value of *h* is a hint to the function that can be used to help satisfy the request or ignored.
void construct(pointer *ptr*, const_reference *val*);	Constructs an object of type T at *ptr*.
void deallocate(pointer *ptr*, size_type *num*);	Deallocates *num* objects of type T starting at *ptr*. The value of *ptr* must have been obtained from **allocate( )**.
void destroy(pointer *ptr*);	Destroys the object at *ptr*. Its destructor is automatically called.
size_type max_size( ) const throw( );	Returns the maximum number of objects of type T that can be allocated.

Member Functions of **allocator** **Table 12-1.**

The **allocator** class defines the following types:

const_pointer	A **const** pointer to an object of type **value_type**.
const_reference	A **const** reference to an object of type **value_type**.
difference_type	Can represent the difference between two addresses.
pointer	A pointer to an object of type **value_type**.
reference	A reference to an object of type **value_type**.
size_type	Capable of holding the size of the largest possible object that can be allocated.
value_type	The type of object being allocated.

12

Most of the time, you will not use the default allocator directly. It is used internally by the container classes. However, there is one member function that you may occasionally find useful: **max_size( )**. For any given container, this function returns the number of elements that can be allocated before free memory is exhausted. Since the size of an item depends upon what type of elements the container is holding, this value must be computed for each type of element. Here is a program that demonstrates **max_size( )**:

```cpp
// Demonstrate allocator's max_size() function.
#include <iostream>
#include <vector>
using namespace std;

int main()
{
  vector<short int>::allocator_type si_a;
  vector<int>::allocator_type i_a;
  vector<long int>::allocator_type li_a;
  vector<float>::allocator_type f_a;
  vector<double>::allocator_type d_a;

  cout << "Here are the number of objects that can be allocated.\n";
  cout << "short integers: ";
  cout << si_a.max_size() << endl;

  cout << "integers: ";
  cout << i_a.max_size() << endl;

  cout << "long integers: ";
  cout << li_a.max_size() << endl;

  cout << "floats: ";
  cout << f_a.max_size() << endl;

  cout << "doubles: ";
  cout << d_a.max_size() << endl;

  return 0;
}
```

Here is sample output. Of course, your output may differ depending upon the compiler that you use and the execution environment.

```
Here are the number of objects that can be allocated.
short integers: 2147483647
integers: 1073741823
long integers: 1073741823
floats: 1073741823
doubles: 536870911
```

In the program, notice how an allocator object for each container was obtained. As described earlier in this book, one of the standard types defined by all of the built-in containers is **allocator_type**. Using this type name, you can create the type of allocator object used by the container.

Custom Allocator Requirements

A custom allocator must provide the same interface as that supplied by **allocator**. Specifically, all allocators must define the required type names, such as **pointer** and **size_type**. Second, they must provide the same member functions. Although the precise implementation of those functions can differ from that provided by the default allocator, their external effects must be the same. Finally, the operations **==** and **!=** must also be defined.

The Raw Storage Iterator

Use raw a storage iterator when operating on uninitialized storage.

Although we discussed iterators in the preceding chapter, there is one additional built-in iterator that relates to memory allocation: **raw_storage_iterator**. The raw storage iterator should be used to copy objects into uninitialized storage, such as memory allocated using **malloc( )**, or perhaps that set aside in an array. Normally, when an algorithm copies an object, it does so using the object's assignment operator. This assumes, however, that the target of the assignment is a previously initialized object. Of course, this will not be the case if the target of an algorithm is uninitialized memory. The **raw_storage_iterator** solves this problem. It creates the required target object in the process of copying by calling the object's copy constructor.

12

The **raw_storage_iterator** template specification is shown here:

```
template <class OutIter, class T>
  class raw_storage_iterator:
    public iterator<output_iterator_tag, void, void, void, void>
```

Here, **OutIter** specifies an output iterator for the object being stored and **T** is the type of data being stored. The **raw_storage_iterator** class is defined in the header **<memory>**, not **<iterator>** like the other built-in iterator classes.

The **raw_storage_iterator** class defines the following constructor:

```
explicit raw_storage_iterator(OutIter ob);
```

Here, *ob* is an iterator to the uninitialized memory. This may be a normal pointer.

The following fragment shows the effects of using **raw_storage_iterator**:

```
// Demonstrate raw storage iterators.
#include <iostream>
#include <deque>
#include <memory>
#include <algorithm>
using namespace std;

class X {
  int a, b;
  int sum;
public:
  X() { a = b = 0; sum = 0; }
  X(int x, int y) { a = x; b = y; }

  // copy constructor
  X(const X &o) {
   a = o.a; b = o.b;
   sum = o.sum; // assign sum
  }

  // overloaded assignment
  X operator=(const X &o) {
    a = o.a; b = o.b;
```

```
        // do not assign sum
        return *this;
    }

    void setsum() { sum = a+b; }

    void show() {
      cout << a << "," << b;
      cout << " Sum is: " << sum << endl;
    }
};

int main()
{
  unsigned char raw1[100], raw2[100];
  X *p;
  deque<X> q(5);
  int i;

  for(i=0; i<5; i++) {
    q[i] = X(i, i);
    q[i].setsum();
  }

  // store deque in uninitialized memory the wrong way
  copy(q.begin(), q.end(), (X *)raw1);

  cout << "Contents of raw memory (incorrect):\n";
  p = (X *) raw1;
  for(i=0; i<5; i++)
    p[i].show();

  // store deque in uninitialized memory the right way
  copy(q.begin(), q.end(),
    raw_storage_iterator<X *, X>((X *)raw2));

  cout << "Contents of raw memory (correct):\n";
  p = (X *) raw2;
  for(i=0; i<5; i++)
    p[i].show();

  return 0;
}
```

12

The output from the program is shown here:

```
Contents of raw memory (incorrect):
0,0 Sum is: 4270196
1,1 Sum is: 4226262
2,2 Sum is: 4292496
3,3 Sum is: 4292200
4,4 Sum is: 7802464
Contents of raw memory (correct):
0,0 Sum is: 0
1,1 Sum is: 2
2,2 Sum is: 4
3,3 Sum is: 6
4,4 Sum is: 8
```

Let's look closely at the program. First, the class **X** defines a default constructor, a parameterized constructor, and a copy constructor. It also overloads the assignment operator. Pay special attention to **operator=( )** and the copy constructor. Notice that the assignment operator *does not* copy the **sum** member, but the copy constructor does. Inside **main( )**, two character arrays called **raw1** and **raw2** are declared. These are used as regions of uninitialized memory that will receive **X** objects. Next, a deque of **X** objects (called **q**) is created and given initial values.

Then, the contents of the **q** are copied into **raw1** without the use of a raw storage iterator. This means that the objects are copied using the assignment operator. Notice the output that is produced. Since the assignment operator does not copy the **sum** member, it contains a garbage value in the target array. However, when **q** is copied into **raw2**, a raw storage iterator is used. This causes the **X**'s copy constructor to be called, and the **sum** member is copied, resulting in the correct outcome.

While the raw storage iterator is not something that most programmers will use on a day-to-day basis, you may find it valuable in certain specialized situations.

Arrays as Containers

By design, standard arrays are compatible with the STL. They are, in essence, simply containers of limited capabilities. For example, they support no member functions and are not dynamic in nature. Despite their restrictions, arrays can be used in conjunction with the STL algorithms. Of course, when using the STL, it is usually easier to employ **vector** when an array-like object

Arrays are limited-capability containers.

is needed. Nevertheless, standard arrays and the STL are compatible. We haven't made use of this fact prior to this point because this book is about the STL, proper. However, there is no reason that you cannot use a standard array as a container when your application allows it.

For standard arrays, an iterator is a pointer.

As applied to an array, an iterator and a pointer are one-and-the-same. Thus, to obtain an iterator to the start of an array, use the address of its first element. By definition, iterators to an array are random-access.

The following program shows how an array can be used as a target or a source in an algorithm:

```cpp
// Using an array as a container.
#include <iostream>
#include <list>
#include <algorithm>
using namespace std;

int main()
{
  list<int> lst(10);
  list<int>::iterator p;
  int *ip, *ip_end;
  int nums[10] = { 0, 1, 2, 3, 4, 5, 6, 7, 8, 9};
  int i;

  cout << "Initial contents of nums: ";
  for(i=0; i<10; i++)
    cout << nums[i] << " ";
  cout << endl;


  // copy nums array to list
  copy(nums, &nums[9], lst.begin());

  cout << "Contents of lst after copy: ";
  for(p=lst.begin(); p!=lst.end(); p++)
    cout << *p << " ";
  cout << endl;
```

12

```
  // remove elements that are less than 5
  ip_end = remove_copy_if(lst.begin(), lst.end(),
            nums, bind2nd(less<int>(), 5));

  cout << "Contents of nums after remove_copy_if(): ";
  for(ip=nums; ip!=ip_end; ip++)
    cout << *ip << " ";

  return 0;
}
```

Here is the output from the program:

```
Initial contents of nums: 0 1 2 3 4 5 6 7 8 9
Contents of lst after copy: 0 1 2 3 4 5 6 7 8 0
Contents of nums after remove_copy_if(): 5 6 7 8
```

In the program, the integer array **nums** is initialized with the values 0 through 9. Then, **nums** is used with the **copy( )** algorithm to copy those values to **lst**, which is an object of type **list**. Notice that the addresses of the first and the last elements in **nums** are the first two parameters to **copy( )**. As explained, pointers to array elements are iterators. Next, elements that are less than 5 are removed from **lst** and the result is put into **nums**. Here, a pointer to the first element in **nums** is passed to **remove_copy_if( )** and a pointer to the last element in the range copied to **nums** is returned.

Since vectors provide a superior alternative, most programmers will use them rather than standard arrays when implementing STL-based solutions. However, don't overlook algorithms as a handy means of managing arrays. Although more or less a side benefit, the ability of the STL to operate on arrays is a convenience that you should not ignore.

bitset

The International Standard for C++ includes in its description of containers one that was not part of the original STL specification: **bitset**. It was not discussed earlier because it is not a fully formed container. However, since the C++ standard includes it in its section on containers, it merits inclusion in this book.

bitset is a
container of
bits.

The **bitset** class supports operations on a set of bits. Its template
specification is

    template <size_t N> class bitset;

Here, N specifies the length of the bitset, in bits. It has the following
constructors:

    bitset( );

    bitset(unsigned long *bits*);

    explicit bitset(const string &*s*, size_t i = 0, size_t *num* = npos);

The first form constructs an empty bitset. The second form constructs a bitset
that has its bits set according to those specified in *bits*. The third form
constructs a bitset using the string *s*, beginning at *i*. The string must contain
only 1s and 0s. Only *num* or *s*.**size( )**-*i* values are used, whichever is less. The
constant **npos** is a value that is sufficiently large to describe the maximum
length of *s*. To use **bitset**, include the header **<bitset>**.

The output operators **<<** and **>>** are defined for **bitset**.

The **bitset** class contains the member functions shown in Table 12-2.

The **iterator** type is not defined for **bitset**. Thus, you cannot use iterators to
access the elements in a bitset and functions such as **begin( )** or **end( )** are
not defined. This limits the number of algorithms in which a bitset may be
used directly.

Member	Description
bool any( ) const;	Returns **true** if any bit in the invoking bitset is 1. It returns **false**, otherwise.
size_type count( ) const;	Returns the number of 1 bits.
bitset<N> &flip( );	Reverses the state of all bits in the invoking bitset and returns ***this**.
bitset<N> &flip(size_t i);	Reverses the bit in position i in the invoking bitset and returns ***this**.

The **bitset**
Member
Functions
Table 12-2.

12

Member	Description
bool none( ) const;	Returns **true** if no bits are set in the invoking bitset.
bool operator !=(const bitset<N> &*op2*) const;	Returns **true** if the invoking bitset differs from the one specified by right-hand operator, *op2*.
bool operator ==(const bitset<N> &*op2*) const;	Returns **true** if the invoking bitset is the same as the one specified by right-hand operator, *op2*.
bitset<N> &operator &=(const bitset<N> &*op2*);	ANDs each bit in the invoking bitset with the corresponding bit in *op2* and leaves the result in the invoking bitset. It returns ***this**.
bitset<N> &operator ^=(const bitset<N> &*op2*);	XORs each bit in the invoking bitset with the corresponding bit in *op2* and leaves the result in the invoking bitset. It returns ***this**.
bitset<N> &operator |=(const bitset<N> &*op2*);	ORs each bit in the invoking bitset with the corresponding bit in *op2* and leaves the result in the invoking bitset. It returns ***this**.
bitset<N> &operator ~=( ) const;	Reverses the state of all bits in the invoking bitset and returns the result.
bitset<N> &operator <<(size_t *num*);	Left-shifts each bit in the invoking bitset *num* positions and returns the result.
bitset<N> &operator >>(size_t *num*);	Right-shifts each bit in the invoking bitset *num* positions and returns the result.
bitset<N> &operator <<=(size_t *num*);	Left-shifts each bit in the invoking bitset *num* positions and leaves the result in the invoking bitset. It returns ***this**.
bitset<N> &operator >>=(size_t *num*);	Right-shifts each bit in the invoking bitset *num* positions and leaves the result in the invoking bitset. It returns ***this**.

The **bitset**
Member
Functions
(continued)
Table 12-2.

Member	Description
reference operator [ ](size_type *i*);	Returns a reference to bit *i* in the invoking bitset.
bitset<N> &reset( );	Clears all bits in the invoking bitset and returns ***this**.
bitset<N> &reset(size_t *i*);	Clears the bit in position *i* in the invoking bitset and returns ***this**.
bitset<N> &set( );	Sets all bits in the invoking bitset and returns ***this**.
bitset<N> &set(size_t *i*, int *val* = 1);	Sets the bit in position *i* to the value specified by *val* in the invoking bitset and returns ***this**. Any nonzero value for *val* is assumed to be 1.
size_t size( ) const;	Returns the number of bits that the bitset can hold.
bool test(size_t *i*) const;	Returns the state of the bit in position *i*.
string to_string( ) const;	Returns a string that contains a representation of the bit pattern in the invoking bitset.
unsigned long to_ulong( ) const;	Converts the invoking bitset into an unsigned long integer.

The **bitset** Member Functions *(continued)*
Table 12-2.

Here is a program that demonstrates **bitset** and several of its member functions:

```
// Demonstrate bitset
#include <iostream>
#include <bitset>
using namespace std;

int main()
{
  bitset<16> b(32);
  bitset<16> b2(0);
```

12

```
    cout << "Original bits:              ";
    cout << b;
    cout << endl;

    // assign bits
    b[0] - 1;
    b[2] = 1;
    b[10] = 1;
    b[12] = 1;

    cout << "Bits after assignment:   ";
    cout << b;
    cout << endl;

    // rotate bits
    b <<= 2;
    cout << "Bits after left rotate: ";
    cout << b;
    cout << endl;

    // flip bits
    cout << "After flipping bits:     ";
    b.flip();
    cout << b;
    cout << endl;

    // see if any bits set
    if(b.any()) cout << "b has at least 1 bit set.\n";

    // count set bits
    cout << "b has " << b.count();
    cout << " bits set.\n";

    // test bits three different ways
    if(b[0] == 1)
      cout << "bit 0 is on\n";
    if(b.test(1))
      cout << "bit 1 is on\n";
    if(b.at(2) == 1)
      cout << "bit 2 is on\n";

    // can add bits to integers
    cout << "Add 11 to bit 0: " << b[0] + 11 << endl;

    return 0;
}
```

Here is the output produced by the program:

```
Original bits:          0000000000100000
Bits after assignment:  0001010000100101
Bits after left rotate: 0101000010010100
After flipping bits:    1010111101101011
b has at least 1 bit set.
b has 11 bits set.
bit 0 is on
bit 1 is on
Add 11 to bit 0: 12
```

Bitsets provide a useful alternative to bitfields and their container-like qualities make using them very convenient for STL-versed programmers. They are, as mentioned earlier, not full-featured containers and they cannot participate in most algorithms.

Custom Containers

As has been mentioned many times in this book, the STL is extensible. You can create your own algorithms (as shown in Chapter 9), your own allocators, and even your own containers. While it might seem a daunting task at first, creating your own container can be quite easy—especially if only limited capabilities are required. The remainder of this chapter describes the process. We will begin by examining the container requirements. We will conclude by creating a container, showing how it can be fully integrated into the STL landscape.

Container Requirements

Before designing a container, it is necessary to know precisely what it must provide. According to Standard C++, all containers must supply a prescribed set of types, operators, and member functions. In addition to these common elements, both sequence and associative containers add several specific requirements.

12

General Requirements

Every container must provide an allocator. Typically, you can use the default allocator provided by **allocator**.

Every container must provide these types:

iterator	const_iterator	reference	const_reference
value_type	size_type	difference_type	

A reversible
container
supports
bidirectional
iterators.

A reversible container (one that supports bidirectional iterators) must also supply these types:

reverse_iterator	const_reverse_iterator

All containers must provide a default constructor, which creates a zero-length container, a copy constructor, and parameterized constructors, the precise form of which differs between sequence and associative containers. A destructor is also required.

The following member functions must be supported:

begin( )	clear( )	empty( )	end( )
erase( )	insert( )	max_size( )	rbegin( )
rend( )	size( )	swap( )	

Of course, **rbegin( )** and **rend( )** are only needed by reversible containers. Some functions require one or more overloaded forms. The forms of the member functions can be determined by looking at any of the built-in containers described earlier.

The fact that a container must define the iterator functions, such as **begin( )**, implies that the container must support all required iterator operations.

The following operators must be supported by all containers:

=	= =	!=	>
<	<=	>=	

One other point: the complexity of the various elements of a container is also specified by Standard C++ and is the same as those for the built-in containers.

Additional Sequence Container Requirements

In addition to a default constructor and a copy constructor, a sequence container must supply a constructor that creates and initializes a specified number of elements. It must also provide a constructor that creates and initializes an object given a range of elements. That is, the following forms of constructors must be supported:

Cnt( )

Cnt(c)

Cnt(num, val)

Cnt(start, end)

Here, *c* is an object of type *Cnt*, *num* is an integer specifying a count, *val* is a value compatible with the type of objects stored in *Cnt*, and *start* and *end* are iterators to a range of elements that will be used to initialize the container.

Standard C++ defines the following optional member functions for sequence containers:

at( )	back( )	front( )	pop_back( )
pop_front( )	push_back( )	push_front( )	

The subscript operator **[ ]** is also optional. Of course, you can also add other member functions of your own design.

Additional Associative Container Requirements

All associative containers must define these additional types:

key_compare	key_type	value_compare

Along with a default constructor and a copy constructor, an associative container must supply constructors that allow you to specify a comparison function. You must also define a constructor that creates and initializes an object given a range of elements. One version of this constructor must use

12

the default comparison function. Another must allow the user to specify the comparison function. That is, the following forms of constructors must be supported:

Cnt( )

Cnt(c)

Cnt(comp)

Cnt(start, end)

Cnt(start, end, comp)

Here, *c* is an object of type *Cnt*, *start* and *end* are iterators to a range of elements that will be used to initialize the container, and *comp* is a comparison function.

Associative containers must provide these additional member functions:

count( )	equal_range( )	find( )	key_comp( )
lower_bound( )	upper_bound( )	value_comp( )	

Creating A Negative-Indexable Array Container

To conclude this book, we will develop a custom container that supports a special type of dynamic array. While the example shown here illustrates the creation of a sequence container, most of the concepts can be applied to the implementation of associative containers, as well.

As you know, in C++, all arrays begin at zero and negative indexes are not allowed. However, some applications would benefit from an array that allows negative indexes. Consider the Cartesian coordinate plane. Each axis is a line that has both positive and negative values. A convenient way to represent such a line in a program would be to use an array that allows negative as well as positive indexes. For example, given a line that runs from –5 to 5, you would like to use an array that could be indexed as shown here:

| -5 | -4 | -3 | -2 | -1 | 0 | 1 | 2 | 3 | 4 | 5 |

In this section, we will develop a container that supports just such an array.

The container developed is called **NP_Array**, which is short for Negative-Positive Array. It is a dynamic container that allows the array to grow in both the positive and negative directions. It can be indexed using both positive and negative values. It supports all of the required sequence container operations, plus the optional **[ ]** operator.

Using **NP_Array**, you can write code like this:

```
NP_Array<int> o(5, 3); // array that runs from -3 to 4

// load the values -3 to 4 into o
for(i = -3; i<5; i++) o[i] = i;
o[-2] = 99;
o[0] = 0[-1];
```

As you can guess, the first line constructs an **NP_Array** object that runs from –3 to 4. **NP_Array** allows you to construct objects by specifying the positive and negative extents of each index. That is, **NP_Array** allows the following form of constructor:

  NP_Array(*positive_extent*, *negative_extent*)

By convention, the positive extent includes the zero index, so the one shown above runs from –3 to 4. Once the array has been constructed, it can be indexed by any value that is within its range. This means that negative indexes are allowed.

Because **NP_Array** is dynamic, it allows elements to be inserted or removed. When either of these operations occurs, the array grows or shrinks as needed. The key point, however, is that the array grows or shrinks in either direction. If an element is added to the negative side, the negative side grows. If an element is removed from the positive side, the positive shrinks. However, in all cases, an insertion or deletion does not disrupt the zero point of the array.

Before starting, it is necessary to point out that the implementation of the **NP_Array** container is, by intent, not optimized for high performance. Its purpose is to clearly show the steps required to create a custom container. As such, it is designed for ease of understanding and straightforwardness of implementation. You might find it enjoyable to expand and optimize its performance on your own.

12

The Entire NP_Array Class

We will begin by showing the entire **NP_Array** class and its relational operators. As you will find when you create your own container classes, even a simple container turns into a fairly large class. The reason for this is, of course, that there are several requirements that must be met. While no single requirement is difficult, combined they still present a fair bit of code. Don't be intimidated; we will look at each part, piece by piece.

```
/* A simplified, custom container that implements an
   array that allows both positive and negative indexes.

   Call this file np_a.h
*/
#include <iostream>
#include <iterator>
#include <algorithm>
using namespace std;

template<class T, class Allocator = allocator<T> >
class NP_Array {
  T *c; // pointer to array of elements
  unsigned zero; // hold location of zero index
  unsigned pos_extent; // extent in positive direction
  unsigned neg_extent; // extent in negative direction
  Allocator a; // allocator
public:
  typedef T value_type;
  typedef Allocator allocator_type;
  typedef Allocator::reference reference;
  typedef Allocator::const_reference const_reference;
  typedef Allocator::size_type size_type;
  typedef Allocator::difference_type difference_type;
  typedef Allocator::pointer pointer;
  typedef Allocator::const_pointer const_pointer;

  // forward iterators
  typedef T * iterator;
  typedef const T * const_iterator;
  /* This container does not support reverse iterators,
     but you can add them if you like. */
```

```
// ********  Constructors and Destructor **************

// default constructor
NP_Array()
{
  pos_extent = neg_extent = 0;
  zero = 0;
  c = a.allocate(0, 0);
}

// construct object of specified dimensions
NP_Array(unsigned p, unsigned n, const T &t=T())
{
  c = a.allocate(p+n, 0);
  pos_extent = p;
  neg_extent = n;
  zero = n;
  for(int i=0; i<size(); i++) a.construct(&c[i], t);
}

// construct from range
NP_Array(iterator start, iterator stop)
{
  c = a.allocate(stop-start, 0);
  pos_extent = stop-start;
  neg_extent = 0;
  zero = 0;
  for(int i=0; i<size(); i++)
    a.construct(&c[i], *start++);
}

// copy constructor
NP_Array(const NP_Array &o)
{
  c = a.allocate(o.size(), 0);
  pos_extent = o.pos_extent;
  neg_extent = o.neg_extent;
  zero = o.zero;
  for(int i=0; i<size(); i++)
    c[i] = o.c[i];
}

// destructor
~NP_Array()
{
```

12

```
  for(int i=0; i<size(); i++) a.destroy(&c[i]);
  a.deallocate(c, size());
}

// ********  Operator Functions **************

T &operator[](int i)
{
  return c[zero+i];
}

const T &operator[](int i) const
{
  return c[zero+i];
}

NP_Array &operator=(const NP_Array &o)
{
  a.deallocate(c, size());
  c = a.allocate(o.size(), 0);
  pos_extent = o.pos_extent;
  neg_extent = o.neg_extent;
  zero = o.zero;
  for(int i=0; i<size(); i++)
    a.construct(&c[i], o.c[i]);
  return *this;
}

// ********  Insert Functions **************
iterator insert(iterator p, const T &val)
{
  iterator q;
  T *tmp = a.allocate(size()+1, 0);
  register int i, j;

  /* copy existing elements to new array, inserting
     new element if possible */
  for(i=j=0; i<size(); i++, j++) {
    if(&c[i] == p) {
      tmp[j] = val;
      j++;
      q = &tmp[j];
    }
    tmp[j] = c[i];
  }
```

```
      if(p == end()) { // new element goes on end
        tmp[j] = val;
        q = &tmp[j];
      }

      // adjust zero point as needed
      if(p < &c[zero]) {
        zero++;
        neg_extent++;
      }
      else
        pos_extent++;

      a.deallocate(c, size());

      c = tmp;

      return q;
    }

    void insert(iterator p, int num, const T &val)
    {
      for(; num>0; num--) p = insert(p, val);
    }

    void insert(iterator p, iterator start, iterator stop)
    {
      while(start != stop) {
        p = insert(p, *start);
        start++;
      }
    }

    // ********  Erase Functions **************
    iterator erase(iterator p)
    {
      iterator q = p;

      if(p != end()) a.destroy(p);

      // adjust zero point as needed
      if(p < &c[zero]) {
        neg_extent--;
        zero--;
      }
```

12

```cpp
    else
      pos_extent--;

    // compact remaining elements
    for( ; p<end(); p++)
      *p = *(p+1);

    return q;
}

iterator erase(iterator start, iterator stop)
{
  iterator p = end();
  int i;

  for(i=stop-start; i>0; i--)
    p = erase(start);

  return p;
}

// ********  Push and Pop Functions *************
void push_back(const T &val)
{
  insert(end(), val);
}

void pop_back()
{
  erase(end()-1);
}

// ********  Iterator Functions *************
iterator begin()
{
  return &c[0];
}

iterator end()
{
  return &c[pos_extent+neg_extent];
}

const_iterator begin() const
{
```

```
    return &c[0];
  }

  const_iterator end() const
  {
    return &c[pos_extent+neg_extent];
  }

  // ********  Misc. Functions **************
  size_type size() const
  {
    return end()-begin();
  }

  bool empty()
  {
    return size() == 0;
  }

  void swap(NP_Array &b)
  {
    NP_Array<T> tmp;

    tmp = *this;
    *this = b;
    b = tmp;
  }

  void clear()
  {
    for(int i=0; i<size(); i++) {
      a.destroy(&c[i]);
    }
    pos_extent = neg_extent = 0;
  }

  // return extents
  int get_neg_ext()
  {
    return neg_extent;
  }

  int get_pos_ext()
  {
    return pos_extent;
  }
```

12

```cpp
   // ******** Options To Add *****************
   /* For fun, try adding the following features:
       . reverse iterators
       . rbegin() and rend()
       . the at() function
       . pop_front() and push_front()
   */
};


// ********  Relational Operators **************

template<class T, class Allocator>
  bool operator==(const NP_Array<T, Allocator> &a,
                  const NP_Array<T, Allocator> &b)
{
  if(a.size() != b.size()) return false;

  return equal(a.begin(), a.end(), b.begin());
}


template<class T, class Allocator>
  bool operator!=(const NP_Array<T, Allocator> &a,
                  const NP_Array<T, Allocator> &b)
{
  return !equal(a.begin(), a.end(), b.begin());
}


template<class T, class Allocator>
  bool operator<(const NP_Array<T, Allocator> &a,
                 const NP_Array<T, Allocator> &b)
{
  return lexicographical_compare(a.begin(), a.end(),
                                 b.begin(), b.end());
}


template<class T, class Allocator>
  bool operator>(const NP_Array<T, Allocator> &a,
                 const NP_Array<T, Allocator> &b)
{
  return b < a;
}


template<class T, class Allocator>
  bool operator<=(const NP_Array<T, Allocator> &a,
                  const NP_Array<T, Allocator> &b)
```

```
{
  return !(a > b);
}

template<class T, class Allocator>
  bool operator>=(const NP_Array<T, Allocator> &a,
                  const NP_Array<T, Allocator> &b)
{
  return !(a < b);
}
```

As the comment at the top indicates, you should put all of this code into a file called **np_a.h**. It will be used by the sample programs shown later.

A Close Look at the NP_Array Class

Let's examine each part of the **NP_Array** class in detail. Like all of the built-in sequence containers, **NP_Array** begins with the following template specification:

> template<class T, class Allocator = allocator<T> >

As expected, **T** is the type of data stored in the container and **Allocator** is the allocator, which defaults to the standard allocator.

The Private Members

The **NP_Array** array class begins with the following private declarations:

```
T *c; // pointer to array of elements
unsigned zero; // hold location of zero index
unsigned pos_extent; // extent in positive direction
unsigned neg_extent; // extent in negative direction
Allocator a; // allocator
```

The pointer **c** stores a pointer to the memory that will contain an array of elements of type **T**. That is, the memory pointed to by **c** will store the elements held by an object of type **NP_Array**. This array will be indexed as usual, from zero to *N*. Indexes to an **NP_Array** object will be translated into zero-based indexes into the array pointed to by **c**.

Although an **NP_Array** container can grow in both the positive and negative directions, it requires that one index be fixed so as to provide a frame of reference for the translation of indexes. The one location that all arrays will have is zero. The **zero** member stores the index of where the zero

12

element is located in the array pointed to by **c**. As you will see, much use is made of this member.

The positive and negative extents of the array are stored in **pos_extent** and **neg_extent**, respectively. For our purposes, zero is counted as a positive value.

The allocator for the container is stored in **a**.

The Required Type Definitions

After the private members, **NP_Array** defines the various **typedef**s required by all sequence containers. They are shown here:

```
typedef T value_type;
typedef Allocator allocator_type;
typedef Allocator::reference reference;
typedef Allocator::const_reference const_reference;
typedef Allocator::size_type size_type;
typedef Allocator::difference_type difference_type;
typedef Allocator::pointer pointer;
typedef Allocator::const_pointer const_pointer;

// forward iterators
typedef T * iterator;
typedef const T * const_iterator;
/* This container does not support reverse iterators,
   but you can add them if you like. */
```

These are similar to the ones used by the built-in containers described in earlier chapters. Notice that the forward iterators are simply pointers to objects of type **T**. This is sufficient for the purpose of **NP_Array**, but might not be for more complicated containers. Also, reverse iterators are not provided, but you might want to try adding them as an interesting exercise.

The NP_Array Constructors and Destructor

To create a compliant container, you must support a variety of constructors. The ones required by **NP_Array** are shown here:

```
// default constructor
NP_Array()
{
  pos_extent = neg_extent = 0;
  zero = 0;
  c = a.allocate(0, 0);
}
```

```
// construct object of specified dimensions
NP_Array(unsigned p, unsigned n, const T &t=T())
{
  c = a.allocate(p+n, 0);
  pos_extent = p;
  neg_extent = n;
  zero = n;
  for(int i=0; i<size(); i++) a.construct(&c[i], t);
}

// construct from range
NP_Array(iterator start, iterator stop)
{
  c = a.allocate(stop-start, 0);
  pos_extent = stop-start;
  neg_extent = 0;
  zero = 0;
  for(int i=0; i<size(); i++)
    a.construct(&c[i], *start++);
}

// copy constructor
NP_Array(const NP_Array &o)
{
  c = a.allocate(o.size(), 0);
  pos_extent = o.pos_extent;
  neg_extent = o.neg_extent;
  zero = o.zero;
  for(int i=0; i<size(); i++)
    c[i] = o.c[i];
}
```

The default constructor creates an empty object. One of the constraints specified by the STL is that the result of calling **size( )** on a default object must be zero. Therefore, the default constructor sets the positive and negative extents to zero. It also sets **zero** to zero and constructs a zero-length array using the **allocate( )** function provided by the allocator. The last two steps ensure that a fully formed object exists in all cases.

The next constructor creates an object with a specified range. The positive extent is specified in the first parameter and the negative extent is specified

12

in the second. As stated, the zero index is assumed to be part of the positive extent. Thus, this statement

```
NP_Array<char> ch(10, 2);
```

creates a negative-positive array that begins at –2 and runs through 9. The array is allocated using **allocate( )**. To be a compliant container, you must use the allocator functions, rather than calling **new**, to obtain memory required by the container. Once allocated, each element in the array is constructed using either the value passed as the third parameter or by using the default constructor for the elements. The construction is accomplished using the allocator function **construct( )**.

The third constructor creates a new object from a range of values. In this case, the array is created such that it begins at zero.

Last is the copy constructor. It allocates memory for the new object and then copies the extents, zero location, and elements from the source object. Thus, the copy uses its own memory but is otherwise identical to the source.

The **NP_Array** destructor is shown here:

```
// destructor
~NP_Array()
{
  for(int i=0; i<size(); i++) a.destroy(&c[i]);
  a.deallocate(c, size());
}
```

It first destroys each element in the array by calling the allocator's **destroy( )** function, which by default calls **delete**. It then frees the memory used by the array.

The NP_Array Operator Functions

There are three member operator functions defined by **NP_Array**. The first two are the **operator[ ]( )** functions shown here:

```
T &operator[](int i)
{
  return c[zero+i];
}
```

```
const T &operator[](int i) const
{
  return c[zero+i];
}
```

For a fully formed container, both **const** and non-**const** versions of the **[ ]** operator are required. While quite short, these functions provide the mechanism by which the **NP_Array** can be indexed with positive and negative values. Since **zero** holds the index of the value within the array pointed to by **c** that corresponds to the location of the zero index within the negative-positive array, the value of **zero** is simply added to the index passed in **i**, providing the needed translation.

The **operator=( )** function shown here is a bit more complex:

```
NP_Array &operator=(const NP_Array &o)
{
  a.deallocate(c, size());
  c = a.allocate(o.size(), 0);
  pos_extent = o.pos_extent;
  neg_extent = o.neg_extent;
  zero = o.zero;
  for(int i=0; i<size(); i++)
    a.construct(&c[i], o.c[i]);
  return *this;
}
```

It first frees the memory used by the previous contents of the target object. It then allocates sufficient memory to hold the contents of the source object. It sets the member variables appropriately and then copies the elements. Notice that the elements are constructed as they are inserted into the target array.

The Insert Functions

The STL requires that a sequence container support three forms of **insert( )**: one that inserts a value, one that inserts multiple copies of a value, and one that inserts a range. The versions of **insert( )** defined for **NP_Array** are shown here:

12

```
iterator insert(iterator p, const T &val)
{
  iterator q;
  T *tmp = a.allocate(size()+1, 0);
  register int i, j;
```

```
    /* copy existing elements to new array, inserting
       new element if possible */
    for(i=j=0; i<size(); i++, j++) {
      if(&c[i] == p) {
        tmp[j] = val;
        j++;
        q = &tmp[j];
      }
      tmp[j] = c[i];
    }
    if(p == end()) { // new element goes on end
      tmp[j] = val;
      q = &tmp[j];
    }

    // adjust zero point as needed
    if(p < &c[zero]) {
      zero++;
      neg_extent++;
    }
    else
      pos_extent++;

    a.deallocate(c, size());

    c = tmp;

    return q;
  }

  void insert(iterator p, int num, const T &val)
  {
    for(; num>0; num--) p = insert(p, val);
  }

  void insert(iterator p, iterator start, iterator stop)
  {
    while(start != stop) {
      p = insert(p, *start);
      start++;
    }
  }
```

As you can see, the second two versions of **insert( )** are defined in terms of the first. The first version inserts an element at the location specified by the iterator passed as its first parameter. It returns an iterator to the inserted element. It operates by allocating a new segment of memory that is large enough to hold all of the existing elements plus the new one. It then copies the existing elements to the newly allocated memory, inserting the new element at the proper location. It then deallocates the original memory used by the object, updates the object's member variables appropriately, assigns a pointer to the new memory to **c**, and returns a pointer to the inserted object.

Notice the code that updates the **pos_extent** and **neg_extent** variables. Remember: the array can grow in either the positive or negative direction, based upon whether the new element is inserted on the positive side or the negative side of the array. Thus, it is necessary to determine where the insertion takes place and change the proper extent. This is determined by comparing the iterator passed in **p** to the address of the zero element. If the iterator is less than the zero element, then the negative side is expanding; otherwise, the positive end is growing.

The Erase Functions

Sequence containers must support two **erase( )** functions: one that removes the element pointed to by an iterator and one that removes a range of elements. Both functions return an iterator to the element immediately after the one removed, or **end( )** if the last element is removed. The **NP_Array** versions of these functions are shown here:

```
iterator erase(iterator p)
{
  iterator q = p;

  if(p != end()) a.destroy(p);

  // adjust zero point as needed
  if(p < &c[zero]) {
    neg_extent--;
    zero--;
  }
  else
    pos_extent--;

  // compact remaining elements
  for( ; p<end(); p++)
    *p = *(p+1);
```

12

```
    return q;
}

iterator erase(iterator start, iterator stop)
{
  iterator p = end();
  int i;

  for(i=stop-start; i>0; i--)
    p = erase(start);

  return p;
}
```

The second version is framed in terms of the first. The first version operates by destroying the deleted element, adjusting the positive and negative extent values appropriately, and then compacting the remaining elements.

The Push and Pop Functions
NP_Array implements **push_back( )** and **pop_back( )**. They are shown here. As you can see, they are implemented in terms of **insert( )** and **erase( )**.

```
void push_back(const T &val)
{
  insert(end(), val);
}

void pop_back()
{
  erase(end()-1);
}
```

For fun, you might want to implement **push_front( )** and **pop_front( )**. They are only slight variations on the ones shown.

The Iterator Functions
Because iterators for the **NP_Array** container are simply pointers into the memory pointed to by **c**, the iterator functions **begin( )** and **end( )** are trivial. However, notice that both **const** and non-**const** versions are required.

```
iterator begin()
{
  return &c[0];
}

iterator end()
{
  return &c[pos_extent+neg_extent];
}

const_iterator begin() const
{
  return &c[0];
}

const_iterator end() const
{
  return &c[pos_extent+neg_extent];
}
```

Miscellaneous Functions

All sequence containers must implement **size( )**, **empty( )**, **swap( )**, and **clear( )**. **NP_Array** also provides **get_neg_ext( )** and **get_pos_ext( )**, which allow the user to obtain the negative and positive extents, respectively. These functions are shown here. Their operation is straightforward.

```
size_type size() const
{
  return end()-begin();
}

bool empty()
{
  return size() == 0;
}

void swap(NP_Array &b)
{
  NP_Array<T> tmp;

  tmp = *this;
  *this = b;
  b = tmp;
}
```

12

```
void clear()
{
  for(int i=0; i<size(); i++) {
    a.destroy(&c[i]);
  }
  pos_extent = neg_extent = 0;
}

// return extents
int get_neg_ext()
{
  return neg_extent;
}

int get_pos_ext()
{
  return pos_extent;
}
```

The Relational Operators

The relational operators defined for **NP_Array** are shown here:

```
template<class T, class Allocator>
  bool operator==(const NP_Array<T, Allocator> &a,
                  const NP_Array<T, Allocator> &b)
{
  if(a.size() != b.size()) return false;

  return equal(a.begin(), a.end(), b.begin());
}

template<class T, class Allocator>
  bool operator!=(const NP_Array<T, Allocator> &a,
                  const NP_Array<T, Allocator> &b)
{
  return !equal(a.begin(), a.end(), b.begin());
}

template<class T, class Allocator>
  bool operator<(const NP_Array<T, Allocator> &a,
                 const NP_Array<T, Allocator> &b)
{
  return lexicographical_compare(a.begin(), a.end(),
```

```
                                          b.begin(), b.end());
}

template<class T, class Allocator>
  bool operator>(const NP_Array<T, Allocator> &a,
                 const NP_Array<T, Allocator> &b)
{
  return b < a;
}

template<class T, class Allocator>
  bool operator<=(const NP_Array<T, Allocator> &a,
                  const NP_Array<T, Allocator> &b)
{
  return !(a > b);
}

template<class T, class Allocator>
  bool operator>=(const NP_Array<T, Allocator> &a,
                  const NP_Array<T, Allocator> &b)
{
  return !(a < b);
}
```

Both **operator=( )** and **operator!=( )** use the **equal( )** algorithm to determine equality. As defined by **equal( )**, two objects are the same if each contains the same elements, in the same order.

The **<** operator uses **lexicographical_compare( )** to determine when one object is less than another. The use of this function is recommended by Standard C++. It operates by comparing corresponding elements in the two sequences, searching for the first mismatch. If a mismatch is found, it returns **true** if the element from the first range is less than the element from the second range. It returns **false** otherwise.

Some NP_Array Sample Programs

12

To demonstrate **NP_Array**, three sample programs are shown. Here is the first one. It exercises the various member functions. It also employs three algorithms, a function object, and a function adaptor.

```
// Demonstrate basic NP_Array operations.
#include <iostream>
#include <algorithm>
```

```
#include <functional>
#include "np_a.h"
using namespace std;

// display integers
void display(int v)
{
  cout << v << " ";
}

int main()
{
  NP_Array<int> ob(5, 5);
  NP_Array<int>::iterator p;
  int i, sum;

  cout << "Size of ob is: " << ob.size() << endl;

  cout << "Initial contents of ob:\n";
  for(i=-5; i<5; i++) cout << ob[i] << " ";
  cout << endl;

  // give ob some values
  for(i=-5; i<5; i++) ob[i] = i;

  cout << "New values for ob: \n";
  p = ob.begin();
  do {
    cout << *p++ << " ";
  } while (p!=ob.end());
  cout << endl;

  // display sum of negative indexes
  sum = 0;
  for(i = -ob.get_neg_ext(); i<0; i++)
    sum += ob[i];
  cout << "Sum of values with negative subscripts is: ";
  cout << sum << "\n\n";

  // use copy() to copy one object to another
  cout << "Copy ob to ob2 using copy() algorithm.\n";
  NP_Array<int> ob2(ob.get_pos_ext(), ob.get_neg_ext());
  copy(ob.begin(), ob.end(), ob2.begin());
```

```
// use for_each() algorithm to display ob2
cout << "Contents of ob2: \n";
for_each(ob2.begin(), ob2.end(), display);
cout << endl;

// use remove_copy_if() to remove those values less than 0
cout << "Remove values less than zero and";
cout << " put result into ob3.\n";
NP_Array<int> ob3(ob.get_pos_ext(), ob.get_neg_ext());
replace_copy_if(ob.begin(), ob.end(), ob3.begin(),
                bind2nd(less<int>(), 0), 0);
cout << "Contents of ob3: \n";
for_each(ob3.begin(), ob3.end(), display);
cout << "\n\n";

cout << "Swap ob and ob3.\n";
ob.swap(ob3); // swap ob and ob3
cout << "Here is ob3:\n";
for_each(ob3.begin(), ob3.end(), display);
cout << endl;
cout << "Swap again to restore.\n";
ob.swap(ob3); // restore
cout << "Here is ob3 after second swap:\n";
for_each(ob3.begin(), ob3.end(), display);
cout << "\n\n";

// use insert() member functions
cout << "Element at ob[0] is " << ob[0] << endl;
cout << "Insert values into ob.\n";
ob.insert(ob.end(), -9999);
ob.insert(&ob[1], 99);
ob.insert(&ob[-3], -99);
for_each(ob.begin(), ob.end(), display);
cout << endl;
cout << "Element at ob[0] is " << ob[0] << endl;
cout << endl;

cout << "Insert -7 three times to front of ob.\n";
ob.insert(ob.begin(), 3, -7);
for_each(ob.begin(), ob.end(), display);
cout << endl;
cout << "Element at ob[0] is " << ob[0] << endl;
cout << endl;
```

12

```cpp
// use push_back() and pop_back()
cout << "Push back the value 40 onto ob.\n";
ob.push_back(40);
for_each(ob.begin(), ob.end(), display);
cout << endl;
cout << "Pop back two values from ob.\n";
ob.pop_back(); ob.pop_back();
for_each(ob.begin(), ob.end(), display);
cout << "\n\n";

// use erase()
cout << "Erase element at 0.\n";
p = ob.erase(&ob[0]);
for_each(ob.begin(), ob.end(), display);
cout << endl;
cout << "Element at ob[0] is " << ob[0] << endl;
cout << endl;

cout << "Erase many elements in ob.\n";
p = ob.erase(&ob[-2], &ob[3]);
for_each(ob.begin(), ob.end(), display);
cout << endl;
cout << "Element at ob[0] is " << ob[0] << endl;
cout << endl;

cout << "Insert ob4 into ob.\n";
NP_Array<int> ob4(3, 0);
for(i=0; i<3; i++) ob4[i] = i+100;
ob.insert(&ob[0], ob4.begin(), ob4.end());
for_each(ob.begin(), ob.end(), display);
cout << endl;
cout << "Element at ob[0] is " << ob[0] << endl;
cout << endl;

cout << "Here is ob shown with its indices:\n";
for(i=-ob.get_neg_ext(); i<ob.get_pos_ext(); i++)
  cout << "[" << i << "]: " << ob[i] << endl;
cout << endl;

cout << "Make a copy of ob2.\n";
NP_Array<int> ob5(ob2);
for_each(ob5.begin(), ob5.end(), display);
cout << "\n\n";
```

```
      cout << "Clear ob.\n";
      ob.clear();
      for_each(ob.begin(), ob.end(), display);
      cout << "Size of ob after clear: " << ob.size();
      cout << "\n\n";

      cout << "Construct object from a range.\n";
      NP_Array<int> ob6(&ob2[-2], ob2.end());
      cout << "Size of ob6: " << ob6.size() << endl;
      for_each(ob6.begin(), ob6.end(), display);
      cout << endl;

      return 0;
    }
```

The output from this program is shown here:

```
Size of ob is: 10
Initial contents of ob:
0 0 0 0 0 0 0 0 0 0
New values for ob:
-5 -4 -3 -2 -1 0 1 2 3 4
Sum of values with negative subscripts is: -15

Copy ob to ob2 using copy() algorithm.
Contents of ob2:
-5 -4 -3 -2 -1 0 1 2 3 4
Remove values less than zero and put result into ob3.
Contents of ob3:
0 0 0 0 0 0 1 2 3 4

Swap ob and ob3.
Here is ob3:
-5 -4 -3 -2 -1 0 1 2 3 4
Swap again to restore.
Here is ob3 after second swap:
0 0 0 0 0 0 1 2 3 4

Element at ob[0] is 0
Insert values into ob.
-5 -4 -99 -3 -2 -1 0 99 1 2 3 4 -9999
Element at ob[0] is 0

Insert -7 three times to front of ob.
-7 -7 -7 -5 -4 -99 -3 -2 -1 0 99 1 2 3 4 -9999
```

12

```
Element at ob[0] is 0

Push back the value 40 onto ob.
-7 -7 -7 -5 -4 -99 -3 -2 -1 0 99 1 2 3 4 -9999 40
Pop back two values from ob.
-7 -7 -7 -5 -4 -99 -3 -2 -1 0 99 1 2 3 4

Erase element at 0.
-7 -7 -7 -5 -4 -99 -3 -2 -1 99 1 2 3 4
Element at ob[0] is 99

Erase many elements in ob.
-7 -7 -7 -5 -4 -99 -3 3 4
Element at ob[0] is 3

Insert ob4 into ob.
-7 -7 -7 -5 -4 -99 -3 100 101 102 3 4
Element at ob[0] is 100

Here is ob shown with its indices:
[-7]: -7
[-6]: -7
[-5]: -7
[-4]: -5
[-3]: -4
[-2]: -99
[-1]: -3
[0]: 100
[1]: 101
[2]: 102
[3]: 3
[4]: 4

Make a copy of ob2.
-5 -4 -3 -2 -1 0 1 2 3 4

Clear ob.
Size of ob after clear: 0

Construct object from a range.
Size of ob6: 7
-2 -1 0 1 2 3 4
```

The next sample program demonstrates the relational operators:

```cpp
// Demonstrate the relational operators.
#include <iostream>
using namespace std;

#include "np_a.h"

// display integers
void display(int v)
{
  cout << v << " ";
}

int main()
{
  NP_Array<int> ob1(2, 3), ob2(2, 3), ob3(4, 4);
  int i;

  // give ob1 and ob2 some values
  for(i=-3; i<2; i++) {
    ob1[i] = i;
    ob2[i] = i;
  }

  cout << "Contents of ob1 and ob2:\n";
  for(i=-3; i<2; i++)
    cout << ob1[i] << " ";
  cout << endl;
  for(i=-3; i<2; i++)
    cout << ob2[i] << " ";
  cout << "\n\n";

  if(ob1 == ob2) cout << "ob1 == ob2\n";
  if(ob1 != ob2) cout << "error\n";
  cout << endl;

  cout << "Assign ob1[-1] the value 99\n";
  ob1[-1] = 99;
  cout << "Contents of ob1 is now:\n";
  for(i=-3; i<2; i++)
    cout << ob1[i] << " ";
  cout << endl;
```

12

```
   if(ob1 == ob2) cout << "error\n";
   if(ob1 != ob2) cout << "ob1 != ob2\n";
   cout << endl;

   if(ob1 < ob2) cout << "ob1 < ob2\n";
   if(ob1 <= ob2) cout << "ob1 <= ob2\n";
   if(ob1 > ob2) cout << "ob1 > ob2\n";
   if(ob1 >= ob2) cout << "ob1 >= ob2\n";

   if(ob2 < ob1) cout << "ob2 < ob1\n";
   if(ob2 <= ob1) cout << "ob2 <= ob1\n";
   if(ob2 > ob1) cout << "ob2 > ob1\n";
   if(ob2 >= ob1) cout << "ob2 >= ob1\n";
   cout << endl;

   // compare objects of differing sizes
   if(ob3 != ob1) cout << "ob3 != ob1";
   if(ob3 == ob1) cout << "ob3 == ob1";

   return 0;
}
```

Its output is shown here:

```
Contents of ob1 and ob2:
-3 -2 -1 0 1
-3 -2 -1 0 1

ob1 == ob2

Assign ob1[-1] the value 99
Contents of ob1 is now:
-3 -2 99 0 1
ob1 != ob2

ob1 > ob2
ob1 >= ob2
ob2 < ob1
ob2 <= ob1

ob3 != ob1
```

The following program stores class objects in an **NP_Array**. It also illustrates when the constructor and destructor functions are called when various operations take place.

```cpp
// Store class objects in an NP_Array.
#include <iostream>
#include "np_a.h"
using namespace std;

class test {
public:
  int a;
  test() { cout << "constructing\n"; a=0; }
  test(const test &o) {
    cout << "copy constructor\n";
    a = o.a;
  }
  ~test() { cout << "destructing\n"; }
};

int main()
{
  NP_Array<test> t(2, 3);
  int i;

  for(i=-3; i<2; i++) t[i].a = i;

  for(i=-3; i<2; i++) cout << t[i].a << " ";
  cout << endl;

  // copy to new container
  NP_Array<test> t2(4, 7);
  copy(t.begin(), t.end(), &t2[-2]);

  cout << "Contents of t2:\n";
  for(i=-7; i<4; i++) cout << t2[i].a << " ";
  cout << endl;

  NP_Array<test> t3(t.begin()+1, t.end()-1);
  cout << "Contents of t3:\n";
  for(i=t3.get_neg_ext(); i<t3.get_pos_ext(); i++)
                      cout << t3[i].a << " ";
  cout << endl;
```

12

```
  t.clear();

  cout << "Size after clear(): " << t.size() << endl;

  // assign container objects
  t = t3;
  cout << "Contents of t:\n";
  for(i=t.get_neg_ext(); i<t.get_pos_ext(); i++) cout << t[i].a << " ";
  cout << endl;

  return 0;
}
```

The output from this program is shown here:

```
constructing
copy constructor
copy constructor
copy constructor
copy constructor
copy constructor
destructing
-3 -2 -1 0 1
constructing
copy constructor
copy constructor
copy constructor
copy constructor
copy constructor
copy constructor
copy constructor
copy constructor
copy constructor
copy constructor
copy constructor
destructing
Contents of t2:
0 0 0 0 0 -3 -2 -1 0 1 0
copy constructor
copy constructor
copy constructor
Contents of t3:
-2 -1 0
destructing
```

```
destructing
destructing
destructing
destructing
Size after clear(): 0
copy constructor
copy constructor
copy constructor
Contents of t:
-2 -1 0
destructing
destructing
destructing
destructing
destructing
destructing
destructing
destructing
destructing
destructing
destructing
destructing
destructing
destructing
destructing
destructing
destructing
destructing
```

Things to Try

You might want to try experimenting with the **NP_Array** class. As the comments in **np_a.h** suggest, you can add reverse iterators: the **at( )**, **rbegin( )**, **rend( )**, **push_front( )**, and **pop_front( )** functions. Here are some other ideas. Try optimizing the container. For example, try allocating a little more memory than needed when constructing objects so that not all insert operations force a reallocation. As stated, the code in **NP_Array** was designed for transparency of operation, not for speed, so it can be easily improved. Try creating member functions that convert the negative-positive array into a standard, zero-based array. Try adding a constructor that takes a standard array and an index as a parameter. Have the constructor convert the array into a negative-positive array. Use the index as the location of zero. Finally, as an extra challenge, on your own, try creating an associative container.

12

Building a Container Adaptor

Sometimes it may be easier to create a container adaptor rather than an actual container. The advantage is that you do not need to implement all of the container requirements yourself. You can use those elements from the adapted container instead. It is actually quite easy to create a container adaptor. Simply design a template class that takes as one of its template arguments a container. For the required **typedef**s, adapt those provided by the container. Then, implement each of the adaptor's functions in terms of the container being adapted. For example, here is a partial skeleton for a sequence container adaptor:

```cpp
// A partial container adaptor skeleton.
template<class T, class Cont = vector<T> >
class C_Adaptor {
  Cont c; // store an instance of container being adapted
  // ...
 public:
  typedef Cont::value_type value_type;
  typedef Cont::allocator_type allocator_type;
  typedef Cont::reference reference;
  typedef Cont::const_reference const_reference;
  typedef Cont::size_type size_type;
  typedef Cont::difference_type difference_type;
  typedef Cont::iterator iterator;
  typedef Cont::const_iterator const_iterator;
  typedef Cont::reverse_iterator reverse_iterator;
  typedef Cont::const_reverse_iterator const_reverse_iterator;

  // some skeletal constructors
  C_Adaptor() {
    c = Cont();
    // ...
  }

C_Adaptor(int n, const T &t = T()) {
    c = Cont(n, t);
  }
```

```
  // a few example member functions
  T &operator[](int i) {
    return c[i];
  }

  iterator insert(iterator p, const T &v) {
    return c.insert(p, v);
  }

  iterator begin() {
    return c.begin();
  }

  iterator end() {
    return c.end();
  }

  // fill in the rest
};
```

As this skeleton shows, you must store an instance of the container being adapted and then use this object to hold the elements that you will be storing. Write all member functions in terms of the adapted container. In essence, creating a container adaptor simply involves calling the appropriate functions in the underlying container. Of course, you can enhance or restrict the operations that you allow.

Once you have created an adaptor, simply pass the type of container that you want to use as a template parameter. For example, the following creates an object that adapts **deque**:

```
C_Adaptor<int, deque<int> > ob(5);
```

As the skeleton does, it is usually best to supply a default container. In this case, the default is **vector**. Thus, the following statement adapts a vector by default:

```
C_Adaptor<int> ob(5);
```

Creating a container adaptor is often faster and easier than creating a stand-alone container. Consider implementing an adaptor the next time you need a custom container.

12

What Next?

As you have seen throughout the 12 chapters that comprise this book, the STL is a remarkably powerful yet easy-to-use subsystem defined by Standard C++. As the art of programming continues to evolve, you can expect STL-based solutions to increase. Aside from the obvious convenience of the built-in containers, using the STL lets you program at a higher level, which is more efficient. But the genius of the STL is that you can still utilize low-level code where needed. You can take advantage of the benefits provided by the abstraction inherent in the STL without yielding full control over your program. In fact, you can even "hand optimize" STL-based code in much the same way that you would low-level C++ routines. The STL keeps you, the programmer, firmly in charge. And this is just where C++ programmers want to be!

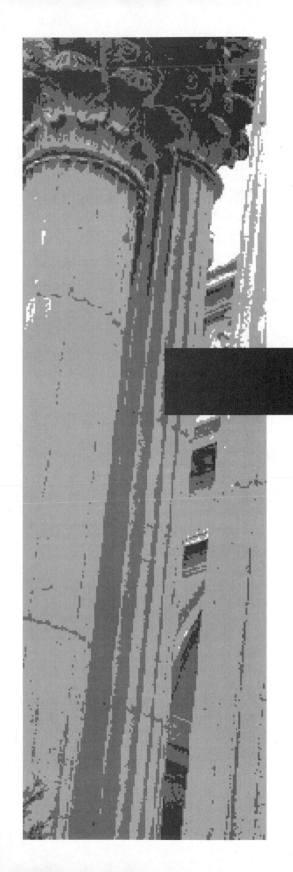

APPENDIX A

The STL Algorithms

The algorithms defined by the standard template library are described here. These algorithms operate on containers through iterators. All of the algorithms are template functions. Here are descriptions of the generic type names used by the algorithms.

Generic Name	Represents
BiIter	Bidirectional iterator
ForIter	Forward iterator
InIter	Input iterator
OutIter	Output iterator
RandIter	Random access iterator
T	Some type of data
Size	Some type of integer
Func	Some type of function
Generator	A function that generates objects
BinPred	Binary predicate
UnPred	Unary predicate
Comp	Comparison function

adjacent_find

```
template <class ForIter>
  ForIter adjacent_find(ForIter start, ForIter end);
template <class ForIter, class BinPred>
  ForIter adjacent_find(ForIter start, ForIter end, BinPred pfn);
```

The **adjacent_find( )** algorithm searches for adjacent matching elements within a sequence specified by *start* and *end* and returns an iterator to the first element. If no adjacent pair is found, *end* is returned. The first version looks for equivalent elements. The second version lets you specify your own method for determining matching elements.

binary_search

```
template <class ForIter, class T>
  bool binary_search(ForIter start, ForIter end, const T &val);
template <class ForIter, class T, class Comp>
  bool binary_search(ForIter start, ForIter end, const T &val,
                     Comp cmpfn);
```

The **binary_search( )** algorithm performs a binary search on an ordered sequence beginning at *start* and ending with *end* for the value specified by *val*. It returns true if the *val* is found and false otherwise. The first version compares the elements in the specified sequence for equality. The second version allows you to specify your own comparison function.

copy

```
template <class InIter, class OutIter >
  OutIter copy(InIter start, InIter end, OutIter result);
```

The **copy( )** algorithm copies a sequence beginning at *start* and ending with *end*, putting the result into the sequence pointed to by *result*. It returns a pointer to the end of the resulting sequence. The range to be copied must not overlap with *result*.

copy_backward

```
template <class BiIter1, class BiIter2>
  BiIter2 copy_backward(BiIter1 start, BiIter1 end, BiIter2 result);
```

The **copy_backward( )** algorithm is the same as **copy( )** except that it moves the elements from the end of the sequence first.

count

```
template <class InIter, class T>
  size_t count(InIter start, InIter end, const T &val);
```

A

The **count( )** algorithm returns the number of elements in the sequence beginning at *start* and ending at *end* that match *val*.

count_if

```
template <class InIter, class UnPred>
  size_t count(InIter start, InIter end, UnPred pfn);
```

The **count_if( )** algorithm returns the number of elements in the sequence beginning at *start* and ending at *end* for which the unary predicate *pfn* returns true.

equal

```
template <class InIter1, class InIter2>
  bool equal(InIter1 start1, InIter1 end1, InIter2 start2);
template <class InIter1, class InIter2, class BinPred>
  bool equal(InIter1 start1, InIter1 end1, InIter2 start2,
             BinPred pfn);
```

The **equal( )** algorithm determines if two ranges are the same. The range determined by *start1* and *end1* is tested against the sequence pointed to by *start2*. If the ranges are the same, true is returned. Otherwise, false is returned.

The second form allows you to specify a binary predicate that determines when two elements are equal.

equal_range

```
template <class ForIter, class T>
  pair<ForIter, ForIter> equal_range(ForIter start, ForIter end,
                                     const T &val);
template <class ForIter, class T, class Comp>
  pair<ForIter, ForIter> equal_range(ForIter start, ForIter end,
                                     const T &val, Comp cmpfn);
```

The **equal_range( )** algorithm returns a range in which an element can be inserted into a sequence without disrupting the ordering of the sequence. The region in which to search for such a range is specified by *start* and *end*. The value is passed in *val*. To specify your own search criteria, specify the comparison function *cmpfn*.

The template class **pair** is a utility class that can hold a pair of objects in its **first** and **second** members.

fill and fill_n

```
template <class ForIter, class T>
  void fill(ForIter start, ForIter end, const T &val);
template <class ForIter, class Size, class T>
  void fill_n(ForIter start, Size num, const T &val);
```

The **fill( )** and **fill_n( )** algorithms fill a range with the value specified by *val*. For **fill( )** the range is specified by *start* and *end*. For **fill_n( )**, the range begins at *start* and runs for *num* elements.

find

```
template <class InIter, class T>
  InIter find(InIter start, InIter end, const T &val);
```

The **find( )** algorithm searches the range *start* to *end* for the value specified by *val*. It returns an iterator to the first occurrence of the element or to *end* if the value is not in the sequence.

find_end

```
template <class ForIter1, class ForIter2>
  ForIter1 find_end(ForIter1 start1, ForIter1 end1,
                    ForIter2 start2, ForIter2 end2);
template <class ForIter1, class ForIter2, class BinPred>
  ForIter1 find_end(ForIter1 start1, ForIter1 end1,
                    ForIter2 start2, ForIter2 end2, BinPred pfn);
```

The **find_end( )** algorithm finds the last iterator of the subsequence defined by *start2* and *end2* within the range *start1* and *end1*. If the sequence is found, an iterator to the last element in the sequence is returned. Otherwise, the iterator *end1* is returned.

The second form allows you to specify a binary predicate that determines when elements match.

A

find_first_of

```
template <class ForIter1, class ForIter2>
  FwdIter1 find_first_of(ForIter1 start1, ForIter1 end1,
                         ForIter2 start2, ForIter2 end2);
template <class ForIter1, class ForIter2, class BinPred>
  FwdIter1 find_first_of(ForIter1 start1, ForIter1 end1,
                         ForIter2 start2, ForIter2 end2,
                         BinPred pfn);
```

The **find_first_of( )** algorithm finds the first element within the sequence defined by *start1* and *end1* that matches an element within the range *start2* and *end2*. If no matching element is found, the iterator *end1* is returned.

The second form allows you to specify a binary predicate that determines when elements match.

find_if

```
template <class InIter, class UnPred>
  InIter find_if(InIter start, InIter end, UnPred pfn);
```

The **find_if( )** algorithm searches the range *start* to *end* for an element for which the unary predicate *pfn* returns true. It returns an iterator to the first occurrence of the element or to *end* if the value is not in the sequence.

for_each

```
template <class InIter, class Func>
  Func for_each(InIter start, InIter end, Func fn);
```

The **for_each( )** algorithm applies the function *fn* to the range of elements specified by *start* and *end*. It returns *fn*.

generate and generate_n

```
template <class ForIter, class Generator>
  void generate(ForIter start, ForIter end, Generator fngen);
template <class OutIter, class Size, class Generator>
  void generate_n(OutIter start, Size num, Generator fngen);
```

The algorithms **generate( )** and **generate_n( )** assign to elements in a range the values returned by a generator function. For **generate( )**, the range being assigned is specified by *start* and *end*. For **generate_n( )**, the range begins at *start* and runs for *num* elements. The generator function is passed in *fngen*. It has no parameters.

includes

```
template <class InIter1, class InIter2>
  bool includes(InIter1 start1, InIter1 end1,
                InIter2 start2, InIter2 end2);
template <class InIter1, class InIter2, class Comp>
  bool includes(InIter1 start1, InIter1 end1,
                InIter2 start2, InIter2 end2, Comp cmpfn);
```

The **includes( )** algorithm determines if the sequence defined by *start1* and *end1* includes all of the elements in the sequence defined by *start2* and *end2*. It returns true if the elements are all found and false otherwise.

The second form allows you to specify a comparison function that determines when one element is less than another.

inplace_merge

```
template <class BiIter>
  void inplace_merge(BiIter start, BiIter mid, BiIter end);
template <class BiIter, class Comp>
  void inplace_merge(BiIter start, BiIter mid, BiIter end,
                     Comp cmpfn);
```

Within a single sequence, the **inplace_merge( )** algorithm merges the range defined by *start* and *mid* with the range defined by *mid* and *end*. Both ranges must be sorted in increasing order. After executing, the resulting sequence is sorted in increasing order.

The second form allows you to specify a comparison function that determines when one element is less than another.

A

iter_swap

```
template <class ForIter1, class ForIter2>
  void iter_swap(ForIter1 i, ForIter2 j)
```

The **iter_swap( )** algorithm exchanges the values pointed to by its two
iterator arguments.

lexicographical_compare

```
template <class InIter1, class InIter2>
  bool lexicographical_compare(InIter1 start1, InIter1 end1,
                               InIter2 start2, InIter2 end2);
template <class InIter1, class InIter2, class Comp>
  bool lexicographical_compare(InIter1 start1, InIter1 end1,
                               InIter2 start2, InIter2 end2,
                               Comp cmpfn);
```

The **lexicographical_compare( )** algorithm alphabetically compares the
sequence defined by *start1* and *end1* with the sequence defined by *start2* and
end2. It returns true if the first sequence is lexicographically less than the
second (that is, if the first sequence would come before the second using
dictionary order).

The second form allows you to specify a comparison function that
determines when one element is less than another.

lower_bound

```
template <class ForIter, class T>
  ForIter lower_bound(ForIter start, ForIter end, const T &val);
template <class ForIter, class T, class Comp>
  ForIter lower_bound(ForIter start, ForIter end, const T &val,
                      Comp cmpfn);
```

The **lower_bound( )** algorithm finds the first point in the sequence defined
by *start* and *end* that is not less than *val*. It returns an iterator to this point.

The second form allows you to specify a comparison function that
determines when one element is less than another.

make_heap

```
template <class RandIter>
  void make_heap(RandIter start, RandIter end);
template <class RandIter, class Comp>
  void make_heap(RandIter start, RandIter end, Comp cmpfn);
```

The **make_heap( )** algorithm constructs a heap from the sequence defined by *start* and *end*.

The second form allows you to specify a comparison function that determines when one element is less than another.

max

```
template <class T>
  const T &max(const T &i, const T &j);
template <class T, class Comp>
  const T &max(const T &i, const T &j, Comp cmpfn);
```

The **max( )** algorithm returns the maximum of two values.

The second form allows you to specify a comparison function that determines when one element is less than another.

max_element

```
template <class ForIter>
  ForIter max_element(ForIter start, ForIter last);
template <class ForIter, class Comp>
  ForIter max_element(ForIter start, ForIter last, Comp cmpfn);
```

A

The **max_element( )** algorithm returns an iterator to the maximum element within the range *start* and *last*.

The second form allows you to specify a comparison function that determines when one element is less than another.

merge

```
template <class InIter1, class InIter2, class OutIter>
  OutIter merge(InIter1 start1, InIter1 end1,
                InIter2 start2, InIter2 end2,
                OutIter result);
template <class InIter1, class InIter2, class OutIter, class Comp>
  OutIter merge(InIter1 start1, InIter1 end1,
                InIter2 start2, InIter2 end2,
                OutIter result, Comp cmpfn);
```

The **merge( )** algorithm merges two ordered sequences, placing the result into a third sequence. The sequences to be merged are defined by *start1*, *end1* and *start2*, *end2*. The result is put into the sequence pointed to by *result*. An iterator to the end of the resulting sequence is returned.

The second form allows you to specify a comparison function that determines when one element is less than another.

min

```
template <class T>
  const T &min(const T &i, const T &j);
template <class T, class Comp>
  const T &min(const T &i, const T &j, Comp cmpfn);
```

The **min( )** algorithm returns the minimum of two values.

The second form allows you to specify a comparison function that determines when one element is less than another.

min_element

```
template <class ForIter>
  ForIter min_element(ForIter start, ForIter last);
template <class ForIter, class Comp>
  ForIter min_element(ForIter start, ForIter last, Comp cmpfn);
```

The **min_element( )** algorithm returns an iterator to the minimum element within the range *start* and *last*.

The second form allows you to specify a comparison function that determines when one element is less than another.

mismatch

```
template <class InIter1, class InIter2>
  pair<InIter1, InIter2> mismatch(InIter1 start1, InIter1 end1,
                                  InIter2 start2);
template <class InIter1, class InIter2, class BinPred>
  pair<InIter1, InIter2> mismatch(InIter1 start1, InIter1 end1,
                                  InIter2 start2, BinPred pfn);
```

The **mismatch( )** algorithm finds the first mismatch between the elements in two sequences. Iterators to the two elements are returned. If no mismatch is found, iterators to the last element in each sequence are returned.

The second form allows you to specify a binary predicate that determines when one element is equal to another.

The **pair** template class contains two data members called **first** and **second** that hold the pair of values.

next_permutation

```
template <class BiIter>
  bool next_permutation(BiIter start, BiIter end);
template <class BiIter, class Comp>
  bool next_permutation(BiIter start, BiIter end, Comp cmfn);
```

The **next_permutation( )** algorithm constructs the next permutation of a sequence. The permutations are generated assuming a sorted sequence: from low to high represents the first permutation. If the next permutation does not exist, **next_permutation( )** sorts the sequence as its first permutation and returns false. Otherwise, it returns true.

The second form allows you to specify a comparison function that determines when one element is less than another.

nth_element

```
template <class RandIter>
  void nth_element(RandIter start, RandIter element, RandIter end);
template <class RandIter, class Comp>
  void nth_element(RandIter start, RandIter element,
                    RandIter end, Comp cmpfn);
```

The **nth_element( )** algorithm arranges the sequence specified by *start* and *end* such that all elements less than *element* come before that element and all elements greater than *element* come after it.

The second form allows you to specify a comparison function that determines when one element is greater than another.

partial_sort

```
template <class RandIter>
  void partial_sort(RandIter start, RandIter mid, RandIter end);
template <class RandIter, class Comp>
  void partial_sort(RandIter start, RandIter mid,
                    RandIter end, Comp cmpfn);
```

The **partial_sort( )** algorithm sorts the range *start* to *end.* However, after execution, only elements in the range *start* to *mid* will be in sorted order.

The second form allows you to specify a comparison function that determines when one element is less than another.

partial_sort_copy

```
template <class InIter, class RandIter>
  RandIter partial_sort_copy(InIter start, InIter end,
                              RandIter res_start, RandIter res_end);
template <class InIter, class RandIter, class Comp>
  RandIter partial_sort_copy(InIter start, InIter end,
                              RandIter res_start, RandIter res_end,
                              Comp cmpfn);
```

The **partial_sort_copy( )** algorithm sorts the range *start* to *end* and then copies as many elements as will fit into the resulting sequence defined by *res_start* and *res_end*. It returns an iterator to the last element copied into the resulting sequence.

The second form allows you to specify a comparison function that determines when one element is less than another.

partition

```
template <class BiIter, class UnPred>
  BiIter partition(BiIter start, BiIter end, UnPred pfn);
```

The **partition( )** algorithm arranges the sequence defined by *start* and *end* such that all elements for which the predicate specified by *pfn* returns true come before those for which the predicate returns false. It returns an iterator to the beginning of the elements for which the predicate is false.

pop_heap

```
template <class RandIter>
  void pop_heap(RandIter start, RandIter end);
template <class RandIter, class Comp>
  void pop_heap(RandIter start, RandIter end, Comp cmpfn);
```

The **pop_heap( )** exchanges the *first* and *last*–1 elements and then rebuilds the heap.

The second form allows you to specify a comparison function that determines when one element is less than another.

A

prev_permutation

```
template <class BiIter>
  bool prev_permutation(BiIter start, BiIter end);
template <class BiIter, class Comp>
  bool prev_permutation(BiIter start, BiIter end, Comp cmpfn);
```

The **prev_permutation( )** algorithm constructs the previous permutation of a sequence. The permutations are generated assuming a sorted sequence: from low to high represents the first permutation. If the previous permutation does not exist, **prev_permutation( )** sorts the sequence as its final permutation and returns false. Otherwise, it returns true.

The second form allows you to specify a comparison function that determines when one element is less than another.

push_heap

```
template <class RandIter>
  void push_heap(RandIter start, RandIter end);
template <class RandIter, class Comp>
  void push_heap(RandIter start, RandIter end, Comp cmpfn);
```

The **push_heap( )** algorithm pushes an element onto the end of a heap. The range specified by *start* and *end* is assumed to represent a valid heap.

The second form allows you to specify a comparison function that determines when one element is less than another.

random_shuffle

```
template <class RandIter>
  void random_shuffle(RandIter start, RandIter end);
template <class RandIter, class Generator>
  void random_shuffle(RandIter start, RandIter end,
                      Generator rand_gen);
```

The **random_shuffle( )** algorithm randomizes the sequence defined by *start* and *end*.

The second form specifies a custom random number generator. This function must have the following general form:

rand_gen(*num*);

It must return a random number between zero and *num*.

remove, remove_if, remove_copy, and remove_copy_if

```
template <class ForIter, class T>
  ForIter remove(ForIter start, ForIter end, const T &val);
template <class ForIter, class UnPred>
  ForIter remove_if(ForIter start, ForIter end,  UnPred pfn);
template <class ForIter, class OutIter, class T>
  OutIter remove_copy(InIter start, InIter end,
                        OutIter result, const T &val);
template <class ForIter, class OutIter, class UnPred>
  OutIter remove_copy_if(InIter start, InIter end,
                        OutIter result, UnPred pfn);
```

The **remove( )** algorithm removes elements from the specified range that are equal to *val*. It returns an iterator to the end of the remaining elements.

The **remove_if( )** algorithm removes elements from the specified range for which the predicate *pfn* is true. It returns an iterator to the end of the remaining elements.

The **remove_copy( )** algorithm copies elements from the specified range that are equal to *val* and puts the result into the sequence pointed to by *result*. It returns an iterator to the end of the result.

The **remove_copy_if( )** algorithm copies elements from the specified range for which the predicate *pfn* is true and puts the result into the sequence pointed to by *result*. It returns an iterator to the end of the result.

replace, replace_copy, replace_if, and replace_copy_if

A

```
template <class ForIter, class T>
  void replace(ForIter start, ForIter end,
               const T &old, const T &new);
template <class ForIter, class UnPred, class T>
  void replace_if(ForIter start, ForIter end,
                  UnPred pfn, const T &new);
template <class ForIter, class OutIter, class T>
  OutIter replace_copy(InIter start, InIter end, OutIter result,
                        const T &old, const T &new);
template <class ForIter, class OutIter, class UnPred, class T>
  OutIter replace_copy_if(InIter start, InIter end, OutIter result,
                        UnPred pfn, const T &new);
```

Within the specified range, the **replace( )** algorithm replaces elements with the value *old* with elements that have the value *new*.

Within the specified range, the **replace_if( )** algorithm replaces those elements for which the predicate *pfn* is true with elements that have the value *new*.

Within the specified range, the **replace_copy( )** algorithm copies elements to *result*. In the process it replaces elements that have the value *old* with elements that have the value *new*. The original range is unchanged. An iterator to the end of *result* is returned.

Within the specified range, the **replace_copy_if( )** algorithm copies elements to *result*. In the process it replaces elements for which the predicate *pfn* returns true with elements that have the value *new*. The original range is unchanged. An iterator to the end of *result* is returned.

reverse and reverse_copy

```
template <class BiIter>
  void reverse(BiIter start, BiIter end);
template <class BiIter, class OutIter>
  OutIter reverse_copy(BiIter first, BiIter last, OutIter result);
```

The **reverse( )** algorithm reverses the order of the range specified by *start* and *end*.

The **reverse_copy( )** algorithm copies in reverse order the range specified by *start* and *end* and stores the result in *result*. It returns an iterator to the end of *result*.

rotate and rotate_copy

```
template <class ForIter>
  void rotate(ForIter start, ForIter mid, ForIter end);
template <class ForIter, class OutIter>
  OutIter rotate_copy(ForIter start, ForIter mid, ForIter end,
                      OutIter result);
```

The **rotate( )** algorithm left-rotates the elements in the range specified by *start* and *end* so that the element specified by *mid* becomes the new first element.

The **rotate_copy( )** algorithm copies the range specified by *start* and *end,* storing the result in *result*. In the process it left-rotates the elements so that the element specified by *mid* becomes the new first element. It returns an iterator to the end of *result*.

search

```
template <class ForIter1, class ForIter2>
  ForIter1 search(ForIter1 start1, ForIter1 end1,
                  ForIter2 start2, ForIter2 end2);
template <class ForIter1, class ForIter2, class BinPred>
  ForIter1 search(ForIter1 start1, ForIter1 end1,
                  ForIter2 start2, ForIter2 end2, BinPred pfn);
```

The **search( )** algorithm searches for a subsequence within a sequence. The sequence being searched is defined by *start1* and *end1*. The subsequence is specified by *start2* and *end2*. If the subsequence is found, an iterator to its beginning is returned. Otherwise, *end1* is returned.

The second form allows you to specify a binary predicate that determines when one element is equal to another.

search_n

```
template <class ForIter, class Size, class T>
  ForIter search_n(ForIter start, ForIter end,
                   Size num, const T &val);
template <class ForIter, class Size, class T, class BinPred>
  ForIter search_n(ForIter start, ForIter end,
                   Size num, const T &val, BinPred pfn);
```

A

The **search_n( )** algorithm searches for a sequence of *num* elements equal to *val* within a sequence. The sequence being searched is defined by *start1* and *end1*. If the subsequence is found, an iterator to its beginning is returned. Otherwise, *end* is returned.

The second form allows you to specify a binary predicate that determines when one element is equal to another.

set_difference

```
template <class InIter1, class InIter2, class OutIter>
  OutIter set_difference(InIter1 start1, InIter1 end1,
          InIter2 start2, InIter2 last2, OutIter result);
template <class InIter1, class InIter2, class OutIter, class Comp>
  OutIter set_difference(InIter1 start1, InIter1 end1,
          InIter2 start2, InIter2 last2,
          OutIter result, Comp cmpfn);
```

The **set_difference( )** algorithm produces a sequence that contains the difference between the two ordered sets defined by *start1*, *end1* and *start2*, *end2*. That is, the set defined by *start2*, *end2* is subtracted from the set defined by *start1*, *end1*. The result is ordered and put into *result*. It returns an iterator to the end of the result.

The second form allows you to specify a comparison function that determines when one element is less than another.

set_intersection

```
template <class InIter1, class InIter2, class OutIter>
  OutIter set_intersection(InIter1 start1, InIter1 end1,
          InIter2 start2, InIter2 last2, OutIter result);
template <class InIter1, class InIter2, class OutIter, class Comp>
  OutIter set_intersection(InIter1 start1, InIter1 end1,
          InIter2 start2, InIter2 last2,
          OutIter result, Comp cmpfn);
```

The **set_intersection( )** algorithm produces a sequence that contains the intersection of the two ordered sets defined by *start1*, *end1* and *start2*, *end2*. These are the elements common to both sets. The result is ordered and put into *result*. It returns an iterator to the end of the result.

The second form allows you to specify a comparison function that determines when one element is less than another.

set_symmetric_difference

```
template <class InIter1, class InIter2, class OutIter>
  OutIter set_symmetric_difference(InIter1 start1, InIter1 end1,
          InIter2 start2, InIter2 last2, OutIter result);
```

```
template <class InIter1, class InIter2, class OutIter, class Comp>
  OutIter set_symmetric_difference(InIter1 start1, InIter1 end1,
          InIter2 start2, InIter2 last2, OutIter result,
          Comp cmpfn);
```

The **set_symmetric_difference( )** algorithm produces a sequence that contains the symmetric difference between the two ordered sets defined by *start1*, *end1* and *start2*, *end2*. That is, the resultant set contains only those elements that are not common to both sets. The result is ordered and put into *result*. It returns an iterator to the end of the result.

The second form allows you to specify a comparison function that determines when one element is less than another.

set_union

```
template <class InIter1, class InIter2, class OutIter>
  OutIter set_union(InIter1 start1, InIter1 end1,
          InIter2 start2, InIter2 last2, OutIter result);
template <class InIter1, class InIter2, class OutIter, class Comp>
  OutIter set_union(InIter1 start1, InIter1 end1,
          InIter2 start2, InIter2 last2, OutIter result,
          Comp cmpfn);
```

The **set_union( )** algorithm produces a sequence that contains the union of the two ordered sets defined by *start1*, *end1* and *start2*, *end2*. Thus, the resultant set contains those elements that are in both sets. The result is ordered and put into *result*. It returns an iterator to the end of the result.

The second form allows you to specify a comparison function that determines when one element is less than another.

A

sort

```
template <class RandIter>
  void sort(RandIter start, RandIter end);
template <class RandIter, class Comp>
  void sort(RandIter start, RandIter end, Comp cmpfn);
```

The **sort( )** algorithm sorts the range specified by *start* and *end*.

The second form allows you to specify a comparison function that determines when one element is less than another.

sort_heap

```
template <class RandIter>
  void sort_heap(RandIter start, RandIter end);
template <class RandIter, class Comp>
  void sort_heap(RandIter start, RandIter end, Comp cmpfn);
```

The **sort_heap( )** algorithm sorts a heap within the range specified by *start* and *end*.

The second form allows you to specify a comparison function that determines when one element is less than another.

stable_partition

```
template <class BiIter, class UnPred>
  BiIter stable_partition(BiIter start, BiIter end, UnPred pfn);
```

The **stable_partition( )** algorithm arranges the sequence defined by *start* and *end* such that all elements for which the predicate specified by *pfn* returns true come before those for which the predicate returns false. The partitioning is stable. This means that the relative ordering of the sequence is preserved. It returns an iterator to the beginning of the elements for which the predicate is false.

stable_sort

```
template <class RandIter>
  void stable_sort(RandIter start, RandIter end);
template <class RandIter, class Comp>
  void stable_sort(RandIter start, RandIter end, Comp cmpfn);
```

The **sort( )** algorithm sorts the range specified by *start* and *end*. The sort is stable. This means that equal elements are not rearranged.

The second form allows you to specify a comparison function that determines when one element is less than another.

swap

```
template <class T>
  void swap(T &i, T &j);
```

The **swap( )** algorithm exchanges the values referred to by *i* and *j*.

swap_ranges

```
template <class Forter1, class ForIter2>
  ForIter2 swap_ranges(ForIter1 start1, ForIter1 end1,
                       ForIter2 start2);
```

The **swap_ranges( )** algorithm exchanges elements in the range specified by *start1* and *end1* with elements in the sequence beginning at *start2*. It returns a pointer to the end of the sequence specified by *start2*.

transform

```
template <class InIter, class OutIter, class Func>
  OutIter transform(InIter start, InIter end,
                    OutIter result, Func unaryfunc);
template <class InIter1, class InIter2, class OutIter, class Func>
  OutIter transform(InIter1 start1, InIter1 end1,
                    InIter2 start2, OutIter result,
                    Func binaryfunc);
```

The **transform( )** algorithm applies a function to a range of elements and stores the outcome in *result*. In the first form, the range is specified by *start* and *end*. The function to be applied is specified by *unaryfunc*. This function receives the value of an element in its parameter and it must return its transformation.

In the second form, the transformation is applied using a binary operator function that receives the value of an element from the sequence to be transformed in its first parameter and an element from the second sequence as its second parameter.

Both versions return an iterator to the end of the resulting sequence.

A

unique and unique_copy

```
template <class ForIter>
  ForIter unique(ForIter start, ForIter end);
template <class ForIter, class BinPred>
  ForIter unique(ForIter start, ForIter end, BinPred pfn);
template <class ForIter, class OutIter>
  OutIter unique_copy(ForIter start, ForIter end, OutIter result);
template <class ForIter, class OutIter, class BinPred>
  OutIter unique_copy(ForIter start, ForIter end, OutIter result,
                      BinPred pfn);
```

The **unique( )** algorithm eliminates consecutive duplicate elements from the specified range. The second form allows you to specify a binary predicate that determines when one element is equal to another. **unique( )** returns an iterator to the end of the range.

The **unique_copy( )** algorithm copies the range specified by *start1* and *end1*, eliminating consecutive duplicate elements in the process. The outcome is put into *result*. The second form allows you to specify a binary predicate that determines when one element is equal to another. **unique_copy( )** returns an iterator to the end of the range.

upper_bound

```
template <class ForIter, class T>
  ForIter upper_bound(ForIter start, ForIter end, const T &val);
template <class ForIter, class T, class Comp>
  ForIter upper_bound(ForIter start, ForIter end, const T &val,
                      Comp cmpfn);
```

The **upper_bound( )** algorithm finds the last point in the sequence defined by *start* and *end* that is not greater than *val*. It returns an iterator to this point.

The second form allows you to specify a comparison function that determines when one element is less than another.

APPENDIX B

The basic_string Class

This appendix describes the Standard C++ string class. As you know, C++ supports character strings two ways. The first is as a null-terminated character array. This is sometimes referred to as a *C string*. The second way is as a class object of type **basic_string**. There are two specializations of **basic_string**: **string**, which supports **char** strings, and **wstring**, which supports **wchar_t** (wide character) strings. Most often, you will use string objects of type **string**.

As mentioned in Chapter 2, **basic_string** is essentially a container. Although not part of the STL proper, **basic_string** is still compatible with it. This means that iterators and the STL algorithms can operate on strings. Since **basic_string** works with the STL, it is described here.

A class used by **basic_string** is **char_traits**, which defines several attributes of the characters that comprise a string. It is important to understand that while the most common strings are made up of either **char** or **wchar_t** characters, **basic_string** can operate on any object that can be used to represent a text character. Both **basic_string** and **char_traits** are described here.

The basic_string Class

The template specification for **basic_string** is

```
template <class CharType, class Attr = char_traits<CharType>,
        class Allocator = allocator<T> > class basic_string
```

Here, **CharType** is the type of character being used, **Attr** is the class that describes the character's traits, and **Allocator** specifies the allocator. **basic_string** has the following constructors:

```
explicit basic_string(const Allocator &a = Allocator( ));

basic_string(size_type len, CharType ch ,
        const Allocator &a = Allocator( ));

basic_string(const CharType *str;  const Allocator &a = Allocator( ));

basic_string(const CharType *str; size_type len,
        const Allocator &a = Allocator( ));

basic_string(const basic_string &str, size_type indx = 0,
        size_type len=npos, const Allocator &a = Allocator( ));

template <class InIter> basic_string(InIter start, InIter end,
        const Allocator &a = Allocator( ));
```

The first form constructs an empty string. The second form constructs a string that has *len* characters of value *ch*. The third form constructs a string from the one pointed to by *str*. The fourth form constructs a string that contains a substring of *str* that begins at zero and is *len* characters long. The fifth form constructs a string from another **basic_string** using the substring that begins at *indx* that is *len* characters long. The sixth form constructs a string that contains the elements in the range specified by *start* and *end*.

The following comparison operators are defined for **basic_string**:

   ==, <, <=, !=, >, >=

Also defined is the + operator, which yields the result of concatenating one string with another and the I/O operators << and >>, which can be used to input and output strings.

The + operator can be used to concatenate a string object with another string object or a string object with a C-style string. That is, the following variations are supported:

   string + string

   string + C-string

   C-string + string

The + operator can also be used to concatenate a character onto the end of a string.

The **basic_string** class defines the constant **npos**, which is usually –1. This constant represents the length of the longest possible string.

In the descriptions, the generic type **CharType** represents the type of character stored by a string. Since the names of the placeholder types in a template class are arbitrary, **basic_string** declares **typedef**ed versions of these types. This makes the type names concrete. The types defined by **basic_string** are shown here:

B

size_type	Some integral type loosely equivalent to **size_t**.
reference	A reference to a character.
const_reference	A **const** reference to a character.
iterator	An iterator.
const_iterator	A **const** iterator.
reverse_iterator	A reverse iterator.

const_reverse_iterator	A **const** reverse iterator.
value_type	The type of character stored in a string.
allocator_type	The type of the allocator.
pointer	A pointer to a character within a string.
const_pointer	A **const** pointer to a character within a string.
traits_type	A **typedef** for **char_traits<CharType>**.
difference_type	A type that can store the difference between two addresses.

The member functions defined by **basic_string** are shown in Table B-1. To keep the table easy to read, the functions are shown in terms of **string** rather than the unwieldy template specification **basic_string<CharType, Attr, Allocator>**. Of course, the functions apply to any type of **basic_string**, including objects of type **wstring**.

Member	Description
string &append(const string &*str*);	Appends *str* onto the end of the invoking string. Returns ***this**.

string &append(const string &*str*,
                 size_type *indx*,
                 size_type *len*);
	Appends a substring of *str* onto the end of the invoking string. The substring being appended begins at *indx* and runs for *len* characters. Returns ***this**.

string &append(const CharType **str*);	Appends *str* onto the end of the invoking string. Returns ***this**.
string &append(const CharType **str*, size_type *num*);	Appends the first *num* characters from *str* onto the end of the invoking string. Returns ***this**.
string &append(size_type *len*, CharType *ch*);	Appends *len* characters specified by *ch* to the end of the invoking string. Returns ***this**.

The
basic_string
Member
Functions

Table B-1.

Member	Description
template<class InIter> string &append(InIter *start*, InIter *end*);	Appends the sequence specified by *start* and *end* onto the end of the invoking string. ***this** is returned.
string &assign(const string &*str*);	Assigns *str* to the invoking string. Returns ***this**.
string &assign(const string &*str*, size_type *indx*, size_type *len*);	Assigns a substring of *str* to the invoking string. The substring being assigned begins at *indx* and runs for *len* characters. Returns ***this**.
string &assign(const CharType **str*);	Assigns *str* to the invoking string. Returns *** this**.
string &assign(const CharType **str*, size_type *len*);	Assigns the first *len* character from *str* to the invoking string. Returns ***this**.
string &assign(size_type *len*, CharType *ch*);	Assigns *len* characters specified by *ch* to the end of the invoking string. Returns ***this**.
template<class InIter> string &assign(InIter *start*, InIter *end*);	Assigns the sequence specified by *start* and *end* to the invoking string. ***this** is returned.
reference at(size_type *indx*); const_reference at(size_type *indx*) const;	Returns a reference to the character specified by *indx*.
iterator begin( ); const_iterator begin( ) const;	Returns an iterator to the first element in the string.
const CharType *c_str( ) const;	Returns a pointer to a C-style (i.e., null-terminated) version of the invoking string.
size_type capacity( ) const;	Returns the current capacity of the string. This is the number of characters it can hold before it will need to allocate more memory.

The
basic_string
Member
Functions
(continued)
Table B-1.

B

Member	Description
int compare(const string &*str*) const;	Compares *str* to the invoking string. It returns one of the following: Less than zero if ***this** < *str* Zero if ***this** == *str* Greater than zero if ***this** > *str*
int compare(size_type *indx*, size_type *len*, const string &*str*) const;	Compares *str* to a substring within the invoking string. The substring begins at *indx* and is *len* characters long. It returns one of the following: Less than zero if ***this** < *str* Zero if ***this** == *str* Greater than zero if ***this** > *str*
int compare(size_type *indx*, size_type *len*, const string &*str*, size_type *indx2*, size_type *len2*) const;	Compares a substring of *str* to a substring within the invoking string. The substring in the invoking string begins at *indx* and is *len* characters long. The substring in *str* begins at *indx2* and is *len2* characters long. It returns one of the following: Less than zero if ***this** < *str* Zero if ***this** == *str* Greater than zero if ***this** > *str*
int compare(const CharType **str*) const;	Compares *str* to the invoking string. It returns one of the following: Less than zero if ***this** < *str* Zero if ***this** == *str* Greater than zero if ***this** > *str*

The
basic_string
Member
Functions
(continued)
Table B-1.

Member	Description
int compare(size_type *indx*, size_type *len*, const CharType **str*, size_type *len2* = npos) const;	Compares a substring of *str* to a substring within the invoking string. The substring in the invoking string begins at *indx* and is *len* characters long. The substring in *str* begins at zero and is *len2* characters long. It returns one of the following: Less than zero if ***this** < *str* Zero if ***this** == *str* Greater than zero if ***this** > *str*
size_type copy(CharType **str*, size_type *len*, size_type *indx* = 0) const;	Beginning at *indx*, copies *len* characters from the invoking string into the character array pointed to by *str*. Returns the number of characters copied.
const CharType *data( ) const;	Returns a pointer to the first character in the invoking string.
bool empty( ) const;	Returns **true** if the invoking string is empty and **false** otherwise.
iterator end( ); const_iterator end( ) const;	Returns an iterator to the end of the string.
iterator erase(iterator *i*);	Removes character pointed to by *i*. Returns an iterator to the character after the one removed.
iterator erase(iterator *start*, iterator *end*);	Removes characters in the range *start* to *end*. Returns an iterator to the character after the last character removed.

The
basic_string
Member
Functions
(continued)
Table B-1.

B

Member	Description
string &erase(size_type *indx* = 0, size_type *len* = npos);	Beginning at *indx*, removes *len* characters from the invoking string. Returns ***this**.
size_type find(const string &*str*, size_type *indx* = 0) const;	Returns the index of the first occurrence of *str* within the invoking string. The search begins at index *indx*. **npos** is returned if no match is found.
size_type find(const CharType **str*, size_type *indx* = 0) const;	Returns the index of the first occurrence of *str* within the invoking string. The search begins at index *indx*. **npos** is returned if no match is found.

size_type find(const CharType **str*,
                 size_type *indx*,
                 size_type *len*) const;
	Returns the index of the first occurrence of the first *len* characters of *str* within the invoking string. The search begins at index *indx*. **npos** is returned if no match is found.

size_type find(CharType *ch*, size_type *indx* = 0) const;	Returns the index of the first occurrence of *ch* within the invoking string. The search begins at index *indx*. **npos** is returned if no match is found.
size_type find_first_of(const string &*str*, size_type *indx* = 0) const;	Returns the index of the first character within the invoking string that matches any character in *str*. The search begins at index *indx*. **npos** is returned if no match is found.
size_type find_first_of(const CharType **str*, size_type *indx* = 0) const;	Returns the index of the first character within the invoking string that matches any character in *str*. The search begins at index *indx*. **npos** is returned if no match is found.

The
basic_string
Member
Functions
(continued)
Table B-1.

Member	Description
size_type find_first_of(const CharType *str, size_type indx, size_type len) const;	Returns the index of the first character within the invoking string that matches any character in the first len characters of str. The search begins at index indx. **npos** is returned if no match is found.
size_type find_first_of(CharType ch, size_type indx = 0) const;	Returns the index of the first occurrence of ch within the invoking string. The search begins at index indx. **npos** is returned if no match is found.
size_type find_first_not_of(const string &str, size_type indx = 0) const;	Returns the index of the first character within the invoking string that does not match any character in str. The search begins at index indx. **npos** is returned if no mismatch is found.
size_type find_first_not_of(const CharType *str, size_type indx = 0) const;	Returns the index of the first character within the invoking string that does not match any character in str. The search begins at index indx. **npos** is returned if no mismatch is found.
size_type find_first_not_of(const CharType *str, size_type indx, size_type len) const;	Returns the index of the first character within the invoking string that does not match any character in the first len characters of str. The search begins at index indx. **npos** is returned if no mismatch is found.
size_type find_first_not_of(CharType ch, size_type indx = 0) const;	Returns the index of the first character within the invoking string that does not match ch. The search begins at index indx. **npos** is returned if no mismatch is found.

The **basic_string** Member Functions *(continued)* **Table B-1.**

B

Member	Description
size_type find_last_of(const string &*str*, size_type *indx* = npos) const;	Returns the index of the last character within the invoking string that matches any character in *str*. The search begins at index *indx*. **npos** is returned if no match is found.
size_type find_last_of(const CharType **str*, size_type *indx* = npos) const;	Returns the index of the last character within the invoking string that matches any character in *str*. The search begins at index *indx*. **npos** is returned if no match is found.
size_type find_last_of(const CharType **str*, size_type *indx*, size_type *len*) const;	Returns the index of the last character within the invoking string that matches any character in the first *len* characters of *str*. The search begins at index *indx*. **npos** is returned if no match is found.
size_type find_last_of(CharType *ch*, size_type *indx* = npos) const;	Returns the index of the last occurrence of *ch* within the invoking string. The search begins at index *indx*. **npos** is returned if no match is found.
size_type find_last_not_of(const string &*str*, size_type *indx* = npos) const;	Returns the index of the last character within the invoking string that does not match any character in *str*. The search begins at index *indx*. **npos** is returned if no mismatch is found.
size_type find_last_not_of(const CharType **str*, size_type *indx* = npos) const;	Returns the index of the last character within the invoking string that does not match any character in *str*. The search begins at index *indx*. **npos** is returned if no mismatch is found.

The
basic_string
Member
Functions
(continued)
Table B-1.

Member	Description
size_type find_last_not_of(const CharType *str, size_type *indx*, size_type *len*) const;	Returns the index of the last character within the invoking string that does not match any character in the first *len* characters of *str*. The search begins at index *indx*. **npos** is returned if no mismatch is found.
size_type find_last_not_of(CharType *ch*, size_type *indx* = npos) const;	Returns the index of the last character within the invoking string that does not match *ch*. The search begins at index *indx*. **npos** is returned if no mismatch is found.
allocator_type get_allocator( ) const;	Returns the string's allocator.
iterator insert(iterator *i*, const CharType &*ch*);	Inserts *ch* immediately before the character specified by *indx*. An iterator to the character is returned.
string &insert(size_type *indx*, const string &*str*);	Inserts *str* into the invoking string at the index specified by *indx*. Returns ***this**.
string &insert(size_type *indx1*, const string &*str*, size_type *indx2*, size_type *len*);	Inserts a substring of *str* into the invoking string at the index specified by *indx1*. The substring begins at *indx2* and is *len* characters long. Returns ***this**.
string &insert(size_type *indx*, const CharType *str*);	Inserts *str* into the invoking string at the index specified by *indx*. Returns ***this**.
string &insert(size_type *indx*, const CharType *str*, size_type *len*);	Inserts the first *len* characters of *str* into the invoking string at the index specified by *indx*. Returns ***this**.

The
basic_string
Member
Functions
(continued)
Table B-1.

B

Member	Description

string &insert(size_type *indx*,
                   size_type *len*,
                   CharType *ch*);
	Inserts *len* characters of value *ch* into the invoking string at the index specified by *indx*. Returns ***this**.

void insert(iterator *i*, size_type *len*, const CharType &*ch*)	Inserts *len* copies of *ch* immediately before the element specified by *i*.

template <class InIter>
    void insert(iterator *i*, InIter *start*,
                   InIter *end*);
	Inserts the sequence defined by *start* and *end* immediately before the element specified by *i*.

size_type length( ) const;	Returns the number of characters in the string.
size_type max_size( ) const;	Returns the maximum number of characters that the string can hold.
reference operator[ ](size_type *indx*) const; const_reference operator[ ](size_type *indx*) const;	Returns a reference to the character specified by *indx*.

string &operator=(const string &*str*);
string &operator=(const CharType **str*);
string &operator=(CharType *ch*);
	Assigns the specified string or character to the invoking string. Returns ***this**.

string &operator+=(const string &*str*);
string &operator+=(const CharType **str*);
string &operator+=(CharType *ch*);
	Appends the specified string or character onto the end of the invoking string. Returns ***this**.

reverse_iterator rbegin( ); const_reverse_iterator rbegin( ) const;	Returns a reverse iterator to the end of the string.
reverse_iterator rend( ); const_reverse_iterator rend( ) const;	Returns a reverse iterator to the start of the string.

string &replace(size_type *indx*,
                   size_type *len*,
                   const string &*str*);
	Replaces up to *len* characters in the invoking string, beginning at *indx* with the string in *str*. Returns ***this**.

The
basic_string
Member
Functions
(continued)
Table B-1.

Member	Description
string &replace(size_type *indx1*, size_type *len1*, const string &*str*, size_type *indx2*, size_type *len2*);	Replaces up to *len1* characters in the invoking string beginning at *indx1* with the *len2* characters from the string in *str* that begin at *indx2*. Returns ***this**.
string &replace(size_type *indx*, size_type *len*, const CharType **str*);	Replaces up to *len* characters in the invoking string, beginning at *indx* with the string in *str*. Returns ***this**.
string &replace(size_type *indx1*, size_type *len1*, const CharType **str*, size_type *len2*);	Replaces up to *len1* characters in the invoking string beginning at *indx1* with the *len2* characters from the string in *str* that begin at *indx2*. Returns ***this**.
string &replace(size_type *indx*, size_type *len1*, size_type *len2*, CharType *ch*);	Replaces up to *len1* characters in the invoking string beginning at *indx* with *len2* characters specified by *ch*. Returns ***this**.
string &replace(iterator *start*, iterator *end*, const string &*str*);	Replaces the range specified by *start* and *end* with *str*. Returns ***this**.
string &replace(iterator *start*, iterator *end*, const CharType **str*);	Replaces the range specified by *start* and *end* with *str*. Returns ***this**.
string &replace(iterator *start*, iterator *end*, const CharType **str*, size_type *len*);	Replaces the range specified by *start* and *end* with the first *len* characters from *str*. Returns ***this**.
string &replace(iterator *start*, iterator *end*, size_type *len*, CharType *ch*);	Replaces the range specified by *start* and *end* with the *len* characters specified by *ch*. Returns ***this**.

The **basic_string** Member Functions *(continued)* **Table B-1.**

B

Member	Description

template <class InIter>
    string &replace(iterator *start1*,
                            iterator *end1*,
                            InIter *start2,*
                            InIter *end2*);
	Replaces the range specified by *start1* and *end1* with the characters specified by *start2* and *end2*. Returns ***this**.

void reserve(size_type *num* = 0);	Sets the capacity of the string so that it is equal to at least *num*.
void resize(size_type *num*) void resize(size_type *num*, CharType *ch*);	Changes the size of the string to that specified by *num*. If the string must be lengthened, then elements with the value specified by *ch* are added to the end.
size_type rfind(const string &*str*, size_type *indx* = npos) const;	Returns the index of the last occurrence of *str* within the invoking string. The search begins at index *indx*. **npos** is returned if no match is found.
size_type rfind(const CharType **str*, size_type *indx* = npos) const;	Returns the index of the last occurrence of *str* within the invoking string. The search begins at index *indx*. **npos** is returned if no match is found.

size_type rfind(const CharType **str*,
                    size_type *indx*,
                    size_type *len*) const;
	Returns the index of the last occurrence of the first *len* characters of *str* within the invoking string. The search begins at index *indx*. **npos** is returned if no match is found.

size_type rfind(CharType *ch*, size_type *indx* = npos) const;	Returns the index of the last occurrence *ch* within the invoking string. The search begins at index *indx*. **npos** is returned if no match is found.

The
basic_string
Member
Functions
(continued)
Table B-1.

Member	Description
size_type size( ) const;	Returns the number of characters currently in the string.
string substr(size_type *indx* = 0, size_type *len* = npos) const;	Returns a substring of *len* characters beginning at *indx* within the invoking string.
void swap(string &*str*)	Exchanges the characters stored in the invoking string with those in *str*.

The **basic_string** Member Functions *(continued)*
Table B-1.

The char_traits Class

The class **char_traits** describes several attributes associated with a character. Its template specification is shown here:

> template<class CharType> struct char_traits

Here, **CharType** specifies the type of the character.

The C++ library provides two specializations of **char_traits**: one for **char** characters and one for **wchar_t** characters. The **char_traits** class defines the following five data types:

char_type	The type of the character. This is a **typedef** for **CharType**.
int_type	An integer type that can hold a character of type **char_type** or the EOF character.
off_type	An integer type that can represent an offset in a stream.
pos_type	An integer type that can represent a position in a stream.
state_type	An object type that stores the conversion state (applies to multibyte characters).

B

The member functions of **char_traits** are shown in Table B-2.

Member	Description
static void assign(char_type &*ch1*, const char_type &*ch2*);	Assigns *ch2* to *ch1*.
static char_type *assign(char_type **str*, size_t *num*, char_type *ch2*);	Assigns *ch2* to the first *num* characters in *str*. Returns *str*.
static int compare(const char_type **str1*, const char_type **str2*, size_t *num*);	Compare *num* characters in *str1* to those in *str2*. Returns zero if the strings are thesame. Otherwise, returns less than zero if *str1* is less than *str2* or greater than zero if *str1* is greater than *str2*.
static char_type *copy(char_type **to*, const char_type **from*, size_t *num*);	Copies *num* characters from *from* to *to*. Returns *to*.
static int_type eof( );	Returns the end-of-file character.
static bool eq(const char_type &*ch1*, const char_type &*ch2*);	Compares *ch1* to *ch2* and returns **true** if the characters are the same and **false** otherwise.
static bool eq_int_type(const int_type &*ch1*, const int_type &*ch2*);	Returns **true** if *ch1* equals *ch2* and **false** otherwise.
static const char_type *find(const char_type **str*, size_t *num*, const char_type *ch*);	Returns a pointer to the first occurrence of *ch* in *str*. Only the first *num* characters are examined. Returns a null pointer on failure.
static size_t length(const char_type **str*);	Returns the length of *str*.

The Member
Functions of
char_traits

Table B-2.

Member	Description
static bool lt(const char_type &*ch1*, const char_type &*ch2*);	Returns **true** if *ch1* is less than *ch2* and **false** otherwise.
static char_type *move(char_type **to*, const char_type **from*, size_t *num*);	Copies *num* characters from *from* to *to*. Returns *to*.
static int_type not_eof(const int_type &*ch*);	If *ch* is not the EOF character, then *ch* is returned. Otherwise, the EOF character is returned.
static state_type get_state(pos_type *pos*);	Returns the conversion state.
static char_type to_char_type(const int_type &*ch*);	Converts *ch* into a **char_type** and returns the result.
static int_type to_int_type(const char_type &*ch*);	Converts *ch* into an **int_type** and returns the result.

The Member
Functions of
char_traits
(continued)
Table B-2.

B

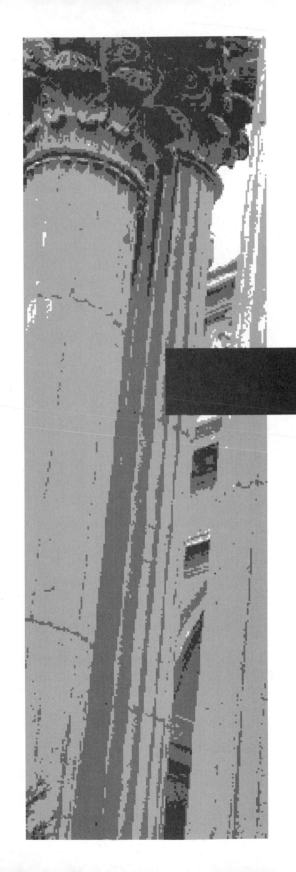

APPENDIX C

The valarray Class

The header **<valarray>** defines a number of classes that support numeric arrays. The main class is **valarray**, and it defines a one-dimensional array that holds numeric values. While **valarray** is not a fully formed container, it provides a more efficient way of storing and manipulating numeric data than does a **vector**. That is, a **valarray** is designed expressly for numeric processing. Although not part of the STL, and not fully compatible with it, **valarray** may be an important option for some programmers. For this reason, a brief overview is presented here.

The **valarray** class has this template specification:

    template <class T> class valarray

It defines the following constructors:

    valarray( );

    explicit valarray (size_t *num*);

    valarray(const T &*v*, size_t *num*);

    valarray(const T **ptr*, size_t *num*);

    valarray(const valarray<T> &*ob*);

    valarray(const slice_array<T> &*ob*);

    valarray(const gslice_array<T> &*ob*);

    valarray(const mask_array<T> &*ob*);

    valarray(const indirect_array<T> &*ob*);

Here, the first constructor creates an empty object. The second creates a **valarray** of length *num*. The third creates a **valarray** of length *num* initialized to *v*. The fourth creates a **valarray** of length *num* and initializes it with the elements pointed to by *ptr*. The fifth form creates a copy of *ob*. The next four constructors create a **valarray** from one of **valarray**'s helper classes. These constructors are not used by your program, but are automatically called when certain **valarray** operations take place.

The following operators are defined for **valarray**:

+	–	*	/
–=	+=	/=	*=

=	==	!=	<<
>>	<<=	>>=	^
^=	%	%=	~
!	|	|=	&
&=	[ ]		

These operators have several overloaded forms which are described in the accompanying tables.

The member functions and operators defined by **valarray** are shown in Table C-1. The non-member operator functions defined for **valarray** are shown it Table C-2. The transcendental functions defined for **valarray** are shown in Table C-3.

The following program demonstrates a few of the many capabilities of **valarray**:

```
// Demonstrate valarray
#include <iostream>
#include <valarray>
#include <cmath>
using namespace std;

int main()
{
  valarray<int> v(10);
  int i;

  for(i=0; i<10; i++) v[i] = i;

  cout << "Original contents: ";
  for(i=0; i<10; i++)
    cout << v[i] << " ";
  cout << endl;

  v = v.cshift(3);

  cout << "Shifted contents: ";
  for(i=0; i<10; i++)
    cout << v[i] << " ";
  cout << endl;

  valarray<bool> vb = v < 5;
  cout << "Those elements less than 5: ";
```

C

```
    for(i=0; i<10; i++)
      cout << vb[i] << " ";
    cout << endl << endl;

    valarray<double> fv(5);
    for(i=0; i<5; i++) fv[i] = (double) i;

    cout << "Original contents: ";
    for(i=0; i<5; i++)
      cout << fv[i] << " ";
    cout << endl;

    fv = sqrt(fv);

    cout << "Square roots: ";
    for(i=0; i<5; i++)
      cout << fv[i] << " ";
    cout << endl;

    fv = fv + fv;
    cout << "Double the square roots: ";
    for(i=0; i<5; i++)
      cout << fv[i] << " ";
    cout << endl;

    fv = fv - 10.0;
    cout << "After subtracting 10 from each element:\n";
    for(i=0; i<5; i++)
      cout << fv[i] << " ";
    cout << endl;

    return 0;
}
```

Its output is shown here:

```
Original contents: 0 1 2 3 4 5 6 7 8 9
Shifted contents: 3 4 5 6 7 8 9 0 1 2
Those elements less than 5: 1 1 0 0 0 0 0 1 1 1

Original contents: 0 1 2 3 4
Square roots: 0 1 1.41421 1.73205 2
Double the square roots: 0 2 2.82843 3.4641 4
After subtracting 10 from each element:
-10 -8 -7.17157 -6.5359 -6
```

Function	Description
valarray<T> apply(T *func*(T)) const; valarray<T> apply(T *func*(const T &*ob*)) const;	Applies *func( )* to the invoking array and returns an array containing the result.
valarray<T> cshift(int *num*) const;	Left-rotates the invoking array *num* places. (That is, it performs a circular shift left.) Returns an array containing the result.
T max( ) const;	Returns the maximum value in the invoking array.
T min( ) const	Returns the minimum value in the invoking array.
valarray<T> &operator=(const valarray<T> &*ob*);	Assigns the elements in *ob* to the corresponding elements in the invoking array. Returns a reference to the invoking array.
valarray<T> &operator=(const T &*v*);	Assigns each element in the invoking array the value *v*. Returns a reference to the invoking array.
valarray<T> &operator=(const slice_array<T> &*ob*);	Assigns a subset. Returns a reference to the invoking array.
valarray<T> &operator=(const gslice_array<T> &*ob*);	Assigns a subset. Returns a reference to the invoking array.
valarray<T> &operator=(const mask_array<T> &*ob*);	Assigns a subset. Returns a reference to the invoking array.
valarray<T> &operator=(const indirect_array<T> &*ob*);	Assigns a subset. Returns a reference to the invoking array.
valarray<T> operator+( ) const;	Unary plus applied to each element in the invoking array. Returns the resulting array.
valarray<T> operator–( ) const;	Unary minus applied to each element in the invoking array. Returns the resulting array.

The Member Functions of **valarray**
Table C-1.

C

Function	Description
valarray<T> operator~( ) const;	Unary bitwise NOT applied to each element in the invoking array. Returns the resulting array.
valarray<T> operator!( ) const;	Unary logical NOT applied to each element in the invoking array. Returns the resulting array.
valarray<T> &operator+=(const T &v) const;	Adds *v* to each element in the invoking array. Returns a reference to the invoking array.
valarray<T> &operator-=(const T &v) const;	Subtracts *v* from each element in the invoking array. Returns a reference to the invoking array.
valarray<T> &operator/=(const T &v) const;	Divides each element in the invoking array by *v*. Returns a reference to the invoking array.
valarray<T> &operator*=(const T &v) const;	Multiplies each element in the invoking array by *v*. Returns a reference to the invoking array.
valarray<T> &operator%=(const T &v) const;	Assigns each element in the invoking array the remainder of a division by *v*. Returns a reference to the invoking array.
valarray<T> &operator^=(const T &v) const;	XORs *v* with each element in the invoking array. Returns a reference to the invoking array.
valarray<T> &operator&=(const T &v) const;	ANDs *v* with each element in the invoking array. Returns a reference to the invoking array.
valarray<T> &operator|=(const T &v) const;	ORs *v* to each element in the invoking array. Returns a reference to the invoking array.
valarray<T> &operator<<=(const T &v) const;	Left-shifts each element in the invoking array *v* places. Returns a reference to the invoking array.

The Member Functions of **valarray** *(continued)*
Table C-1.

Function	Description
valarray<T> &operator>>=(const T &v) const;	Right-shifts each element in the invoking array *v* places. Returns a reference to the invoking array.
valarray<T> &operator+=(const valarray<T> &ob) const;	Corresponding elements of the invoking array and *ob* are added together. Returns a reference to the invoking array.
valarray<T> &operator–=(const valarray<T> &ob) const;	The elements in *ob* are subtracted from their corresponding elements in the invoking array. Returns a reference to the invoking array.
valarray<T> &operator/=(const valarray<T> &ob) const;	The elements in the invoking array are divided by their corresponding elements in *ob*. Returns a reference to the invoking array.
valarray<T> &operator*=(const valarray<T> &ob) const;	Corresponding elements of the invoking array and *ob* are multiplied together. Returns a reference to the invoking array.
valarray<T> &operator%=(const valarray<T> &ob) const;	The elements in the invoking array are divided by their corresponding elements in *ob* and the remainder is stored. Returns a reference to the invoking array.
valarray<T> &operator^=(const valarray<T> &ob) const;	The XOR operator is applied to corresponding elements in *ob* and the invoking array. Returns a reference to the invoking array.
valarray<T> &operator&=(const valarray<T> &ob) const;	The AND operator is applied to corresponding elements in *ob* and the invoking array. Returns a reference to the invoking array.

The Member Functions of **valarray** *(continued)*
Table C-1.

C

Function	Description
valarray<T> &operator|=(const valarray<T> &*ob*) const;	The OR operator is applied to corresponding elements in *ob* and the invoking array. Returns a reference to the invoking array.
valarray<T> &operator<<=(const valarray<T> &*ob*) const;	Elements in the invoking array are left-shifted by the number of places specified in the corresponding elements in *ob*. Returns a reference to the invoking array.
valarray<T> &operator>>=(const valarray<T> &*ob*) const;	Elements in invoking array are right- shifted by the number of places specified in the corresponding elements in *ob*. Returns a reference to the invoking array.
T &operator[ ] (size_t *indx*) ;	Returns a reference to the element at the specified index.
T operator[ ] {size_t *indx*) const;	Returns the value at the specified index.
slice_array<T> operator[ ](slice *ob*);	Returns the specified subset.
valarray<T> operator[ ](slice *ob*) const;	Returns the specified subset.
gslice_array<T> operator[ ](const gslice &*ob*);	Returns the specified subset.
valarray<T> operator[ ](const gslice &*ob*) const;	Returns the specified subset.
mask_array<T> operator[ ](valarray<bool> &*ob*);	Returns the specified subset.
valarray<T> operator[ ](valarray<bool> &*ob*) const;	Returns the specified subset.
indirect_array<T> operator[ ](const valarray<size_t> &*ob*);	Returns the specified subset.
valarray<T> operator[ ](const valarray<size_t> &*ob*) const;	Returns the specified subset.

The Member
Functions of
valarray
(continued)
Table C-1.

Function	Description
void resize(size_t *num*, T *v* = T( ));	Resizes the invoking array. If elements must be added, they are assigned the value of *v*.
size_t size( ) const;	Returns the size (i.e., the number of elements) of the invoking array.
valarray<T> shift(int *num*) const;	Shifts the invoking array left *num* places. Returns an array containing the result.
T sum( ) const;	Returns the sum of the values stored in the invoking array.

The Member Functions of **valarray** *(continued)* **Table C-1.**

Function	Description
template <class T> valarray<T> operator+(const valarray<T> *ob*, const T &*v*);	Adds *v* to each element of *ob*. Returns an array containing the result.
template <class T> valarray<T> operator+(const T &*v*, const valarray<T> *ob)*;	Adds *v* to each element of *ob*. Returns an array containing the result.
template <class T> valarray<T> operator+(const valarray<T> *ob1*, const valarray<T> &*ob2*);	Adds each element in *ob1* to its corresponding element in *ob2*. Returns an array containing the result.
template <class T> valarray<T> operator–(const valarray<T> *ob*, const T &*v*);	Subtracts *v* from each element of *ob*. Returns an array containing the result.
template <class T> valarray<T> operator–(const T &*v*, const valarray<T> *ob)*;	Subtracts each element of *ob* from *v*. Returns an array containing the result.
template <class T> valarray<T> operator–(const valarray<T> *ob1*, const valarray<T> &*ob2*);	Subtracts each element in *ob2* from its corresponding element in *ob1*. Returns an array containing the result.

The Non-member Operator Functions Defined for **valarray** **Table C-2.**

C

Function	Description

template <class T> valarray<T>
    operator*(const valarray<T> *ob*,
        const T &*v*);
	Multiplies each element in *ob* by *v*. Returns an array containing the result.

template <class T> valarray<T>
    operator*(const T &*v*,
        const valarray<T> *ob*);
	Multiplies each element in *ob* by *v*. Returns an array containing the result.

template <class T> valarray<T>
    operator*(const valarray<T> *ob1*,
        const valarray<T> &*ob2*);
	Multiplies corresponding elements in *ob1* by those in *ob2*. Returns an array containing the result.

template <class T> valarray<T>
    operator/(const valarray<T> *ob*,
        const T &*v*);
	Divides each element in *ob* by *v*. Returns an array containing the result.

template <class T> valarray<T>
    operator/(const T &*v*,
        const valarray<T> *ob*);
	Divides *v* by each element in *ob*. Returns an array containing the result.

template <class T> valarray<T>
    operator/(const valarray<T> *ob1*,
        const valarray<T> &*ob2*);
	Divides each elements in *ob1* by its corresponding element in *ob2*. Returns an array containing the result.

template <class T> valarray<T>
    operator%(const valarray<T> *ob*,
        const T &*v*);
	Returns the remainder that results from dividing each element in *ob* by *v*. Returns an array containing the result.

template <class T> valarray<T>
    operator%(const T &*v*,
        const valarray<T> *ob*);
	Returns the remainder that results from dividing *v* by each element in *ob*. Returns an array containing the result.

template <class T> valarray<T>
    operator%(const valarray<T> *ob1*,
        const valarray<T> &*ob2*);
	Returns the remainder that results from dividing each element in *ob1* by its corresponding element in *ob2*. Returns an array containing the result.

The
Non-member
Operator
Functions
Defined for
valarray
(continued)
Table C-2.

Function	Description

template <class T> valarray<T>
  operator^(const valarray<T> *ob*,
    const T &*v*);
	XORs each element in *ob* with *v*. Returns an array containing the result.

template <class T> valarray<T>
  operator^(const T &*v*,
    const valarray<T> *ob*);
	XORs each element in *ob* with *v*. Returns an array containing the result.

template <class T> valarray<T>
  operator^(const valarray<T> *ob1*,
    const valarray<T> &*ob2*);
	XORs each element in *ob1* with its corresponding element in *ob2*. Returns an array containing the result.

template <class T> valarray<T>
  operator&(const valarray<T> *ob*,
    const T &*v*);
	ANDs each element in *ob* with *v*. Returns an array containing the result.

template <class T> valarray<T>
  operator&(const T &*v*,
    const valarray<T> *ob*);
	ANDs each element in *ob* with *v*. Returns an array containing the result.

template <class T> valarray<T>
  operator&(const valarray<T> *ob1*,
    const valarray<T> &*ob2*);
	ANDs each element in *ob1* with its corresponding element in *ob2*. Returns an array containing the result.

template <class T> valarray<T>
  operator|(const valarray<T> *ob*,
    const T &*v*);
	ORs each element in *ob* with *v*. Returns an array containing the result.

template <class T> valarray<T>
  operator|(const T &*v*,
    const valarray<T> *ob*);
	ORs each element in *ob* with *v*. Returns an array containing the result.

template <class T> valarray<T>
  operator|(const valarray<T> *ob1*,
    const valarray<T> &*ob2*);
	ORs each element in *ob1* with its corresponding element in *ob2*. Returns an array containing the result.

template <class T> valarray<T>
  operator<<(const valarray<T> *ob*,
    const T &*v*);
	Left-shifts each element in *ob* by the number of places specified by *v*. Returns an array containing the result.

The
Non-member
Operator
Functions
Defined for
valarray
(continued)
Table C-2.

Function	Description

template <class T> valarray<T>
    operator<<(const T &v,
        const valarray<T> ob);
	Left-shifts v the number of places specified by the elements in *ob*. Returns an array containing the result.

template <class T> valarray<T>
    operator<<(const valarray<T> ob1,
        const valarray<T> &ob2);
	Left-shifts each element in *ob1* the number of places specified by its corresponding element in *ob2*. Returns an array containing the result.

template <class T> valarray<T>
    operator>>(const valarray<T> ob,
        const T &v);
	Right-shifts each element in *ob* the number of places specified by v. Returns an array containing the result.

template <class T> valarray<T>
    operator>>(const T &v,
        const valarray<T> ob);
	Right-shifts v the number of places specified by the elements in *ob*. Returns an array containing the result.

template <class T> valarray<T>
    operator>>(const valarray<T> ob1,
        const valarray<T> &ob2);
	Right-shifts each element in *ob1* the number of places specified by its corresponding element in *ob2*. Returns an array containing the result.

template <class T> valarray<bool>
    operator==(const valarray<T> ob,
        const T &v);
	For every i, performs *ob*[i] == v. Returns a Boolean array containing the result.

template <class T> valarray<bool>
    operator==(const T &v,
        const valarray<T> ob);
	For every i, performs v == *ob*[i]. Returns a Boolean array containing the result.

template <class T> valarray<bool>
    operator==(const valarray<T> ob1,
        const valarray<T> &ob2);
	For every i, performs *ob1*[i] == *ob2*[i]. Returns a Boolean array containing the result.

template <class T> valarray<bool>
    operator!=(const valarray<T> ob,
        const T &v);
	For every i, performs *ob*[i] != v. Returns a Boolean array containing the result.

The
Non-member
Operator
Functions
Defined for
valarray
(continued)
Table C-2.

Function	Description

template <class T> valarray<bool>
   operator!=(const T &v,
        const valarray<T> ob);
	For every i, performs *v* != *ob*[i]. Returns a Boolean array containing the result.

template <class T> valarray<bool>
   operator!=(const valarray<T> ob1,
        const valarray<T> &ob2);
	For every i, performs *ob1*[i] != *ob2*[i]. Returns a Boolean array containing the result.

template <class T> valarray<bool>
   operator<(const valarray<T> ob,
        const T &v);
	For every i, performs *ob*[i] < *v*. Returns a Boolean array containing the result.

template <class T> valarray<bool>
   operator<(const T &v,
        const valarray<T> ob);
	For every i, performs *v* < *ob*[i]. Returns a Boolean array containing the result.

template <class T> valarray<bool>
   operator<(const valarray<T> ob1,
        const valarray<T> &ob2);
	For every i, performs *ob1*[i] < *ob2*[i]. Returns a Boolean array containing the result.

template <class T> valarray<bool>
   operator<=(const valarray<T> ob,
        const T &v);
	For every i, performs *ob*[i] <= *v*. Returns a Boolean array containing the result.

template <class T> valarray<bool>
   operator<=(const T &v,
        const valarray<T> ob);
	For every i, performs *v* <= *ob*[i]. Returns a Boolean array containing the result.

template <class T> valarray<bool>
   operator<=(const valarray<T> ob1,
        const valarray<T> &ob2);
	For every i, performs *ob1*[i] <= *ob2*[i]. Returns a Boolean array containing the result.

template <class T> valarray<bool>
   operator>(const valarray<T> ob,
        const T &v);
	For every i, performs *ob*[i] > *v*. Returns a Boolean array containing the result.

template <class T> valarray<bool>
   operator>(const T &v,
        const valarray<T> ob);
	For every i, performs *v* > *ob*[i]. Returns a Boolean array containing the result.

template <class T> valarray<bool>
   operator>(const valarray<T> ob1,
        const valarray<T> &ob2);
	For every i, performs *ob1*[i] > *ob2*[i]. Returns a Boolean array containing the result.

The
Non-member
Operator
Functions
Defined for
valarray
(continued)
Table C-2.

C

Function	Description

template <class T> valarray<bool>
    operator>=(const valarray<T> *ob*,
                const T &*v*);
	For every i, performs *ob*[i] >= *v*.
	Returns a Boolean array
	containing the result.

template <class T> valarray<bool>
    operator>=(const T &*v*,
                const valarray<T> *ob)*;
	For every i, performs *v* >= *ob*[i].
	Returns a Boolean array
	containing the result.

template <class T> valarray<bool>
    operator>=(const valarray<T> *ob1*,
                const valarray<T> &*ob2*);
	For every i, performs *ob1*[i] >=
	ob2[i]. Returns a Boolean array
	containing the result.

template <class T> valarray<bool>
    operator&&(const valarray<T> *ob*,
                const T &*v*);
	For every i, performs *ob*[i] && *v*.
	Returns a Boolean array
	containing the result.

template <class T> valarray<bool>
    operator&&(const T &*v*,
                const valarray<T> *ob)*;
	For every i, performs *v* && *ob*[i].
	Returns a Boolean array
	containing the result.

template <class T> valarray<bool>
    operator&&(const valarray<T> *ob1*,
                const valarray<T> &*ob2*);
	For every i, performs *ob1*[i] &&
	ob2[i]. Returns a Boolean array
	containing the result.

template <class T> valarray<bool>
    operator||(const valarray<T> *ob*,
                const T &*v*);
	For every i, performs *ob*[i] || *v*.
	Returns a Boolean array
	containing the result.

template <class T> valarray<bool>
    operator||(const T &*v*,
                const valarray<T> *ob)*;
	For every i, performs *v* || *ob*[i].
	Returns a Boolean array
	containing the result.

template <class T> valarray<bool>
    operator||(const valarray<T> *ob1*,
                const valarray<T> &*ob2*);
	For every i, performs *ob1*[i] ||
	ob2[i]. Returns a Boolean array
	containing the result.

The
Non-member
Operator
Functions
Defined for
valarray
(continued)
Table C-2.

The slice and gslice Classes

The **<valarray>** header defines two utility classes called **slice** and **gslice**. These classes encapsulate a slice (i.e., a portion) from an array. These classes are used with the subset forms of **valarray**'s **operator[ ]**.

Function	Description
template<class T> valarray<T> abs(const valarray<T> &*ob*);	Obtains the absolute value of each element in *ob* and returns an array containing the result.
template<class T> valarray<T> acos(const valarray<T> &*ob*);	Obtains the arccosine of each element in *ob* and returns an array containing the result.
template<class T> valarray<T> asin(const valarray<T> &*ob*);	Obtains the arcsine of each element in *ob* and returns an array containing the result.
template<class T> valarray<T> atan(const valarray<T> &*ob*);	Obtains the arctangent of each element in *ob* and returns an array containing the result.

template<class T> valarray<T>
    atan2(const valarray<T> &*ob1*,
        const valarray<T> &*ob2*);
	For all i, obtains the arctangent of *ob1*[i] / *ob2*[i] and returns an array containing the result.

template<class T> valarray<T> atan2(const T &*v*, const valarray<T> &*ob*);	For all i, obtains the arctangent of *v* / *ob1*[i] and returns an array containing the result.
template<class T> valarray<T> atan2(const valarray<T> &*ob*, const T &*v*);	For all i, obtains the arctangent of *ob1*[i] / *v* and returns an array containing the result.
template<class T> valarray<T> cos(const valarray<T> &*ob*);	Obtains the cosine of each element in *ob* and returns an array containing the result.
template<class T> valarray<T> cosh(const valarray<T> &*ob*);	Obtains the hyperbolic cosine of each element in *ob* and returns an array containing the result.
template<class T> valarray<T> exp(const valarray<T> &*ob*);	Computes exponential function for each element in *ob* and returns an array containing the result.
template<class T> valarray<T> log(const valarray<T> &*ob*);	Obtains the natural logarithm of each element in *ob* and returns an array containing the result.
template<class T> valarray<T> log10(const valarray<T> &*ob*);	Obtains the common logarithm of each element in *ob* and returns an array containing the result.

Transcendental
Functions
Defined for
valarray
Table C-3.

C

Function	Description

template<class T> valarray<T>
    pow(const valarray<T> &*ob1*,
        const valarray<T> &*ob2*);
	For all i, computes $ob1[i]^{ob2[i]}$ and returns an array containing the result.

template<class T> valarray<T> pow(const T &*v*, const valarray<T> &*ob*);	For all i, computes $v^{ob[i]}$ and returns an array containing the result.
template<class T> valarray<T> pow(const valarray<T> &*ob*, const T &*v*);	For all i, computes $ob1[i]^{v}$ and returns an array containing the result.
template<class T> valarray<T> sin(const valarray<T> &*ob*);	Obtains the sine of each element in *ob* and returns an array containing the result.
template<class T> valarray<T> sinh(const valarray<T> &*ob*);	Obtains the hyperbolic sine of each element in *ob* and returns an array containing the result.
template<class T> valarray<T> sqrt(const valarray<T> &*ob*);	Obtains the square root of each element in *ob* and returns an array containing the result.
template<class T> valarray<T> tan(const valarray<T> &*ob*);	Obtains the tangent of each element in *ob* and returns an array containing the result.
template<class T> valarray<T> tanh(const valarray<T> &*ob*);	Obtains the hyperbolic tangent of each element in *ob* and returns an array containing the result.

Transcendental
Functions
Defined for
valarray
(continued)
Table C-3.

The **slice** class allows you to view a one-dimensional **valarray** as if it were a two-dimensional array. Since **valarrays** are always one-dimensional, **slice** is an important class. The **slice** class is shown here:

```
class slice {
public:
  slice();
  slice(size_t start, size_t len, size_t interval);
  size_t start() const;
  size_t size() const;
  size_t stride();
};
```

The first constructor creates an empty slice. The second constructor creates a slice that specifies the starting element, the number of elements to obtain, and the interval between slices (also called the *stride*). The interval determines the length of a row in the synthesized two-dimensional array. The member functions return these values.

Here is a program that demonstrates **slice**:

```
// Demonstrate slice
#include <iostream>
#include <valarray>
using namespace std;

int main()
{
  valarray<int> v(10), result;
  int i;

  for(i=0; i<10; i++) v[i] = i;

  cout << "Contents of v: ";
  for(i=0; i<10; i++)
    cout << v[i] << " ";
  cout << endl;

  result = v[slice(0,5,2)];

  cout << "Contents of result: ";
  for(i=0; i<result.size(); i++)
    cout << result[i] << " ";

  return 0;
}
```

The output from the program is shown here:

```
Contents of v: 0 1 2 3 4 5 6 7 8 9
Contents of result: 0 2 4 6 8
```

As you can see, the resulting array consists of five elements of **v**, beginning at 0, that are 2 apart. That is, the resulting sequence contains the five elements from the first column of the following two-dimensional array.

0	1
2	3
4	5
6	7
8	9

The **gslice** class is shown here:

```
class gslice {
public:
  gslice();
  gslice()(size_t start, const valarray<size_t> &lens,
           const valarray<size_t> &intervals);
  size_t start() const;
  valarray<size_t> size() const;
  valarray<size_t> stride() const;
};
```

The first constructor creates an empty slice. The second constructor creates a slice that specifies the starting element, an array that specifies the number of elements, and an array that specifies the intervals between elements (that is, the *strides*). The number of lengths and intervals must be the same. The member functions return these parameters. This class is used to create multi-dimensional arrays from a **valarray** (which is alway one-dimensional).

The following program demonstrates **gslice**. It treats the array specified by **v** as if it were a 4 × 3 two-dimensional array and then creates a slice that is the 3 × 3 two-dimensional array formed by the upper left corner.

```
// Demonstrate gslice()
#include <iostream>
#include <valarray>
using namespace std;

int main()
{
  valarray<int> v(16), result;
  valarray<size_t> len(2), interval(2);
  int i;

  for(i=0; i<16; i++) v[i] = i;
```

```
len[0] = 3; len[1] = 3;
interval[0] = 4; interval[1] = 1;

cout << "Contents of v: ";
for(i=0; i<16; i++)
  cout << v[i] << " ";
cout << endl;

result = v[gslice(0,len,interval)];

cout << "Contents of result: ";
for(i=0; i<result.size(); i++)
  cout << result[i] << " ";

return 0;
}
```

The output is shown here:

```
Contents of v: 0 1 2 3 4 5 6 7 8 9 10 11 12 13 14 15
Contents of result: 0 1 2 4 5 6 8 9 10
```

Notice that not all of the elements from **v** are part of the synthesized two-dimensional array. Only the first three elements from each logical row are used. That is, the slice created is shown in bold below.

0	**1**	**2**	3
4	**5**	**6**	7
8	**9**	**10**	11
12	13	14	15

The Helper Classes

The **valarray** class relies upon these "helper" classes, which your program will never instantiate directly: **slice_array**, **gslice_array**, **indirect_array**, and **mask_array**.

The Numeric
Algorithms

The header **<numeric>** defines four numeric algorithms that can be used to process the contents of containers through iterators. Although none are technically part of the STL proper, they are fully compatible with it. Each numeric algorithm is examined here.

accumulate

The **accumulate( )** algorithm computes a summation of all of the elements within a specified range and returns the result. Its prototype is shown here:

> template <class InIter, class T> T accumulate(InIter *start*, InIter *end*, T *v*);

> template <class InIter, class T, class BinFunc>
>   T accumulate(InIter *start*, InIter *end*, T *v*, BinFunc *func*);

Here, **T** is the type of values being operated upon. The first version computes the sum of all elements in the range *start* to *end*. The second version applies *func* to the running total. (That is, *func* specifies how the summation will occur.) The value of *v* provides an initial value to which the running total is added.

Here is an example that demonstrates **accumulate( )**:

```
// Demonstrate accumulate()
#include <iostream>
#include <vector>
#include <numeric>
using namespace std;

int main()
{
  vector<int> v(5);
  int i, total;

  for(i=0; i<5; i++) v[i] = i;

  total = accumulate(v.begin(), v.end(), 0);

  cout << "Summation of v is: " << total;

  return 0;
}
```

The following output is produced:

```
Summation of v is: 10
```

adjacent_difference

The **adjacent_difference( )** algorithm produces a new sequence in which each element is the difference between adjacent elements in the original sequence. (The first element in the result is the same as the original first element.) The template specification for **adjacent_difference( )** is shown here:

```
template <class InIter, class OutIter>
    OutIter adjacent_difference(InIter start, InInter end, OutIter result);

template <class InIter, class OutIter, class BinFunc>
    OutIter adjacent_difference(InIter start, InInter end, OutIter result,
                                BinFunc func);
```

Here, *start* and *end* are iterators to the beginning and ending of the original sequence. The resulting sequence is stored in the sequence pointed to by *result*. In the first form, adjacent elements are subtracted, with the element at location *n* being subtracted from the element at location *n*+1. In the second, the binary function *func* is applied to adjacent elements. An iterator to the end of *result* is returned.

Here is an example that uses **adjacent_difference( )**:

```
// Demonstrate adjacent_difference()
#include <iostream>
#include <vector>
#include <numeric>
using namespace std;

int main()
{
  vector<int> v(10), r(10);
  int i;

  for(i=0; i<10; i++) v[i] = i*2;
  cout << "Original sequence: ";
```

D

```
for(i=0; i<10; i++)
  cout << v[i] << " ";
cout << endl;

adjacent_difference(v.begin(), v.end(), r.begin());

cout << "Resulting sequence: ";
for(i=0; i<10; i++)
  cout << r[i] << " ";

return 0;
}
```

The output produced is shown here:

```
Original sequence: 0 2 4 6 8 10 12 14 16 18
Resulting sequence: 0 2 2 2 2 2 2 2 2 2
```

As you can see, the resulting sequence contains the difference between the values of adjacent elements.

inner_product

The **inner_product( )** algorithm produces a summation of the product of corresponding elements in two sequences and returns the result. It has these template specifications:

> template <class InIter1, class InIter2, class T>
>   T inner_product(InIter1 *start1*, InIter1 *end1*, InIter2 *start2*, T *v*);

> template <class InIter1, class InIter2, class T, class BinFunc1, class BinFunc2>
>   T inner_product(InIter1 *start1*, InIter1 *end1*, InIter2 *start2*, T *v*,
>   BinFunc1 *func2*, BinFunc2 *func2*);

Here, *start1* and *end1* are iterators to the beginning and end of the first sequence. The iterator *start2* is an iterator to the beginning of the second sequence. The value *v* provides an initial value to which the running total is added. In the second form, *func1* specifies a binary function that determines how the running total is computed and *func2* specifies a binary function that determines how the two sequences are multiplied together.

Here is a program that demonstrates **inner_product( )**:

```
// Demonstrate inner_product()
#include <iostream>
#include <vector>
#include <numeric>
using namespace std;

int main()
{
  vector<int> v1(5), v2(5);
  int i, total;

  for(i=0; i<5; i++) v1[i] = i;
  for(i=0; i<5; i++) v2[i] = i+2;

  total = inner_product(v1.begin(), v1.end(),
                        v2.begin(), 0);

  cout << "Inner product is: " << total;

  return 0;
}
```

Here is the output:

```
Inner product is: 50
```

partial_sum

The **partial_sum( )** algorithm sums a sequence of values, putting the current total into each successive element of a new sequence as it goes. (That is, it creates a sequence that is a running total of the original sequence.) The first element in the result is the same as the first element in the original sequence. The template specifications for **partial_sum( )** are shown here.

template <class InIter, class OutIter>
    OutIter partial_sum(InIter *start*, InIter *end*, OutIter *result*);

template <class InIter, class OutIter, class BinFunc>
    OutIter partial_sum(InIter *start*, InIter *end*, OutIter *result*,
                    BinFunc *func*);

D

Here, *start1* and *end1* are iterators to the beginning and end of the original sequence. The iterator *result* is an iterator to the beginning of the resulting sequence. In the second form, *func* specifies a binary function that determines how the running total is computed. An iterator to the end of *result* is returned.

Here is an example of **partial_sum( )**:

```
// Demonstrate partial_sum()
#include <iostream>
#include <vector>
#include <numeric>
using namespace std;

int main()
{
  vector<int> v(5), r(5);
  int i;

  for(i=0; i<10; i++) v[i] = i;
  cout << "Original sequence: ";
  for(i=0; i<5; i++)
    cout << v[i] << " ";
  cout << endl;

  partial_sum(v.begin(), v.end(), r.begin());

  cout << "Resulting sequence: ";
  for(i=0; i<5; i++)
    cout << r[i] << " ";

  return 0;
}
```

Here is its output:

```
Original sequence: 0 1 2 3 4
Resulting sequence: 0 1 3 6 10
```

Index

W